M

MICHAEL POWEL[illegible]

INTERVIEWS

CONVERSATIONS WITH [illegible]
PETER BRUNETTE, GENE[illegible]

Photo credit: courtesy of Thelma Schoonmaker-Powell

MICHAEL POWELL

INTERVIEWS

EDITED BY DAVID LAZAR

UNIVERSITY PRESS OF MISSISSIPPI / JACKSON

www.upress.state.ms.us

Manufactured in the United States of America

11 10 09 08 07 06 05 04 03 4 3 2 1
♾

Library of Congress Cataloging-in-Publication Data
Michael Powell : interviews / edited by David Lazar.
p. cm.—(Conversations with filmmakers series)
Includes index.
ISBN 1-57806-497-X (cloth : alk. paper)—ISBN 1-57806-498-8 (pbk. : alk. paper)
1. Powell, Michael, 1905–1990—Interviews. 2. Motion picture producers and directors—Great Britain—Interviews. I. Lazar, David, 1957– II. Series.
PN1998.3.P69 A5 2003
791.43′0233′092—dc21 2002027038

British Library Cataloging-in-Publication Data available

CONTENTS

INTRODUCTION

THE BELEAGUERED, BEWILDERING, foreshortened, or blighted career is hardly an unfamiliar archetype in the arts and specifically cinema. Names pop up like slightly injured jacks in the box: Eric von Stroheim, Preston Sturges, Orson Welles, James Dean, Judy Holliday, Louise Brooks, Rex Ingram . . . Michael Powell. Not that film owns the market on career travail, but certainly such a collaborative, financially driven, public-dependent art form presents obvious myriad models of attenuation. Michael Powell, one of the least known great directors of sound films, a prototype of the independent filmmaker, and the director of several of the most artful and satisfying films of a period covering, roughly, 1940–1960—*One of Our Aircraft Is Missing, 49th Parallel, The Life and Death of Colonel Blimp, A Matter of Life and Death, I Know Where I'm Going!, The Red Shoes, The Small Back Room, Black Narcissus, Tales of Hoffman, Peeping Tom*—sometimes is presented, and this includes self-presentation, as a poster boy for filmus interruptus.

Interviews with Powell (who created most of his best films with screenwriter Emeric Pressburger, and their production company, The Archers) frequently state as clear and uncontested fact that Powell's career was "destroyed" by the reception of *Peeping Tom* (1960), the first full-length film Powell directed after the dissolution of The Archers' partnership. *Peeping Tom,* a study of scoptophilia (the morbid compulsion to watch), is the story of a young cameraman, Mark Lewis, who films women reacting as he dispatches them with a knife extending from his tripod, a distorting mirror allowing them a grotesque vision of their imminent and actual deaths. It was, indeed, savaged by the critics. Powell takes this up in many of his interviews. In an interview conducted at the Midnight Sun Film Festival, he says, "English critics killed me for making *Peeping Tom.*" To Roland Lacourbe and Danièle Grivel, Powell says, "The film truly ruined me." To the *Times,* Powell quotes two of the reviews: "'The nastiest film I have ever seen,' wrote one, and another said, 'It's a long time since a film disgusted me as much as *Peeping Tom*—beastly picture.'" To William Everson, Powell, with a light sarcasm that frequently shows up in his voice with a kind of muted brio, says about the re-release of *Peeping Tom* in the eighties, "The critics in New York had a good time. They said: 'Here's a marvelous film . . . we heard that our London colleagues tore it apart.'"

But a revulsion, or at least a reaction, to Powell (and Pressburger) had been brewing as distrust for many years. The Archers, it seems, were deemed to have a perverse streak, manifested in their war films' balance, even occasional sympathy to German characters, their mocking of the "Blimp" class of aging military professionals in England, the magistrate in *A Canterbury Tale* who throws glue onto girls' hair, the suggestive invocation of German expressionism in many shots in many films, culminating with the supposed moral and sexual perversion of *Peeping Tom.* After *Peeping Tom,* Powell directed three more feature-length films, all in the 1960s: *The Queen's Guards, They're a Weird Mob,* and *Age of Consent,* the latter two in Australia. None were very popular in the UK, though in Australia, *They're a Weird Mob* was one of the top-ranking box-office films made in Australia at the time. But the questions remain: How much damage did *Peeping Tom* do? Why were English critics so dubious of Powell's and some of The Archers' work? Why, as early as 1950, in "Mr. Powell Replies," do we hear that "the London critics have had a frolic recently over the corpses of Powell and Pressburger, writers, producers, and directors of *Gone to Earth* and of *The Elusive Pimpernel*"?[1]

A few interviewers point out the relationship between *Peeping Tom* and the rest of Powell's career. Frequently forgotten in the consideration of interviews is the contribution of the interviewers, who can run the gamut from cipher to equal partner in dialogue. The unnamed special correspondent for the *Times* tells us, "Themes of horror, we remarked, were not so novel in Mr. Powell's work as some critics had suggested—they occurred in *The Red Shoes* ballet, in *The Tales of Hoffman,* and perhaps particularly relevant to the present instance, in *A Canterbury Tale. . . .*" William Everson takes this issue up even more pointedly and astutely, telling Powell that in his career, at times, it is "almost as though you're tweaking the nose of the public and sort of giving them what they don't want in that kind of film. . . . I just wonder if that's a kind of perverse deliberate trick." Within the context of a discussion of *Peeping Tom,* Everson mentions the blood at the end of *The Red Shoes,* the glue-throwing magistrate in *A Canterbury Tale,* the hawk grabbing a piece of rabbit at the end of *I Know Where I'm Going!* Powell responds, "Oh yes. Of course it is. It's delightful to make the audience shudder." In both cases, Powell doesn't seem particularly inclined to pursue the question. It is good to keep in mind that evasions, partial answers, and simple responses can tell us as much through omission as the most complicated and prolix response.

Ultimately, Powell is somewhat bewildered by the intensity of the response to *Peeping Tom.* He says to Ian Christie, "I don't know why it shocked the critics. I will never understand, never understand that." In some ways, though, Powell answers the question simply, obliquely in a discussion of other films. *The Life and Death of Colonel Blimp, The Small Back Room,* and *Peeping Tom* were explicitly or implicitly subjected to the criterion he suggests as crucial to Everson: "It was a question of timing. Just like when Rex Ingram made *Mare Nostrum* it was five, six years after the Great War, the First World War, and people by that time were fed up with a sort of serious, tragic treatment of the war. So although they said it was a very fine film, they didn't go. And the same thing happened with *The Small Back Room.*" It is impossible to imagine *Peeping Tom* receiving the same critical reception even a few scant years after its initial release in 1960, just as *Blimp* would have raised no eyebrows were it not released during the war. The critical plundering of *Peeping Tom* was made possible by the cultural condition of Britain in the late 1950s.

Despite the fact that both Powell and his interlocutors frequently assert the damage that *Peeping Tom* did to Powell (for example, Powell telling Roland Lacourbe and Danièle Grivel, "It was the end of me with a generation of distributors and cinema owners"), *Million Dollar Movie* tells a slightly different story. Although offers weren't exactly being laid at Michael Powell's door in the 1960s, much of his time was spent developing, proposing, and attempting to advance a variety of projects. Some of these seem in retrospect misguided; some were scotched because Powell, admittedly, had become rather leery of the machinations of film production and would not yield on most points that he considered crucial to his own independence and his guiding vision of what a film, or *the* film should be. Occasionally, Powell went against his instincts and trusted others, Rex Harrison, for example, or

Peter Sellers—who was almost entirely unreliable in his commitment to a film until production actually began—only to have a project evaporate with their withdrawal. However, when one considers that Powell directed three films and several television episodes in the eight years after *Peeping Tom*, these years do not amount to complex exile. Nevertheless, the films were much more difficult to finance—and difficulty created by one's best work can become a rather bitter piece of celluloid. In fact, by *Age of Consent* in 1968, Powell was sixty-three years old and had not directed a film the English public particularly wanted to see for over ten years. On many levels, Powell understood the misfortunes created by vox populi and is magnanimous in self-blame for some of his choices (not signing a long-term deal with John Davis of the Rank organization in the mid-fifties; not anticipating the cruel critical juggernaut awaiting a sensational choice of material on his part; trusting Alexander Korda a second time around, etc.). In any case, lamenting the films that weren't made is a tradition as old as early death.

Peeping Tom is, among other interpretive possibilities, a comment on the war. Karl Boehm's lilting German accent in an Englishman is even stranger than James Mason's English in a German (Van Damm) in *North by Northwest,* which was released the year before (1959). Put together, the two films eerily suggest that any moral optimism to emerge from the defeat of Nazi Germany should be highly tempered. The protagonist killer of *Peeping Tom,* Mark Lewis, is the son of a father whose experiments on his own child suggest Josef Mengele. In *North by Northwest,* George Kaplan, the missing Jew of a red herring, the postwar ghost of a maguffin, is invoked throughout, but has no life other than in the imagination of his creators or their antagonists. In *Peeping Tom,* the son is not evil as much as demented, split, as the ideology of the father gives birth to the psychosis of his son. But as though this weren't enough, narratively, the film frequently moves through color tones, creating a kind of subtext or second text to the film, as if the film, visually, were trying to create both an aesthetic interpretation of violence and a counterpoint to it. Surely the fact that both *Peeping Tom* and *North by Northwest* were written by Jewish screenwriters—Leo Marks with Powell, and Ernest Lehman with Hitchcock—has at least something to do with a Holocaust-informed consciousness. In the "Artists at Work" interview, we are told that "Mr. Marks feels that the sense of sight divorced from the sense of feeling has run riot in the modern world," clearly suggesting a kind of postwar sense of dissociation. The fact that Powell plays the elder Lewis, who films his son's responses to terror, and the boy in the "documentary" footage, who is played by Powell's son Columba, is noted frequently—and the reading of *Peeping Tom* as a comment on the filmmaker's art has been reiterated, at times, too mechanically—but we also learn that Leo Marks suggested most of the torturous surprises. Clearly there is a distinct comment about spectatorship and its relation to women as objects, and the film with its mirrored prefiguring of death, absent mother, and maladapted language (i.e., Teutonicized English) presents a veritable field day for suture theories, perhaps even more directly than in *Psycho, Peeping Tom*'s contemporary. This cinematic self-consciousness appears in earlier Powell works, especially in *A Matter of Life and Death,* but there is a kind of Victorian gothic quality to *Peeping Tom,* which may be the ultimate penny dreadful of metacinema. Certainly it was an ultima Thule for Powell, his last great film.

If Powell did not have many more films in front of him after *Peeping Tom,* at least in his last decade he would experience a retrospective celebration of his career that was an unexpected as its demise. Enter Martin Scorsese. Scorsese, as many of the late interviews note, had admired Powell's films since, as a kid in New York, he had caught *Thief of Bagdad, A Matter of Life and Death, Black Narcissus,* and others on the Million Dollar Movie on television. The Archers' logo, so it seems, was stuck in the middle of his forehead, and the arrow hit the mark. Scorsese helped spark the renewed interest in Powell and The Archers, and introduced Powell to Thelma Schoonmaker, Scorsese's editor who would become Michael Powell's second wife. Many of the late interviews mention the Scorsese connection and the consequent introduction of Powell to Francis Ford Coppola, who named Michael Powell "Senior Director in Residence" at the ill-fated Zoetrope Studios. Plainly, with his personal happiness, his late years on the film festival circuit as something between a revered elder-statesman and a surviving maverick, and the limited but significant advisory role he played for Coppola and Scorsese, Powell was brought back to public life by Scorsese and energized by his interest and friendship.

Despite the sometimes bitter or jeremiadic note Powell sounds in his last several years, being a focal point of interest served him and suited him after his years in the camera obscura of film and public renown. And his service to his own films, but perhaps even more to cinema history, should be noted. In addition to lectures and appearances, the greatest contribution Michael Powell made in the last ten to fifteen years of his life was his rather encyclopedic two-volume autobiography: *A Life in Movies* and *Million Dollar Movie*. These are books crucial both to a consideration of Powell's career and as historical overview of British film through the fifties. Like Charles Lamb's *Elia*, Powell prepared his own epitaph for publication in *Million Dollar Movie*. Clearly, aficionados of Powell's work can engage the most extended version of his written voice in these autobiographies, with their level of seasoned honesty, revealing anecdotal information (the apotheosis of inside dope), directorial insight, and devotion to the art of the cinema, always capital "A." In the interviews, however, one can see Powell's relationship to cinema, his consideration of it, forming over time. To Speakman in 1945, Powell says, "I don't like the word *art*. My view is that the cinema is a craft and while it remains a craft—it's all right—no one need be frightened, but once it becomes an industry. . . ." But by 1972 Powell says definitively to R. Collins and Ian Christie that cinema's "proper form . . . is an art form";[2] to William Everson in 1981, he says, "I regarded myself as the priest of an art"; and in 1987 at Midnight Sun, Michael Powell declares passionately, "I'm talking about art. I'm talking to you as artists. If you're prepared to spend your whole life fighting for your art with people who don't like you, don't understand you, don't help you, then you have my respect and I regard you as a brother."

At other times, however, Powell poses himself as a technician of a very high order. Speaking of *The Wizard of Oz* to Kevin Gough-Yates, Powell says, "Victor Fleming's picture had a big influence on me, yes! . . . Fleming was a great technician and I am, too, quite consciously, a great technician."[3] In several of the interviews, Powell notes with pride that Alexander Korda told him he was the greatest film technician he had worked with. To Collins and Christie, Michael Powell says, "You can only be relaxed if you gather round you such a stupendous team of technicians and craftsmen that they're all contributing just as you are and you're only controlling it all as Lermontov was in *The Red Shoes*."[4] Speaking with Bertrand Tavernier, Powell commits his most distinct and well-known self-evaluation, with audacious humility: "You see, most directors of my generation have their own style, but I don't. Take Hitchcock, for example, or Renoir; these are directors who have found their own style in the cinema. I haven't. I *live* cinema. . . . I am not a film director with a personal style, *I am the cinema*." Powell's argument for himself as a kind of cinematic Auden is somehow elicited by Tavernier, whose director-director interview is one of the most acute.

Further self-evaluations in the interviews frequently return to the importance of collaboration. And though Powell will occasionally assert the primacy of the image and lament the demise of silent film, no other writer-director team in cinema, with perhaps the exception of Wilder-Brackett, had as successful a string of collaborative successes as Powell and Pressburger. As the interviews in this volume make clear, Powell and Pressburger had a unique relationship, a rare partnership of writing (mostly Pressburger, with suggestions from Powell), directing (all Powell, with occasional input from Pressburger), and collaborative producing. Certainly Powell's enthusiastic agreement with The Archers' assertion, "written, directed, and produced by Michael Powell and Emeric Pressburger," represents an all but unprecedented sharing of credit for the production of a film, and Powell, as director more powerful and marketable than any given screenwriter, need not have embraced so unusual a union. But Michael Powell was a connoisseur of the collaboration and understood that the Hungarian émigré, Pressburger, with whom he was paired by Korda, and who had already done much distinguished work in German cinema (and German expressionism shows up frequently as an influence in Archers and Powell films), sparked his own work, as did Powell for Pressburger. The best work the two did has a balance of literate dialogue, technical finesse, and thrilling mise en scène. Nevertheless, we continue to be in the age of the auteur, and Powell and Pressburger's films tend to be regarded as Powell's films, though the interviews continually refer to Pressburger and the importance of their partnership. The story of how Powell and Pressburger agreed to form The Archers shows up in most of the interviews. For example, after explaining to Richard Jameson that Pressburger suggested the formation of a production company, Powell details their public union: "So it came to be: 'written' first, the most important thing in making a film, and 'produced' because you have to find the money and nobody quite knows what a producer does except find the money . . . and then that leaves me: 'directing.' So it came out 'written, produced, and directed by Michael Powell and Emeric Pressburger.'" To Ian Christie, Powell explains that "a big production like *49th Parallel,* which started as just a small idea and grew into a very big film, I don't think one man can do it. Two men—if one of them is a very remarkable one, because it's no good if you haven't got a good story and a good script—two men, as far as we were concerned, could put a film together."

To William Everson, Powell says, "We imagined that a producer was a man who was responsible for the whole thing: finds the story, finds the director, finds the actors, and makes up this wonderful team which then makes a film. We called ourselves producers to stop anybody else from calling themselves producers of our films." Producers, in general, come in for rather a hard time in Powell's estimations, with the exception of Korda. Powell continues, "If you let control get away from you, you'd be surprised how even big things fall quite flat on the cinema." To *Cahiers du cinéma,* he states emphatically that "filmmakers must be independent." To Roland Lacourbe and Danièle Grivet, Michael Powell says, "For me, there is nothing in Hollywood. It's not my life. In England we want to make our films. Not producers' films. . . ."

Powell comments frequently on his aversion to documentary filmmaking and his sense that the use and idea of naturalism are overrated and, in fact, frequently deaden ideological impulses. In addition to his sense of the cinema as a fantastic medium (reiterated implicitly in telling Roger Manvell that Disney is "the greatest genius of us all"[5]), Powell notes the logistical problem of naturalism to Collins and Christie: "Unless we are able to tell a film completely without naturalism, I don't see any future for any budget for any film."[6] The matte paintings, exquisite design work of men like Alfred Junge and Hein Heckroth, were nowhere near as expensive as elaborate location shooting and the work needed to create a visually naturalistic sense of the characters' worlds. Of Powell's major films, *I Know Where I'm Going!* is the most naturalistic, but it tempers a level of naturalistic over-determinism, a critique of intra-British cultural colonialism and class bias, with a slightly surreal frame: hyperkinetic modernism at the beginning, Freudian gothic naturalism in the whirlpool of Corryveckian near the end. The film sits well in the genre of romantic comedy while subtly turning it on its head, expanding its possibilities with a light touch that the transition from naturalism to surrealism seems to buoy. The creation of the whirlpool was clearly a technical turning point for Powell, a sense of ascension into mastery. He says of this sequence, to Kevin Gough-Yates, "After that, we felt we could do anything."[7] But the fantastic is usually grounded in The Archers' films, as it certainly is in *I Know Where I'm Going! The Red Shoes* is grounded in the dogged rigor of Lermontov—Powell's stand in. *Tales of Hoffmann,* the Powell film closest to pure fantasy, is grounded in the sense of theatrical collaboration evident throughout, a subtextual self-evaluation gleaned from Powell's apprenticeship with Rex Ingram. To Everson, Powell says, "But when I look back on it, I realize the thing he had, which was extraordinary, was this sense of theatre, sense of timing, sense of staging. He brought this into films," much as Powell did twenty years later.

At the Midnight Sun Film Festival, Powell recalls: "[After the war] not many color films had been made and we made in succession, *A Matter of Life and Death, Black Narcissus,* and *The Red Shoes,* the most astonishing row of extraordinary films ever made," all films with surreal and/or fantastic qualities. *A Matter of Life and Death* was a war film in a technical sense, commissioned in 1945 when the War Office's propaganda machine turned from mobilizing against Germany to smoothing growing tensions with England's American allies. What Powell and Pressburger created, however, was a genre-smasher. *A Matter of Life and Death* combines romantic comedy, war film, *Metropolis*-inspired fantasy sequences (which Powell frequently insists have psychologically plausible coordinates), psychological drama, and surreal courtroom drama. It sounds absurd, of course, and in a Buñuelian way, it is. Peter Carter (David Niven) is an airman who has mysteriously survived a jump from a burning airplane. In the final moments before he jumps, he makes contact with a radio dispatcher, an American woman, June, played by Kim Hunter. This scene is the linchpin of the film, for in these moments, which he knows to be his last, Peter in his flaming cockpit and June in her antiseptic control room fall in love. In scenes shot in vivid, but naturalistic Technicolor, the plane becomes a flying inferno, as though hell on earth were Peter's final mortal experience. Love becomes the deus ex machina of the film in a way that no one would even attempt today, but Powell creates a doubly-sutured emotional scene: we are pressed into an impossible choice of identifying with the living and dead, man and woman, Englishman and American woman. It is this impossibility which we must nevertheless enact which creates the only possible outcome: Death interacts with life and is effaced, so Love can emerge supreme. How Peter survives is never officially, literally, explained—because we *know* how, unofficially, figuratively. To Kevin Gough-Yates, Powell notes the irony of some critics' complaints about this scene: "But of course they said it's absolutely ridiculous to have a man in this situation with his co-pilot dead and the aeroplane half burned to bits and the wind blowing through,"[8] even though years of war documentaries should have prepared them for the surreal-*seeming* possibility of such a scene. In a reversal of the schema in *The Wizard of Oz, A Matter of Life and Death,* through Pressburger's suggestion, uses color for its earthly scenes, monochrome (undeveloped Technicolor) for its heaven/imaginary scenes, where Peter must defend his desire to stay alive. The film is a Freudian polarization, the life drive extending everywhere, a moving response to the death-full war years. The only significant death in the film that registers emotionally and is rendered dramatically is that of Peter's neurologist, played by Roger Livesey. In a much talked about scene, Livesey surveys *his* village through a camera obscura—which mirrors the film's God's-point-of-view opening when we plunge through space and time towards the earth. In this way, the character is linked to the director—perhaps the only real death is, symbolically, a strategic self-abnegation? But the good doctor's death is Peter's resurrection from the claims of the afterlife. Like Orpheus the doctor brings Peter back, but from the danger on high. *A Matter of Life and Death* is one of the most original and underrated films of the 1940s, and Michael Powell himself refers to it as "perfect" several times, and his own favorite of his films.

The motif of the outsider or misplaced person, the stranger in a strange land, exile, foreigner, or man without a country is a constant motif in Powell's mind and The Archers' films (*Contraband, 49th Parallel, The Spy in Black, A Canterbury Tale, Black Narcissus, A Matter of Life and Death, I Know Where I'm Going!, The Battle of the River Plate, Peeping Tom,* and *They're a Weird Mob*). In *Black Narcissus* we see the English nuns attempt to sustain their habit of sexual repression only to swoon and fall or more wisely retreat when overcome by the erotic/exotic Indian landscape. In the battle between habitat and habit, id trounces super-ego rather roundly. It is only the curiously chaste, but robustly bare-chested English settler (David Farrar) who manages something of a living truce through adaptation, which includes a decidedly hostile attitude to the naively colonizing nuns. In *I Know Where I'm Going!* the Scottish inhabitants of Killoran and their Laird (Roger Livesay) are mere expedients to Joan's (Wendy Hiller's) consummation of wedding vows to her blandly super-powerful industrialist fiancé, who is never seen. His voice, rendered through sporadic radio contacts with the island, provides moments of tonally complex comedy. A version of Blimp on steroids, he is imperturbable, phlegmatically strong-willed, a sort of *homo economus*. The natural world is Joan's unsuspected ally, a feminine counterbalance to the English demigod. It almost seems the hypnotically and sardonically witchy Catriona (Pamela Brown), perhaps the more natural partner to Roger Livesey's Laird, was the force stirring up the fury of the storm that keeps Joan from the island and ironically leads to Joan's betrothal to the Laird (a fantasy of the colony colonizing the empire). The whirlpool that almost drowns Livesey and Hiller—an effect Powell was quite proud of—appears to be a projection of Catriona's psychological Sturm and Drang as much as Joan's.

The clearest evocation of anti-colonial hostility in Powell's films occurs in the courtroom sequence in *A Matter of Life and Death*. The first Revolutionary patriot shot by the British in the beginning of the American Revolution (Raymond Massey) addresses a jury composed entirely of British colonial subjects: the fate of Peter (David Niven), an English poet, is entirely in the hands of those with eternal enmity towards the British Empire. Though this is a Pressburger scene that Powell was never completely satisfied with, this United Nations of anti-imperial feeling and recent colonial history is an extraordinary image. One can only imagine the passing discomfort of an English audience in 1945 for a film that was sponsored to help mend the breech in the Anglo-American alliance. Peter isn't punished for the sins of his fathers, nor can he claim any special privilege based on the historical glories of English history and culture. Powell's own ambivalence about being an English director comes through in many interviews. To Ian Christie he says, "We're far too inclined here to say we've got to create the British cinema. Why? God didn't ordain a British cinema." And at Midnight Sun: "If I hadn't started in Europe, not in England, but in France, with a great American company, Metro-Goldwyn, with a great director, Rex Ingram, I wouldn't have had the high ideals and the vision in front of my eyes that I have had all my life. And you wouldn't have had *Black Narcissus* and *the Red Shoes* and *The Tales of Hoffman*." On the other hand, Powell characterizes himself as very English and was committed to staying in England to make his films.

Each film of Michael Powell's, of The Archers', was a cinematic shot in the dark. The Archers, and Michael Powell solo, were always adding a new twist on an old formula, or a new formula itself: the documentary ghostliness of *Edge of the World*, the three dimensionality of Germans in *The Spy in Black* and *49th Parallel*, the epic satire of *The Life and Death of Colonel Blimp*, the perverse sexual implications in the war film *A Canterbury Tale*, the implicit imperiality and matte painted lushness of *Black Narcissus* (one of the most interesting melodramas of sexual repression), the regional, Hardyish determinism of *Gone to Earth*.

The years 1943–51, when The Archers made *Blimp, A Canterbury Tale, I Know Where I'm Going!, A Matter of Life and Death, Black Narcissus, The Red Shoes, The Small Back Room, Gone to Earth,* and *The Tales of Hoffman,* surely formed one of the more prodigious eras of creativity in twentieth-century cinema. This period combines the concentrated burst of Preston Sturges's films in the forties with the variety of genre and subject that William Wyler covered in his long career and some of the breathtaking use of color in Hitchcock's fifties films.

Michael Powell's encyclopedic memory gives ample due to the production designers, director of photography, editors, and producers who had more than a hand in crafting his films. In a sense, Powell argues for *both* an auteur and collaborative theory of filmmaking; his distinct vision could never have been realized without Pressburger, Junge, Cardiff, and Streeter, yet the images we see are products of his imagination. As he says at Midnight Sun, "My theme is continuity." The major cinematic dramatis personae in Powell's life (Harry Lackman and Rex Ingram, Jerry Jackson, Hitchcock, Joe Rock, Alexander Korda, Emeric Pressburger, David Selznick, Arthur Rank, John Davis, Leo Marks, Martin Scorsese, and Thelma Schoonmaker) form a quirky but continuous historical narrative which represents and transcends the history of film in the twentieth century.

Even the casual reader will note the recurring themes and narratives in interviews with Michael Powell: the importance of silent cinema to Powell's mise en scène; Hitchcock's recognition of the young still photographer and his generosity towards him; a long and somewhat tedious apprenticeship in "quota quickies" followed by the creative freedom granted by and then limited by Alexander Korda and Arthur Rank; the sublime meeting of minds between Powell and Pressburger and the unprecedented decision to present The Archers' films as "Written, produced, and directed by Michael Powell and Emeric Pressburger"; the displeasure of Churchill and the War Office when *Blimp* was in production; Emeric Pressburger's disastrous showing of *The Red Shoes* to Arthur Rank and John David; Leo Marx's cigar, always newly lit when he arrived to meet with Powell; the extension of long-term critical skepticism into moral hostility when *Peeping Tom* was released; the subsequent difficulties of Powell's career; his renaissance, both personally and professionally, through the offices, good will, and love tendered by Martin Scorsese, Francis Ford Coppola, an Thelma Schoonmaker. Other leitmotifs lightly or obsessively weave their place into a public life's narrative.

I find myself longing, at times for more interviewers like William Everson, Ian Christie, Richard Jameson, or Bertrand Tavernier. In many ways, Powell was a director's director, and some of the less skilled or less informed interviewers chase the rabbit of biography and personality too much instead of focusing on the work. But experientially central to reading through interviews is our sense of the questions we want asked, the answers we long to have exposed or explored. For one, I'd like to hear more from Powell on Buñuel, whom he calls, in *Million Dollar Movie,* "My master in the movies."[9] Powell asserts that all films are to some extent surreal in that they present an imaginary two-dimensional narrative with speaking characters, an illusion of living narrative that a director effaces or intensifies—a small step from certain versions of Lacanian film theory. I'd love to be able to read a more expansive version of Powell on surrealism and film, perhaps focusing on those occasions in his films that achieve a direct Brechtian distancing. The other directors Powell lists in his own pantheon—Chaplin, Disney, Hitchcock (the three directors who "saved the film business from going completely off the rails in my time . . ."[10]), Griffith, Murnau—all dovetail with his belief that "images are everything; words are used like music to distill emotion." Reading this, one wants to put in a word for Pressburger, except for the fact that Powell does so himself, insistently asserting his and Pressburger's equal contribution to The Archers' films. Inconsistency, after all, is an autobiographer's prerogative. Any time Powell starts speaking of specific films in depth, his or others', his witty expertise makes me long for more film critiques in the interviews. But as cogent a writer and speaker as Michael Powell was, Powell in print should point to the greater achievement: Powell's films.

Michael Powell was erudite, generous, literate, vexed, curious, fiercely independent, impatient with the business of film business, delighted by collaboration, and terribly loyal to his friends, notably the other Archer, Emeric Pressburger. The argument of innocence shows up repeatedly, poignantly, in many interviews. Speaking of the importance of narrative, Powell says, at Midnight Sun, "I don't think films have changed very much and I know that I haven't changed very much. I'm still the small boy that was determined to make films. I still think that the world as far as telling stories is very much the same." He goes on to speculate about his audience's response: "I'll bet you're just as thrilled now as I was in my mind back in '27, fifty years ago when I envisioned something like that, doing something like that with this wonderful medium of film. Which hasn't changed a sprocket hole since I started in it."

It is the policy of the University Press of Mississippi not to edit published interviews. Nevertheless, because of the transcripted (sometimes confusingly so) nature of some of these texts, some emendations and corrections were necessary, most of which were performed by Thelma Schoonmaker Powell.

I have many people to thank for their participation and cooperation in the production of this book. Foremost and first: Thelma Schoonmaker Powell, who was more than generous in putting her resources and those of the Michael Powell Archives, which she maintains, at my service, and who helped make several of the more important interviews coherent. The custodian of the archives, Marianne Bower, was invaluable in every way in the completion of this manuscript—in addition to her research, transcriptions, and answering a stream of questions from me that ranged from the serious to the ridiculous, Marianne is miraculously tonal, which I appreciated much during the longueurs that inevitably accompany editorial work (What's the weather like on the Upper East Side *now,* Marianne?). Two other members of the Schoonmaker crew, Sarah Feinberg and Justin Bonfiglio, also did yeowoman and yeoman work.

I also owe special thanks to Ian Christie, the central scholar of The Archers' work, for his help and support; to Vicky Mitchell of the BBC Rights Archive; to Mrs. Roy Plomley and her agent for the Roy Plomley estate, April Young; and to Dominique Duvert and Gina Honigsford for their excellent translations.

Whitney Huber Lazar found interviews in corners that I hadn't even thought of looking in and was general counsel to the entire project; I owe her a trip to Florida to count the ways. Robert Miklitsch (my dialectician), Ken Daley, Tony Sanders, George Hartley, Joan Connor, Kasia Marciniak, and Kamil Turowskii helped this and me along, and Max Statland, who took me to see *Jason and the Argonauts* quite a while ago, deserves nothing less than an endnote.

Notes

1. Michael Powell. "Mr. Powell Replies," *Picturegoer,* 30 December 1930.
2. R. Collins and Ian Christie, "Michael Powell," *Monogram* 3 (1972).
3. Kevin Gough-Yates, *Michael Powell,* published on the occasion of Europalia 73, Royal Film Archive of Belgium with the cooperation of the National Film Archive of Great Britain, Filmmuseum/Palais des Beaux-Arts/Brussels.
4. Collins and Christie.
5. Roger Manvell, "Your Questions Answered: Manvell Grills Powell," *The Penguin Film Review, 1946–1949,* vol. 1 (Rowan and Littlefield, 1977).
6. Collins and Christie.

7. Kevin Gough-Yates, *Michael Powell, In Collaboration with Emeric Pressburger* (London: British Film Institute, 1971).

8. Ibid.

9. Michael Powell, *Million Dollar Movie* (London: Mandarin, 1992).

10. Michael Powell, *A Life in Movies: An Autobiography* (London: Heinemann, 1986).

CHRONOLOGY

1905 Michael Latham Powell born in Bekesbourne near Canturbury, Kent, September 30, to Thomas and Mabel Corbett Powell.

1918 Powell's older brother John dies of peritonitis.

1919–21 Staying with his father at his hotel at Cap Ferrat, near Monte Carlo, Michael Powell is introduced to Harry Lachman, who is working with Rex Ingram. Lachman hires Powell, who serves as a grip for *Mare Nostrum* and as an actor and assistant for *The Magician* and *The Garden of Allah.*

1927 Powell is signed by Lachman and appear in a series of short comic films ("Travelaughs").

1928 Powell is hired as stills photographer at Elstree studios, meets Hitchcock and photographs his *Champagne.* Re-edits Lupu Pick's *A Knight in London.*

1929 Co-writes Hitchcock's *Blackmail.*

1931 Directs first film, *Two Crowded Hours,* a "quota qickie." Powell goes on to direct over fifteen additional quota quickies in the next seven years.

1938 Directs *Edge of the World,* Powell's first original full-length film. It opens to strong notices, and he is signed to a one-year contract by Alexander Korda, who brings Powell together with Emeric Pressburger, a Hungarian immigrant with long screenwriting experience in German film.

1939 *The Spy in Black,* first collaboration of Powell and Pressburger.

1940 *Contraband,* a thriller, is released; second collaboration of Powell and Pressburger, and second film with Conrad Veidt. Powell is called in by Alexander Korda to direct parts of *Thief of Bagdad,* already under production.

1941 Powell travels to Canada to scout locations for *49th Parallel,* released that year. Pressburger wins Oscar for script.

1942 *One of Our Aircraft Is Missing.* Powell and Pressburger form The Archers production company, agree to shared credit: written, produced, and directed by Michael Powell and Emeric Pressburger.

1943 *The Silver Fleet* released, an Archers production directed by Vernon C. Sewell. Despite opposition from Winston Churchill and the War Office, and their refusal to release Laurence Oliver for the role of "Sugar" Candy, *The Life and Death of Colonel Blimp* is released, starring Roger Livesey. Marries Frankie Reidy, July 1. Powell has despaired of his pending marriage to Deborah Kerr taking place. (Her contract had been sold to MGM by Gabby Pascal.)

1944 *A Canterbury Tale,* which first raises the hackles of English film critics due to the strangeness of Thomas Culpepper's glue-throwing onto girls' hair. It is the first Archers "failure," with critics and at the box office.

1945 *I Know Where I'm Going!,* his second of three Archers films.

1946 *A Matter of Life and Death,* first Archers color film, following wartime restrictions. Powell considers it his best.

1947 *Black Narcissus* wins Oscar for color cinematography.

1948 *The Red Shoes.* Producer J. Arthur Rank walks out of screening without a word, convinced the film will be a financial disaster. It is booked into a theatre in New York, where it runs for two years.

1949 *The Small Back Room,* Powell and Pressburger's first film back with

Alexander Korda. Powell later says the public was tired of war films at the time, despite the film's quality. It is later regarded as one of The Archers' best films.

1950 *Gone to Earth,* co-produced by Korda and David O. Selznick. Selznick, furious about the final product, hires Rouben Mamoulian to re-shoot footage. *The Elusive Pimpernel.* Powell directs despite misgivings, convinced by Korda. He later says, "It was a complete disaster."

1951 *The Tales of Hoffman.* Special Jury Prize, Cannes.

1952 Powell begins preliminary planning for a film version of *The Tempest,* which despite many attempts, he will never film.

1955 *Oh . . . Rosalinda!,* based on Strauss's *Die Fledermaus.* Considered the least successful of The Archers' "theatrical" films.

1956 Death of Alexander Korda. *The Battle of the River Plate,* special screening at Royal Film Performance. *Ill Met by Moonlight,* last film of The Archers.

1959 *Luna De Miel* (*Honeymoon*): versions of ballets *El Amor Brujo* and *Los Amantes de Teruel.* Special Prize, Cannes.

1960 *Peeping Tom* is savaged by the critics. The film is pulled from theaters and effectively ends Powell's career as a commercial film director. Five months later, *Psycho* opens in England, to much criticism, but commercial success, which Powell later credits to his more pervasive sense of humor.

1961 *The Queen's Guards.*

1962–66 Powell directs episodes of several TV dramas in England and the U.S.

1964 *Bluebeard's Castle,* based on Bartok's opera. Unreleased in Great Britain.

1966 *They're a Weird Mob,* filmed in Australia.

1968 *Age of Consent,* the story of a painter, produced by and starring James Mason. Powell later feels he never got the texture of the paintings themselves right. Last of Michael Powell's full-length films.

1972 *The Boy Who Turned Yellow,* a children's film, and Powell and Pressburger's last cinematic collaboration. Children's Film Foundation Award, 1978.

1973 Powell tries again, unsuccessfully, to find backing for *The Tempest,* with Mia Farrow as his Ariel.

1978 *The Life and Death of Colonel Blimp* reconstructed by the National Film Archive.

1978 Powell and Pressburger retrospective at the National Film Theatre in London.

1983 Frankie Reidy Powell dies July 5.

1984 May 19, Powell marries Thelma Schoonmaker, editor (*Raging Bull, GoodFellas, The Age of Innocence*).

1986 First volume of Powell's autobiography, *A Life in Movies,* published by Heinemann in Great Britain and Knopf in the U.S.

1988 Emeric Pressburger dies February 5.

1990 Michael Powell dies in Avening, Gloucester, February 19.

1992 *Million Dollar Movie,* second volume of Powell's autobiography, completed by Ian Christie and Thelma Schoonmaker, published by Heinemann in Great Britain and Random House in the U.S., with an introduction by Martin Scorsese. Powell imaginatively reconstructs Pressburger's last hours, placing the two of them together, which is where he ends his autobiography.

FILMOGRAPHY

1931
TWO CROWDED HOURS
Director: **Michael Powell**
Screenplay: J. Jefferson Farjeon
Producer: Jerome Jackson, Harry Cohen
Cinematography: Geoffrey Faithfull
Art Director: C. Saunders
Editor: A. Seaborne
Cast: John Longden (Harry Fielding), Jane Welsh (Joyce Danton), Jerry Verno (Jim), Michael Hogan (Scammell), Edward Barber (Tom Murray)
B&W
43 minutes

1932
MY FRIEND THE KING
Director: **Michael Powell**
Screenplay: J. Jefferson Farjeon, from his own story
Producer: Jerome Jackson
Cinematography: Geoffrey Faithfull
Art Director: C. Saunders
Editor: A. Seaborne
Cast: Jerry Verno (Jim), Robert Holmes (Captain Felz), Tracy Holmes (Count Huelin), Eric Pavitt (King Ludwig), Phyllis Loring (Princess Helma), Luli Hohenberg (Countess Zena), H. Saxon Snell (Karl), Victor Fairley (Josef)

B&W
47 minutes

RYNOX
Director: **Michael Powell**
Screenplay: Jerome Jackson, **Michael Powell**, Philip MacDonald, from MacDonald's novel
Producer: Jerome Jackson
Cinematography: Geoffrey Faithfull, Arthur Grant
Art Director: C. Saunders
Editor: A. Seaborne
Cast: Stewart Rome (Boswell Marsh/F. X. Benedik), Edward Willard (Captain James), Charles Paton (Samuel Richforth), Fletcher Lightfoot (Prout), Sybil Grove (Secretary), Leslie Mitchell (Woolrich)
B&W
48 minutes

THE RASP
Director: **Michael Powell**
Screenplay: Philip MacDonald, from his own story
Producer: Jerome Jackson
Cinematography: Geoffrey Faithfull
Art Director: Frank Wells
Cast: Claude Horton (Anthony Gethryn), Phyllis Loring (Lucia Masterson), C. M. Hallard (Sir Arthur Coates), James Raglan (Alan Deacon), Thomas Weguelin (Inspector Boyd), Carol Coombe (Dora Masterson), Leonard Brett (Jimmy Masterson)
B&W
44 minutes

THE STAR REPORTER
Director: **Michael Powell**
Screenplay: Ralph Smart, Philip MacDonald, from MacDonald's story
Producer: Jerome Jackson
Cinematography: Geoffrey Faithfull
Additional Photography: **Michael Powell**
Art Director: Frank Wells

Cast: Harold French (Major Starr), Isla Bevan (Lady Susan Loman), Garry Marsh (Mandel), Spencer Trevor (Lord Longbourne), Anthony Holles (Bonzo), Noel Dainton (Colonel), Elsa Graves (Oliver), Philip Morant (Jeff)
B&W
44 Minutes

HOTEL SPLENDIDE
Director: **Michael Powell**
Screenplay: Ralph Smart, from a story by Philip MacDonald
Producer: Jerome Jackson
Cinematography: Geoffrey Faithfull, Arthur Grant
Editor: A. Seabourne
Art Director: Charles Saunders
Cast: Jerry Verno (Jerry Mason), Anthony Holles ("Mrs. LeGrange"), Edgar Norfolk ("Gentleman Charlie"), Philip Morant (Mr. Meek), Sybil Grove (Mrs. Harkness), Vera Sherborne (Joyce Dacre), Paddy Browne (Mrs. Meek), **Michael Powell** (Eavesdropping Device Operator)
B&W
53 minutes

C.O.D.
Director: **Michael Powell**
Screenplay: Ralph Smart, from a story by Philip MacDonald
Producer: Jerome Jackson
Cinematography: Geoffrey Faithfull
Art Director: Frank Wells
Cast: Garry Marsh (Peter Craven), Hope Davey (Frances), Arthur Stratton (Briggs), Sybil Grove (Mrs. Briggs), Roland Culver (Edward), Peter Gawthorne (Detective), Cecil Ramage (Vyner), Bruce Belfrage (Philip)
B&W
66 minutes

HIS LORDSHIP
Director: **Michael Powell**
Screenplay: Ralph Smart, based on the novel *The Right Honourable*, by Oliver Madox Heuffer
Producer: Jerome Jackson

Cinematography: Geoffrey Faithfull
Music/lyrics: V. C. Clinton-Baddeley and Eric Maschwitz
Art Director: Frank Wells
Cast: Jerry Verno (Bert Gibbs), Janet McGrew (Ilya Myona), Ben Weldon (Washington Lincoln), Polly Ward (Leninia), Peter Gawthorne (Ferguson), Muriel George (Mrs. Gibbs), Michael Hogan (Comrade Curzon), V. C. Clinton-Baddeley (Comrade Howard), Patrick Ludlow (Honourable Grimsthwaite).
B&W
77 minutes

1933
BORN LUCKY
Director: **Michael Powell**
Screenplay: Ralph Smart, from the novel *Mops*, by Oliver Sandys
Producer: Jerome Jackson
Cinematography: Geoffrey Faithfull
Art Director: Ian Campbell-Gray
Cast: Talbot O'Farrell (Turnips), Renee Ray (Mops), John Longden (Frank Dale), Ben Weldon (Harriman), Helen Ferrers (Lady Chard), Barbara Gott (Cook), Paddy Browne (Patty), Roland Gillett (John Chard)
B&W
78 minutes

THE FIRE RAISERS
Director: **Michael Powell**
Screenplay: **Michael Powell**, Jerome Jackson from his original story
Producer: Jerome Jackson
Cinematography: Leslie Rowson
Editor: D. N. Twist
Art Director: Alfred Junge
Cast: Leslie Banks (Jim Bronson), Anne Grey (Arden Brent), Francis L. Sullivan (Stedding), Laurence Anderson (Twist), Harry Caine (Bates), Joyce Kirby (Polly), George Merritt (Sonners), **Michael Powell** (Radio Operator)
B&W
77 minutes

1934
THE NIGHT OF THE PARTY (U.S. TITLE: THE MURDER PARTY)
Director: **Michael Powell**
Screenplay: Ralph Smart, from the play by Roland Pertwee and John Hastings Turner
Producer: Jerome Jackson
Cinematography: Glen MacWilliams
Art Director: Alfred Junge
Cast: Leslie Banks (Sir John Holland), Ian Hunter (Guy Kennington), Jane Baxter (Peggy Studholme), Ernest Thesiger (Chiddiatt), Viola Keats (Joan Holland), Malcolm Keen (Lord Studholme), Jane Millican (Anna Chiddiat), Muriel Aked (Princess Amelta of Corsova), John Turnbull (Ramage), Laurence Anderson (Defense Counsel), W. Graham Brown (General Piddington), Louis Goodrich (Judge), Cecil Ramage (Howard Vernon), Disney Roebuck (Butler), Gerald Barry (Baron Cziatch), Gordon Begg (Miles)
B&W
61 minutes

RED ENSIGN (U.S. TITLE: STRIKE!)
Director: **Michael Powell**
Screenplay: **Michael Powell**, Jerome Jackson
Executive Producer: Michael Balcon
Producer: Jerome Jackson
Cinematography: Leslie Rowson
Editor: Geoffrey Barkas
Art Director: Alfred Junge
Cast: Leslie Banks (David Barr), Carol Goodner (June MacKinnon), Frank Vosper (Lord Dean), Alfred Drayton (Manning), Donald Calthrop (MacLeod), Allan Jeayes (Emerson—"Grierson"), Campbell Gullan (Hannay), Percy Parsons (Casey), Fewlass Llewellyn (Sir Gregory), Henry Oscar (Raglan), Henry Caine (Bassett), John Laurie (Worker), Frederick Piper (Bowler-hatted Man in Bar)
B&W
69 minutes

SOMETHING ALWAYS HAPPENS
Director: **Michael Powell**
Screenplay: Brock Williams

Executive Producer: Irving Asher
Cinematography: Basil Emmott
Editor: Ralph Dawson
Art Director: Peter Proud
Cast: Ian Hunter (Peter Middleton), Nancy O'Neil (Cynthia Hatch), Peter Gawthorne (Benjamin Hatch), John Singer (Billy), Muriel George (Mrs. Badger, Landlady), Barry Livesey (George Hamlin), Millicent Wolf (Glenda), Louie Emery (Mrs. Tremlett), Reg Marcus ("Coster"), George Zucco (Proprietor of Cafe de Paris)
B&W
69 minutes

1935
THE GIRL IN THE CROWD
Director: **Michael Powell**
Screenplay: Brock Williams
Executive Producer: Irving Asher
Cinematography: Basil Emmott
Editor: Bert Bates
Art Director: Peter Proud
Cast: Barry Clifton (David Gordon), Patricia Hilliard (Marian), Googie Withers (Sally), Harold French (Bob), Clarence Blakiston (Mr. Peabody), Margaret Gunn (Joyce), Richard Littledale (Bill Manners), Phyllis Morris (Mrs. Lewis), Patric Knowles (Tom Burrows), Marjorie Corbett (Secretary), Brenda Lawless (Policewoman), Barbara Waring (Mannequin), Eve Lister (Ruby), Betty Lyne (Phyllis), Melita Bell (Assistant Manager), John Wood (Harry)
B&W
52 minutes

THE LOVE NEST
Director: **Michael Powell**
Screenplay: Selwyn Jepson, from a story by Jack Celestin
Producer: Leslie Landau
Cinematography: Arthur Crabtree
Cast: Judy Gunn (Mary Lee), Louis Hayward (John Gregg), Dave Hutcheson (Thompson), Googie Withers (Minnie), Morris Harvey (Company President), Aubrey Dexter (Vice President), Eve Turner (Kathleen), Bernard Miles (Allan),

Jack Knight (Managing Director), Gilbert Davis (Hosiah Smith), Shayle Gardner (Night Watchman), James Craig (Boiler Man), Thorley Walters and Ian Wilson (Chemists)
B&W
65 minutes

THE PHANTOM LIGHT
Director: **Michael Powell**
Screenplay: Ralph Smart, from the play *Haunted Light*, by Evadne Price and Joan Roy Byford
Producer: Jerome Jackson
Cinematography: Roy Kellino
Music: Louis Levy
Art Director: Alex Vetchinsky
Editor: Derek Twist
Cast: Binnie Hale (Alice Bright), Gordon Harker (Sam Higgins), Ian Hunter (Jim Pearce), Donald Calthrop (David Owen), Milton Rosmer (Dr. Carey), Reginald Tate (Tom Evans), Mickey Brantford (Bob Peters), Herbert Lomas (Claff Owen), Fewlass Llewellyn (Griffith Owen), Alice O'Day (Mrs. Owen), Barry O'Neill (Captain Pearce), Edgar K. Bruce (Sergeant Owen), Louie Emery (Station Mistress), John Singer (Cabin Boy)
B&W
76 minutes

THE PRICE OF A SONG
Director: **Michael Powell**
Producer: **Michael Powell**
Screenplay: Anthony Gittens
Cinematography: Jimmy Wilson
Cast: Campbell Gullan (Arnold Grierson), Marjorie Corbett (Margaret Nevern), Gerald Fielding (Michael Hardwicke), Dora Barton (Letty Grierson), Charles Mortimer (Oliver Broom), Oriel Ross (Elsie), Henry Caine (Stringer), Sybil Grove (Mrs. Bancroft), Eric Maturin (Nevern), Felix Aylmer (Graham), Cynthia Stock (Mrs. Bush), Mavis Clair (Maudie Bancroft)
B&W
67 minutes

SOMEDAY
Director: **Michael Powell**
Screenplay: Brock Williams, from the novel *Young Nowhere* by I. A. R. Wylie
Producer: Irving Asher
Cinematography: Basil Emmott and Monty Berman
Art Director: Ian Campbell-Gray
Editor: Bert Bates
Cast: Esmond Knight (Curley Blake), Margaret Lockwood (Emily), Henry Mollison (Canley), Sunday Wilshin (Betty), Raymond Lovell (Carr), Ivor Barnard (Hope), George Pughe (Milkman), Jane Cornell (Nurse)
B&W
68 Minutes

1936
HER LAST AFFAIRE
Director: **Michael Powell**
Screenplay: Ian Dalrymple, from the play *S.O.S.* by Walter Ellis
Producer: Simon Rowson
Cinematography: Geoffrey Faithfull
Editor: Ian Dalrymple
Cast: Hugh Williams (Alan Heriot), Viola Keats (Lady Avril Weyre), Francis L. Sullivan (Sir Julian Weyre), Sophie Stewart (Judy Weyre), Felix Aylmer (Lord Carnforth), Cecil Parker (Sir Arthur Harding), John Gardner (Boxall), Henry Caine (Inspector Marsh), Gerrard Tyrell (Martin)
B&W
78 minutes

THE BROWN WALLET
Director: **Michael Powell**
Screenplay: Ian Dalrymple, from a story by Stacy Aumonier
Executive Producer: Irving Asher
Cinematography: Basil Emmott
Cast: Patric Knowles (John Gillespie), Nancy O'Neil (Eleanor), Henry Caine (Simmonds), Henrietta Watson (Aunt Mary), Charlotte Leigh (Miss Barton), Shayle Gardner (Wotherspoone), Edward Dalby (Minting), Eliot Makeham (Hobday), Bruce Winston (Julian Thorpe), Jane Millican (Miss Bloxham), Louis Goodrich (Coroner), Dick Francis and George Mills (Detectives)

B&W
68 minutes

CROWN V. STEVENS
Director: **Michael Powell**
Screenplay: Brock Williams, from the novel *Third Time Unlucky* by Laurence Meynell
Executive Producer: Irving Asher
Cinematography: Basil Emmott
Editor: Bert Bates
Cast: Beatrix Thompson (Doris Stevens), Patric Knowles (Chris Jansen), Reginald Purdell (Alf), Glennis Lorimer (Molly), Allan Jeayes (Inspector Carter), Frederick Piper (Arthur Stevens), Googie Withers (Ella), Mabel Poulton (Mamie), Morris Harvey (Julius Bayleck), Billy Watts (Joe Andrews), Davina Craig (Maggie)
B&W
66 minutes

THE MAN BEHIND THE MASK
Director: **Michael Powell**
Screenplay: Ian Hay, Sidney Courtenay. Adapted by Jack Byrd from the novel *The Chase of the Golden Plate* by Jacques Futrelle
Producer: Joe Rock
Cinematography: Ernest Palmer
Cast: Hugh Williams (Nick Barclay), Jane Baxter (June Slade), Maurice Schwartz (The Master), Donald Calthrop (Dr. Walpole), Henry Oscar (Officer), Peter Gawthorne (Lord Slade), Kitty Kelly (Miss Weeks), Ronald Ward (Jimmy Slade), George Merritt (Mallory), Reginald Tate (Hayden), Ivor Barnard (Hewitt), Hal Gordon (Sergeant), Gerald Fielding (Harah), Barbara Everest (Lady Slade), Wilfred Caithness (Butler), Moyra Fagan (Nora), Sid Crossley (Postman)
B&W
79 minutes

1937
THE EDGE OF THE WORLD
Director: **Michael Powell**

Screenplay: **Michael Powell**
Producer: Joe Rock
Cinematography: Ernest Palmer, Skeets Kelly, Monty Berman
Production Manager: Gerard Blattner
Music: Cyril Ray, orchestrations by W. L. Williamson
Editor: Derek Twist
Cast: John Laurie (Peter Manson), Belle Chrystall (Ruth Manson), Eric Berry (Robbie Manson), Kitty Kirwan (Jean Manson), Finlay Currie (James Gray), Niall MacGinnis (Andrew Gray), Grant Sutherland (John, the Catechist), Campbell Robson (Dunbar, the Laird), George Summers (Skipper), Margaret Grieg (Baby), **Michael Powell** (Mr. Graham), Frances Reidy (Woman on Boat), Sydney Streeter (Man at Dance)
B&W
81 minutes

1939
THE SPY IN BLACK (U.S. TITLE: U BOAT 29)
Director: **Michael Powell**
Screenplay: Emeric Pressburger, from Roland Pertwee's adaptation of a novel by J. Storer Clouston
Producer: Irving Asher
Cinematography: Bernard Browne
Production Designer: Vincent Korda
Art Director: Frederick Pusey
Music: Miklós Rózsa
Editor: Hugh Stewart
Cast: Conrad Veidt (Captain Ernst Hardt), Valerie Hobson (Frau Tiel, really Jill Blacklock), Sebastian Shaw (Lieutenant Ashington, really Commander David Blacklock), Marius Goring (Lieutenant Schuster), June Duprez (Anne Burnett), Athole Stewart (Reverend Hector Matthews), Agnes Laughlin (Mrs. Matthews), Helen Haye (Mrs. Sedley), Cyril Raymond (Rev. John Harris), Hay Petrie (Engineer), Grant Sutherland (Bob Bratt), Robert Rendel (Admiral), Mary Morris (Chauffeuse), George Summers (Captain Ratter), Margaret Moffatt (Kate), Kenneth Warrington (Commander Dennis), Torin Thatcher (Submarine Officer), Bernard Miles (Hans), Skelton Knaggs (German Orderly), Diana Sinclair-Hall, Esma Cannon
B&W
82 minutes

THE LION HAS WINGS
Director: **Michael Powell**
Screenplay: Adrian Brunel and E. V. H. Emmett, from a story by Ian Dalrymple
Producer: Alexander Korda
Cinematography: Harry Stradling
Art Director: Vincent Korda
Music: Richard Addinsell
Editor: William Hornbeck
Cast: Merle Oberon (Mrs. Richardson), Ralph Richardson (Wing Commander Richardson), June Duprez (June), Robert Douglas (Briefing Officer), Anthony Bushell (Pilot), Derrick de Marney (Bill), Brian Worth (Bobby), Austin Trevor (Schulemburg), Ivan Brandt (Officer), G. H. Mulcaster (Controller), Herbert Lomas (Holveg), Milton Rosmer (Head of Observer Corps), Robert Rendel (Chief of Air Staff), E. V. H. Emmett (Narrator, U.K. version), Lowell Thomas (Narrator, U.S. version), Bernard Miles (Observer), John Longden, Ian Fleming, Miles Malleson, Charles Carson, John Penrose, Frank Tickle, Torin Thatcher.
B&W
76 minutes

1940
CONTRABAND (U.S. TITLE: BLACKOUT)
Director: **Michael Powell**
Screenplay: **Michael Powell**, from original story by Emeric Pressburger
Producer: John Corfield
Cinematography: F. A. Young
Art Director: Alfred Junge
Music: Richard Addinsell
Editor: John Seabourne
Cast: Conrad Veidt (Captain Anderson), Valerie Hobson (Mrs. Sorenson), Hay Petrie (Mate of SS Helving/Chef of "Three Vikings"), Esmond Knight (Mr. Pidgeon), Raymond Lovell (Van Dyne), Charles Victor (Hendrick), Henry Wolston (1st Danish Waiter), Julian Vedey (2nd Danish Waiter), Sydney Moncton (3rd Danish Waiter), Hamilton Keen (4th Danish Waiter), Phoebe Kershaw (Miss Lang), Leo Genn (1st Brother Grimm), Dennis Arundell (Lieman), Harold Warrender (Lt. Commander Ellis RN), Joss Ambler (Lt. Commander

Ashton RNR), Molly Hamley Clifford (Baroness Hekla), Eric Berry (Mr. Abo), Olga Edwardes (Mrs. Abo), Toni Gable (Mrs. Karoly), Desmond Jeans (1st Karoly), Eric Hales (2nd Karoly), Jean Roberts (Hanson), Manning Whiley (Manager of "Mousetrap"), Eric Maturin, John Londen (Passport Officers)
B&W
92 minutes

THE THIEF OF BAGDAD
Directors: Ludwig Berger, **Michael Powell,** Tim Whelan (Uncredited: Zoltan Korda, William Cameron Menzies, Alexander Korda)
Screenplay: Lajos Biró; adaptation/dialogue by Miles Malleson
Producer: Alexander Korda
Cinematography: Georges Périnal
Art Director: Vincent Kalmus, assisted by W. Percy Day, William Cameron Menzies, Frederick Pusey, Ferdinand Bellan
Music: Miklós Rózsa
Special Effects: Lawrence Butler
Editor: William Hornbeck
Cast: Conrad Veidt (Jaffar), Sabu (Abu), June Duprez (Princess), John Justin (Ahmad), Rex Ingram (Djinni), Miles Malleson (Sultan), Morton Selten (King), Mary Morris (Halima), Bruce Winston (Merchant), Hay Petrie (Astrologer), Roy Emerton (Jailer), Allan Jeayes (Storyteller), Adelaide Hall (Singer)
Color
106 minutes

1941
AN AIRMAN'S LETTER TO HIS MOTHER
Producer: **Michael Powell**
Screenplay: **Michael Powell**
Cinematography: **Michael Powell,** with additional photography by Bernard Browne
Narrated by John Gielgud
B&W
5 minutes

49TH PARALLEL (U.S. TITLE: THE INVADERS)
Director: **Michael Powell**
Screenplay: Emeric Pressburger

Producer: **Michael Powell**
Cinematography: Frederick Young
Art Director: David Rawnsley
Music: Ralph Vaughan Williams
Editor: David Lean
Cast: Eric Portman (Lieutenant Hirth), Richard George (Kommandant Bernsdorff), Raymond Lovell (Lt. Kuhnecker), Niall MacGinnis (Vogel), Peter Moore (Kranz), John Chandos (Lohrmann), Basil Appleby (Jahner), Laurence Olivier (Johnnie, the Trapper), Finlay Currie (Factor), Ley On (Nick the Eskimo), Anton Walbrook (Peter), Glynis Johns (Anna), Charles Victor (Andreas), Frederick Piper (David), Leslie Howard (Philip Armstrong Scott), Tawera Moana (George the Indian), Eric Clavering (Art), Carles Rolfe (Bob), Raymond Massey (Andy Brock), Theodore Salt, O. W. Fonger (U.S. Customs Officers)
B&W
104 minutes

1942
ONE OF OUR AIRCRAFT IS MISSING
Director: **Michael Powell**
Screenplay: Emeric Pressburger and **Michael Powell**
Producer: John Corfield, **Michael Powell**, and Emeric Pressburger
Cinematography: Ronald Neame
Art Director: David Rawnsley
Editor: David Lean
Cast: Godfrey Tearle (Sir George Corbett), Eric Portman (Tom Earnshaw), Hugh Williams (Frank Shelley), Bernard Miles (Geoff Hickman), Hugh Burden (John Glyn Haggard), Emrys Jones (Bob Ashley), Pamela Brown (Els Meertens), Joyce Redman (Jet Van Dieren), Googie Withers (Joe de Vries), Hay Petrie (Piet van Dieren, Burgomaster), Selma van Dias (Burgomaster's Wife), Arnold Marle (Pieter Sluys), Robert Helpmann (Julius De Jong), Peter Ustinov (Priest), Alec Clunes (Organist), Hector Abbas (Driver), James Carson (Louis), Bill Akkerman (Willem), Joan Akkerman (Maartje), Peter Schenke (Hendrik), Valerie Moon (Jannie), John Salew (Sentry), William d'Arcy (German Officer), David Ward (First Airman), Robert Duncan (Second Airman), Roland Culver (Naval Officer), Robert Beatty (Hopkins), **Michael Powell** (Dispatching Officer), Stewart Rome (Commander Reynold), David Evans

(Len Martin), John Longden (Man), Gerry Wilmott (Announcer), John Arnold, James Donald, John England, Gordon Jackson
B&W
102 minutes

1943
THE LIFE AND DEATH OF COLONEL BLIMP
Written, produced, and directed by **Michael Powell** and Emeric Pressburger (The Archers)
Cinematography: Georges Périnal
Production Designer: Alfred Junge
Production Manager: Sydney Streeter
Music: Allan Gray
Editor: John Seabourne
Cast: Anton Wilbrook (Theo Kretschmar-Schuldorff), Roger Livesey (Clive Candy), Deborah Karr (Edith Hunter/Barbara Wynne/Angela "Johnny" Cannon), Roland Culver (Colonel Betteridge), James McKechnie (Lieutenant Spud Wilson), Albert Lieven (von Ritter), Arthur Wontner (Counsellor), David Hutcheson (Hoppy), Ursula Jeans (Frau von Kalteneck), John Laurie (John Montgomery Murdoch), Harry Welchman (Major John E. Davis), Reginald Tate (Van Zijl), A. E. Matthews (President of Tribunal), Carle Jaffe (Von Reumann), Valentine Dyall (Von Schonborn), Muriel Aked (Aunt Margaret Hamilton), Felix Aylmer (Bishop), Frith Banbury (Babyface Fitzroy), Neville Mapp (Stuffy Graves), Vincent Holman (Club Porter, 1942), Spencer Trevor (Period Blimp), Dennis Arundel (Cafe Orchestra Leader), James Knight (Club Porter, 1902), David Ward (Kaunitz), Jan van Loewen (Indignant Citizen), Eric Maturin (Colonel Goodhead), Robert Harris (Embassy Secretary), Count Zichy (Colonel Borg), Jane Millican (Nurse Erna), Phyllis Morris (Pebble), Diana Marshall (Sybil), Captain W. H. Barrett (Texan), Corporal Thomas Palmer (Sergeant), Yvonne André (Nun), Marjorie Greasley (Matron), Helen Debroy (Mrs. Wynne), Norman Pierce (Mr. Wynne), Edward Cooper (BBC Official), Joan Swinstead (Secretary), Wally Patch (Sergeant clearing debris), Ferdy Mayne (Prussian Student), John Boxer (Soldier), John Varley, Patrick Macnee
Technicolor
163 minutes

THE VOLUNTEER
Written, produced, and directed by **Michael Powell** and Emeric Pressburger (The Archers)
Cinematography: Freddie Ford
Production Manager: Sydney Streeter
Music: Allan Gray
Editor: John Seabourne
Cast: Ralph Richardson (himself), Pat McGrath (Fred Davey), Laurence Olivier, **Michael Powell**
B&W
46 minutes

1944
A CANTERBURY TALE
Written, produced, and directed by **Michael Powell** and Emeric Pressburger (The Archers)
Cinematography: Erwin Hillier
Production Designer: Alfred Junge
Music: Allan Gray
Editor: John Seabourne
Cast: Eric Portman (Thomas Colpeper, JP), Sheila Sim (Alison Smith), Sgt. John Sweet (Bob Johnson), Dennis Price (Peter Gibbs), Esmond Knight (Narrator/Seven-Sisters Soldier/Village Idiot), Charles Hawtrey (Thomas Duckett), Hay Petrie (Woodcock), George Merritt (Ned Horton), Edward Rigby (Jim Horton), Freda Jackson (Prudence Honeywood), Betty Jardine (Fee Baker), Eliot Makeham (Organist), Harvey Golden (Sgt. Roczinsky), Leonard Smith (Leslie), James Tamsitt (Terry), David Todd (David)
B&W
124 minutes

1945
I KNOW WHERE I'M GOING!
Written, produced, and directed by **Michael Powell** and Emeric Pressburger (The Archers)
Cinematography: Erwin Hillier
Art Director: Alfred Junge
Music: Allan Gray
Editor: John Seabourne

Cast: Wendy Hiller (Joan Webster), Roger Livesy (Torquil MacNeil), George Carney (Mr. Webster), Pamela Brown (Catriona Potts), Walter Hudd (Hunter), Capt. Duncan MacKechnie (Captain "Lochinvar"), Ian Sadler (Iain), Finlay Currie (Ruairidh Mor), Murdo Morrison (Kenny), Margot Fitzsimmons (Bridie), Capt. C. W. R. Knight (Colonel Barnstaple), Donald Strachan (Shepherd), John Rae (Old Shepherd), Duncan McIntyre (Old Shepherd's Son), Jean Cadell (Postmistress), Norman Shelley (Sir Robert Bellinger), Ivy Milton (Peigi), Anthony Eustrel (Hopper), Petula Clark (Cheril), Alec Faversham (Martin), Catherine Lacey (Mrs. Robinson), Valentine Dyall (Mr. Robinson), Nancy Price (Rebecca Crozier), Herbert Lomas (Mr. Campbell), Kitty Kirwan (Mrs. Campbell), John Laurie (John Campbell), Graham Moffat (RAF Sergeant), Boyd Stevens, Maxwell Kennedy, Jean Houston (Singers in Ceildhe), Arthur Chesney (Harmonica Player), Mr. Ramshaw (Torquil, the Eagle)
B&W
92 minutes

1946
A MATTER OF LIFE AND DEATH (U.S. TITLE: STAIRWAY TO HEAVEN)
Written, produced, and directed by **Michael Powell** and Emeric Pressburger (The Archers)
Cinematography: Jack Cardiff
Production Designer: Alfred Junge
Music: Allan Gray
Editor: John Seabourne
Cast: David Niven (Peter Carter), Kim Hunter (June), Marius Goring (Conductor 71), Roger Livesey (Dr. Reeves), Robert Coote (Bob), Kathleen Byron (Angel), Richard Attenborough (English Pilot), Bonar Colleano (American Pilot), Joan Maude (Chief Recorder), Edwin Max (Dr. McEwen), Abraham Sofaer (Judge), Raymond Massey (Abraham Farlan), Robert Atkins (Vicar), Betty Potter (Mrs. Tucker), Bob Roberts (Dr. Gaertler)
Technicolor
104 minutes

1947
BLACK NARCISSUS
Written, produced, and directed by **Michael Powell** and Emeric Pressburger (The Archers)

Cinematography: Jack Cardiff
Production Designer: Alfred Junge
Music: Brian Easdale
Editor: Reginald Mills
Cast: Deborah Kerr (Sister Clodagh), Sabu (Young General), David Farrar (Mr. Dean), Flora Robson (Sister Philippa), Esmond Knight (Old General), Kathleen Byron (Sister Ruth), Jenny Laird (Sister Honey), Judith Furse (Sister Briony), May Hallatt (Angu Ayah), Shaun Noble (Con), Eddie Waley Jr. (Joseph Anthony), Nancy Roberts (Mother Dorothea), Jean Simmons (Kanchi)
Technicolor
100 minutes

1948
THE RED SHOES
Written, produced, and directed by **Michael Powell** and Emeric Pressburger (The Archers)
Cinematography: Jack Cardiff
Production Designer: Hein Heckroth
Art Director: Arthur Lawson
Special Effects: F. George Gunn and D. Hague
Music: Brian Easdale, Sir Thomas Beecham
Choreographer: Robert Helpmann
Editor: Reginald Mills
Cast: Marius Goring (Julian Craster), Anton Walbrook (Boris Lermontov), Moira Shearer (Victoria Page), Léonide Massine (Ljubov), Austin Trevor (Professor Palmer), Esmond Knight (Livy), Eric Berry (Dimitri), Irene Browne (Lady Neston), Ludmilla Tchérina (Boronskaja), Jerry Verno (Stage Door Keeper), Robert Helpmann (Ivan Boleslawsky), Albert Basserman (Ratov), Derek Elphinstone (Lord Oldham), Madame Rambert (herself), Joy Rawlins (Gladys, Victoria's Friend), Jean Short (Terry), Gordon Littmann (Ike), Julia Lang (Balletomane), Bill Shine (Beardie, her companion), Marcel Poncin (M. Boudin), Michel Bazalgette (M. Rideaut), Yvonne André (Victoria's Dresser), Hay Petrie (Boisson), George Woodbridge (Doorman)
Technicolor
133 minutes

1949
THE SMALL BACK ROOM
Produced and directed by **Michael Powell** and Emeric Pressburger (The Archers)
Screenplay: **Michael Powell,** Emeric Pressburger, and Nigel Balchin, from the novel by Nigel Balchin
Cinematography: Christopher Challis
Production Designer: Hein Heckroth
Art Director: John Hoesli
Music: Brian Easdale
Editor: Reginald Mills
Cast: David Farrar (Sammy Rice), Kathleen Byron (Susan), Jack Hawkins (R. B. Waring), Leslie Banks (Colonel Holland), Michael Gough (Stuart), Cyril Cusack (Corporal Taylor), Milton Rosmer (Professor Mair), Walter Fitzgerald (Brine), Emrys Jones (Joe), Michael Goodliffe (Till), Renée Asherson (ATS Corporal), Anthony Bushell (Colonel Strang), Henry Caine (Sgt.-Major Rose), Elwyn Brook-Jones (Gladwin), James Dale (Brigadier), Sam Kydd (Crowhurst), June Elvin (Gillian), David Hutcheson (Norval), Sidney James (Knucksie), Roderick Lovell (Pearson), James Carney (Sgt. Groves), Roddy Hughes (Welsh Doctor), Geoffrey Keen (Pinker), Bryan Forbes (Dying Gunner), Robert Morley (Minister), **Michael Powell** (Gunnery Officer)
B&W
108 minutes

1950
GONE TO EARTH (U.S. TITLE: THE WILD HEART)
Written and directed by **Michael Powell** and Emeric Pressburger (The Archers); screenplay based on the novel by Mary Webb
Producer: David O. Selznick (An Alexander Korda and David O. Selznick presentation)
Cinematography: Christopher Challis
Production Designer: Hein Heckroth
Art Director: Arthur Lawson
Music: Brian Easdale
Editor: Reginald Mills
Cast: Jennifer Jones (Hazel Woodus), David Farrar (Jack Reddin), Cyril Cusack (Edward Marston), Sybil Thorndyke (Mrs. Marston), Edward Chapman (Mr.

James), Esmond Knight (Abel Woodus), Hugh Griffith (Andrew Vessons), George Cole (Albert), Beatrice Varley (Aunt Prowde), Frances Clare (Amelia Comber), Raymond Rollett (Landlord, Hunter's Arms), Gerald Lawson (Road-mender), Bartlett Mullins, Arthur Reynolds (Chapel Elders), Ann Tetheradge (Miss James), Peter Dunlop (Cornet Player), Louis Phillip (Policeman), Valentine Dunn (Martha), Richmond Nairne (Mathias Brooker), Owen Holder (Brother Minister)
Technicolor
110 minutes

1951
THE ELUSIVE PIMPERNEL (U.S. TITLE: THE FIGHTING PIMPERNEL)
Written and directed by **Michael Powell** and Emeric Pressburger (The Archers); screenplay from the novel by Baroness Orczy
Producers: Samuel Goldwyn, Alexander Korda
Cinematography: Christopher Challis
Production Designer: Hein Heckroth
Art Director: Arthur Lawson, Joseph Bato
Special Effects: W. Percy Day
Music: Brian Easdale
Editor: Reginald Mills
Cast: David Niven (Sir Percy Blakeney), Margaret Leighton (Marguerite Blakeney), Jack Hawkins (Prince of Wales), Cyril Cusack (Chauvelin), Robert Coote (Sir Andrew Ffoulkes), Edmond Audran (Armand St. Juste), Danielle Godet (Suzanne de Tournai), Charles Victor (Colonel Winterbotham), David Hutcheson (Lord Anthony Dewhurst), Arlette Marchal (Countesse de Tournai), Gerard Nery (Philippe de Tournai), Eugene Deckers (Captain Merieres), John Longden (Abbot), Arthur Wontner (Lord Grenville), David Oxley (Captain Duroc), Raymond Rollett (Bibot), Philip Stainton (Jellyband), Robert Griffiths (Trubshaw), George de Warfaz (Baron), Jane Gill Davies (Lady Grenville), Richard George (Sir John Coke), Cherry Cottrell (Lady Bristow), John Fitzgerald (Sir Michael Travers), Patrick Macnee (Hon. John Bristow), Terence Alexander (Duke of Dorset), Tommy Duggan (Earl of Sligo), John Fitchen (Nigel Seymour), John Hewitt (Major Pretty), Hugh Kelly (Mr. Fitzdrummond), Richard Nairne (Beau Pepys)
Technicolor
109 minutes

THE TALES OF HOFFMANN
Written, produced, and directed by **Michael Powell** and Emeric Pressburger (The Archers); screenplay from Dennis Arundell's adaptation of the opera by Offenbach; libretto by Jules Barbier
Cinematography: Christopher Challis
Production Designer/Costumes: Hein Heckroth
Art Director: Arthur Lawson
Music: Jacques Offenbach, directed by Sir Thomas Beecham
Choreography: Frederick Ashton
Editor: Reginald Mills
Singers: Robert Rounseville, Owen Brannigan, Monica Sinclair, Rene Soames, Bruce Dargavel, Dorothy Bond, Margherita Grandi, Grahame Clifford, Joan Alexander
Cast:
Prologue and Epilogue: Moira Shearer (Stella), Robert Rounseville (Hoffmann), Robert Helpmann (Lindorff), Pamela Brown (Niklaus), Frederick Ashton (Kleinzack), Meinhart Maur (Luther), Edmond Audran (Cancer)
The Tale of Olympia: Moira Shearer (Olympia), Robert Helpmann (Coppelius), Léonide Massine (Spalanzani)
The Tale of Giulietta: Ludmilla Tchérina (Giulietta), Robert Helpmann (Coppelius), Léonide Massine (Schlemiel)
The Tale of Antonia: Ann Ayars (Antonia), Robert Helpmann (Dr. Miracle), Léonide Massine (Franz)
Technicolor
127 minutes

THE WILD HEART
Shortened version of *Gone to Earth*; released in U.S. with additional direction by Rouben Mamoulian, narration by Joseph Cotten
82 minutes

1955
THE SORCERER'S APPRENTICE
Director: **Michael Powell**
Producer: Harold Voller
Screenplay: Dennis Arundell, based on a story by Goethe
Cinematography: Christopher Challis

Production Designer: Hein Heckroth
Sets: K. H. Joksch
Editor: Reginald Mills
Music: Hamburg State Opera Orchestra
Choreography: Helga Swedlund
Cast: Solo dancer, Sonia Arova
Technicolor
13 minutes

1956
OH . . . ROSALINDA!
Written, produced, and directed by **Michael Powell** and Emeric Pressburger (The Archers); screenplay based on Johann Strauss's operetta *Die Fledermaus*
Lyrics: Dennis Arundell
Cinematography: Christopher Challis
Production Designer: Hein Heckroth
Music: Johann Strauss, music directed by Frederick Lewis
Choreography: Alfred Rodriguez
Editor: Reginald Mills
Cast: Anthony Quayle (General Orlovsky), Anton Walbrook (Dr. Falke, the Fledermaus—singing dubbed by Walter Berry), Richard Marner (Colonel Lebotov), Ludmilla Tchérina (Rosalinda—singing dubbed by Sari Barabas), Michael Redgrave (Colonel Eisenstein), Mel Ferrer (Capt. Alfred Westerman—singing dubbed by Alexander Young), Nicholas Bruce (Hotel Receptionist), Anneliese Rothenberger (Adele), Dennis Price (Major Frank—singing dubbed by Dennis Dowling), Oskar Sima (Frosch)
The Ladies: Barbara Archer, Betty Ash, Joyce Blair, Hildy Christian, Pamela Foster, Jill Ireland, Patricia Garnett, Annette Gibson, Eileen Gourley, Jean Grayston, Grizelda Hervey, Maya Koumani, Olga Lowe, Sara Luzita, Ingrid Marshall, Alicia Massy-Beresford, Eileen Sands, Herta Seydel, Anna Steele, Jennifer Walmsley, Dorothy Whitney, Prudence Hyman
The Gentlemen: Michael Anthony, Igor Barczinsky, Cecil Bates, Richard Bennett, Nicholas Bruce, Ray Buckingham, Denis Carey, Rolf Carston, Terence Cooper, Robert Crewdson, Peter Darrell, Edmund Forsyth, Roger Gage, David Gilbert, Robert Harrold, Jan Lawski, Raymond Lloyd, William Martin, Kenneth Melville, Orest Orloff, Robert Ross, John Schlesinger, Frederick Schrecker, Maurice Metliss, Kenneth Smith, Richard Marner

Technicolor
101 minutes

THE BATTLE OF THE RIVER PLATE (U.S. TITLE: PURSUIT OF THE GRAF SPEE)
Written, produced, and directed by **Michael Powell** and Emeric Pressburger (The Archers)
A production of The Archers and J. Arthur Rank
Cinematography: Christopher Challis
Production Designer: Arthur Lawson
Music: Brian Easdale
Editor: Reginald Mills
Cast: John Gregson (Captain F. S. Bell), Anthony Quayle (Commodore Henry Harwood), Peter Finch (Captain Langsdorff), Ian Hunter (Captain Woodhouse), Jack Gwillim (Captain Parry), Bernard Lee (Captain Patrick Dove), Lionel Murton (Mike Fowler), Anthony Bushell (Mr. Millington-Drake), Peter Illing (Dr. Guani), Michael Goodliffe (Captain McCall), Patric Macnee (Lt. Commander Medley), John Chandos (Dr. Langmann), Douglas Wilmer (Mr. Desmoulins), William Squire (Ray Martin), Roger Delgado (Captain Varela), Andrew Cruickshank (Captain Stubbs), Christopher Lee (Manolo), Edward Atienza (Pop), April Olrich (Dolores), Donald Moffat (Swanston), Maria Mercedes (Madame X), John Schlesinger (German Officer), John Le Mesurier (Padre), Anthony Newley, Nigel Stock (British Officers aboard Graf Spee), Alan Beale (Captain Pottinger), Brian Worth, Ronald Clarke
Technicolor
119 minutes

1957
ILL MET BY MOONLIGHT (U.S. TITLE: NIGHT AMBUSH)
Written, produced, and directed by **Michael Powell** and Emeric Pressburger; screenplay based on the novel by W. Stanley Moss
A production of The Archers and J. Arthur Rank
Cinematography: Christopher Challis
Art Director: Alex Vetchinsky
Special Effects: Bill Warrington
Music: Mikis Theodorakis
Editor: Arthur Stevens
Cast: Dirk Bogarde (Major Paddy Leigh-Femor), Marius Goring (Major Gen-

eral Karl Kreipe), David Oxley (Captain W. Stanley Moss), Cyril Cusack (Sandy), Laurence Payne (Manoli), Wolfe Morris (George), Michael Gough (Andoni Zoidakis), Roland Bartrop (Micky Akoumianakis), Brian Worth (Stratis Saviolkis), Paul Stassino (Yani Katsias), Adeeb Assaly (Zahari), John Cairney (Elias), George Eugeniou (Charis Zographakis), Demitri Andreas (Niko), Theo Moreas (Village Priest), Takis Frangofinos (Michali), Christopher Lee (German Officer at Dentist), Peter Augustine, John Houseman, Phyllia Houseman, Andrea Maladrinos, Christopher Rhodes
B&W
104 minutes

1959
LUNA DE MIEL (ENGLISH TITLE: HONEYMOON)
Director: **Michael Powell**
Screenplay: **Michael Powell**, Luis Escobar
Producers: **Michael Powell**, Cesáreo González
Cinematography: Georges Périnal
Art Director: Ivor Beddoes
Music: Mikis Theodorakis
Ballets:
El amor Brujo, written by Gregorio Martínez Sierra, with music by Manuel de Falla
Choreography: Antonio
Soloist: María Carla Alcalá
Dancer: Léonide Massine
Los amantes de Teruel, music by Mikis Theodorakis, conducted by Sir Thomas Beecham
Choreography: Léonide Massine
Cast: Anthony Steel (Kit Kelly), Ludmilla Tchérina (Anna), Antonio (himself), Léonide Massine ("Der Geist"), Rosita Segovia (Rosita Candelas), Carmen Rojas (Lucia), Antonio's Spanish Ballet Troupe—Juan Carmona, María Gámez, Diego Hurtado

1960
PEEPING TOM
Director: **Michael Powell**
Screenplay: Leo Marks

Producer: **Michael Powell**
Cinematography: Otto Heller
Art Director: Arthur Lawson
Music: Brian Easdale, Wally Stott
Editor: Noreen Ackland
Cast: Carl Boehm (Mark Lewis), Anna Massey (Helen), Maxine Audley (Mrs. Stephens), Moira Shearer (Vivian), Esmond Knight (Arthur Baden), Michael Goodliffe (Don Jarvis), Shirley Anne Field (Diane Ashley), Bartlett Mullins (Mr. Peters), Jack Watson (Inspector Gregg), Nigel Davenport (Sergeant Miller), Pamela Green (Milly), Martin Miller (Dr. Rosan), Brian Wallace (Tony), Brenda Bruce (Dora), Miles Malleson (Elderly Gentleman), Susan Travers (Lorraine), Maurice Durant (Publicity Chief), Brian Worth (Assistant Director), Veronica Hurst (Miss Simpson), Alan Rolfe (Store Detective), **Michael Powell** (Mark's father), Columba Powell (Mark as a child)
Eastman Colour
109 minutes

1961
THE QUEEN'S GUARDS
Director: **Michael Powell**
Screenplay: Roger Milner, from an idea by Simon Harcourt-Smith
Producer: **Michael Powell**
Cinematography: Gerry Turpin
Art Director: Wilfred Shingleton
Music: Brian Easdale
Editor: Noreen Ackland
Cast: Daniel Massey (John Fellowes), Robert Stephens (Henry Wynne Walton), Raymond Massey (Captain Fellowes), Ursula Jeans (Mrs. Fellowes), Judith Stott (Ruth), Elizabeth Shepherd (Susan), Duncan Lamont (Wilkes), Peter Myers (Gordon Davidson), Ian Hunter (Dobbie), Jess Conrad (Dankworth), Patrick Connor (Brewer), William Young (Williams), Jack Allen (Brigadier Cummings), Jack Watling (Captain Shergold), Andrew Crawford (Biggs), Cornel Lucas (Photographer), Nigel Green (Abu Sibdar), Rene Cutforth (Commentator), Jack Watson (Sergeant Johnson), Laurence Payne (Farinda)
Technicolor
110 minutes

1964
HERZOG BLAUBART'S BURG/BLUEBEARD'S CASTLE
Director: **Michael Powell**
Screenplay: Libretto of Béla Bartók's opera *Bluebeard's Castle* by Béla Balázs
Producer: Norman Foster
Cinematography: Hannes Staudinger
Production Designer: Hein Heckroth
Music: Bartók
Cast: Norman Foster (Bluebeard), Anna Raquel Sartre (Judit)
Technicolor
60 minutes

1966
THEY'RE A WEIRD MOB
Director: **Michael Powell**
Screenplay: Richard Imrie [Emeric Pressburger], from a novel by John O'Grady
Producer: **Michael Powell**
Cinematography: Arthur Grant
Art Director: Dennis Gentle
Music: Laurence Leonard, Alan Boustead
Editor: G. Turney-Smith
Cast: Walter Chiari (Nino Culotta), Clare Dunne (Kay Kelly), Chips Rafferty (Harry Kelly), Alida Chelli (Giuliana), Ed Devereaux (Joe), Slim de Grey (Pat), John Meillon (Dennis), Charles Little (Jimmy), Anne Haddy (Barmaid), Jack Allen (Fat Man in Bar), Red Moore (Texture Man), Ray Hartley (Newsboy), Tony Bonner (Lifesaver), Alan Lander (Charlie), Judith Arthy (Dixie), Keith Petersen (Drunk Man on Ferry), Muriel Steinbeck (Mrs. Kelly), Gloria Dawn (Mrs. Chapman), Jeanie Drynan (Betty), Gita Rivera (Maria), Doreen Warburton (Edie), Barry Creyton, Noel Brophy, Graham Kennedy
Eastman Colour
112 minutes

1969
AGE OF CONSENT
Director: **Michael Powell**
Screenplay: Peter Yeldham, based on a novel by Norman Lindsay

Producers: James Mason, **Michael Powell**
Cinematography: Hannes Staudinder
Art Director: Dennis Gentle
Music: Stanley Myers
Editor: Anthony Buckley
Cast: James Mason (Bradley Monahan), Helen Mirren (Cora), Jack MacGowran (Nat Kelly), Neva Carr-Glyn (Ma Ryan), Andonia Katsaros (Isabel Marley), Michael Boddy (Hendricks), Harold Hopkins (Ted Farrell), Slim de Grey (Cooley), Max Meldrum (TV Interviewer), Frank Thring (Godfrey), Dora Hing (Receptionist), Clarissa Kaye (Meg), Judy McGrath (Grace), Lenore Caton (Edna), Diane Strachan (Susie), Roberta Grant (Ivy), Prince Nial (Jasper), Hudson Faucett (New Yorker), Peggy Cass (New Yorker's Wife), Eric Reuman (Art Lover), Tommy Hanlon Jr. (Levi-Strauss), Geoff Cartwright (Newsboy)
Eastman colour
98 minutes

1972
THE BOY WHO TURNED YELLOW
Director: **Michael Powell**
Screenplay: Emeric Pressburger
Producer: Roger Cherrill
Cinematography: Christopher Challis
Art Director: Bernard Sarron
Music: Patrick Gowers, David Vorhaus
Editor: Peter Boita
Cast: Mark Dightam (John), Robert Eddison (Nick), Helen Weir (Mrs. Saunders), Brian Worth (Mr. Saunders), Esmond Knight (Doctor), Laurence Carter (Schoolteacher), Patrick McAliney (Supreme Beefeater), Lem Kitaj (Munro)
Eastman Colour
55 minutes

1978
RETURN TO THE EDGE OF THE WORLD
Director: **Michael Powell**
Screenplay: Sydney Streeter
A return visit to Foula, scene of Powell's *Edge of the World*, commissioned by BBC Television

Cast: **Michael Powell**, John Laurie, Grant Sutherland, Frankie Reidy, Sydney Streeter
85 minutes (including *Edge of the World*)

1983
PAVLOVA—A WOMAN FOR ALL TIME
Powell was Western Version Supervisor of the GB/USSR production, which originated in his idea of a project on the life of Pavlova.

MICHAEL POWELL

INTERVIEWS

Desert Island Discs

ROY PLOMLEY/1942

ANN: *Once again a well-known personality is going to tell us which eight gramophone records he would choose to have with him if he were to be cast away alone on a desert island. The series is devised and presented by Roy Plomley, and here he is to introduce tonight's castaway.*

RP: *Good evening, everyone. Tonight's castaway is a prominent figure in the world of British films—one of our most accomplished directors. His successes have included* 49th Parallel, One of Our Aircraft Is Missing, The Spy in Black *and* Edge of the World, *and he tells me he is at present working on a picture with the promising title* The Life and Death of Colonel Blimp. *His name is Michael Powell. What is your first record, Mr. Powell?*
MP: An arrangement of "The Campbells Are Coming" sung by The Glasgow Orpheus Choir. I'd like you to notice particularly how an instrumental effect is obtained just by the human voices. It's one of the most dramatic records I know and I never get tired of it. That record has already qualified as a desert island disc.

RP: *Don't tell me that you and a gramophone* have *been marooned on a desert island.*
MP: Marooned, yes. Island, yes. Deserted, no. A few years ago I made a film called *Edge of the World.*

A transcript of the BBC radio program, October 8, 1942. Printed by permission of the BBC and Mrs. Diana Plomley.

RP: *About one of the Shetland Islands, wasn't it?*
MP: Yes. In 1930 I came across a newspaper article about the gradual depopulation of the outer Scottish islands, and the way that modern conditions were forcing the inhabitants to the mainland. It caught my imagination. It seemed an ideal subject for a film. I thought out a story and pestered everybody in the film business with it until 1936, when I found someone to back the idea. I persuaded a bunch of unsuspicious people to go with me and we spent the whole summer on the little island of Foula, the westernmost of the Shetlands, about 20 miles from the mainland. Our unit consisted of 24 men and 2 women, our average age was 25. We shot 200,000 feet of film on the island.

RP: *How much of it was used in the finished picture?*
MP: About 7000. We had a desperate struggle to finish and by the end of October we still had a number of vital scenes to make. Every day brought the winter gales nearer and we stood a good chance of being marooned on Foula for the whole winter.

RP: *And were you?*
MP: No, by the skin of our teeth. We were out off for several weeks with no fresh meat, bread, vegetables and worst of all, cigarettes. In those days that seemed like hardship. At the end of October there was a lull in the gales and a relief ship was able to take us off.

RP: *But you had finished the picture?*
MP: Yes—in a 100 mile an hour gale. At night we used to sit in our huts, which were lashed to the ground to stop them blowing away. We would play games, work or talk while the floor heaved under us and sometimes we listened to my portable gramophone. It was our only music. One record I took to Foula was "Tintagel" by Bax—eerie, mystic music that seems to me the very essence of islands and the sea. Often I've propped my gramophone against a streaming wet boulder and heard that music pour out over the mountainside while the actors appeared and disappeared in the mist. I know from experience that these first two records that I have chosen stand the test of constant repetition under very trying circumstances. Also they would remind me of a wonderful year and the fulfilment of an ambition. I don't think I shall ever make another film, however good it may turn out to be,

that will mean as much to me as *The Edge of the World.* So you see, Mr. Plomley, that I have special qualification to be a castaway.

RP: *How did the islanders react to having a film unit dropped into their midst for 4 or 5 months?*
MP: On the wall of my house is a coloured map of Foula. Every member of the unit has one, and it is inscribed "From the men of Foula to the men of *The Edge of the World* in memory of 4 months comradeship."

RP: *Perhaps in one of those stone crofts on Foula, with the galo howling round it, someone is listening to you now.*
MP: I hope so. They are our friends and we have never forgotten them.

RP: *What about Number 3 in your list?*
MP: My third choice is a song from George Gershwin's negro opera *Porgy and Bess.* It's sung by Todd Duncan. "I Got Plenty of Nuttin."

RP: *It seems a nice practical philosophy for a desert island—I got plenty of nothing, and nothing's plenty for me."*
MP: Unless you are one of the Swiss Family Robinson.

RP: *What next?*
MP: Everyone has a popular tune which is associated with a particular time in his or her life. It may mean nothing to anybody else but that's not their business. Mine is a particular record: a concert arrangement (I think that's what they call it) of "Without a Song," played by Victor Young and his Orchestra.

RP: *Without knowing why you're sentimental about it, I think that would always make pleasant listening.*
MP: It's a good record. A Russian one comes next—"Bessarabianka" sung by Peter Lescenco. It's a crazy record, not like any other I know. And I defy you to keep from beating time to the rhythm. If ever I felt I was going crazy on my desert island I should play this record, do a Russian dance on the sands and feel quite sane again. As you can hear, mine are mostly highly coloured, but simple records. If I was a castaway, I don't think I should yearn for Beethoven, Brahms, Sibelius—any of the giants whose works I like to play in

London. On a desert island, or on any island there are mighty orchestrations of wind and sea and wild landscapes at your door. I would want drama, sophistication or some perfect piece of artistry which would be a product of both.

RP: *You ask a good deal there.*

MP: Right. But on my desert island I should have it if I had any one of Chaliapino's records—and he would dwarf the landscapes. . . .

And—although I don't dance, I'd want a waltz.

RP: *Now why a waltz?*

MP: If you must have a reason, because a desert island is about the only place left in the world where there is room to waltz.

The last week or two we have all felt proud of the music of Ralph Vaughan Williams. There's one of his compositions I would be proud to take with me because in a small way I was responsible for it: "The Overture to 49th Parallel."

RP: *Making that picture was another adventure, wasn't it?*

MP: It was a dozen rolled into one. Three months in a freighter going up Labrador coast to Hudson Bay—weeks in a Hutterite settlement—pack-horse trips across the Rockies. That's another part of my life I wouldn't want to forget, and this splendid theme by Vaughan Williams would recapture it for me. The voice that is orchestrated with the music is the voice of Vincent Massey, the High Commissioner for Canada.

RP: *What a wonderful tune. Who spoke those lines at the end?*

MP: The U-boat Commander and his Lieutenant—the scene with which the film opens. Vaughan Williams has talked of developing that theme into a bigger work. I hope he does. It shouldn't die, as a film dies.

RP: *That was your last record, Mr. Powell. Thanks a lot for letting us hear your choice. Next time you make a picture on an island, make sure you put those eight records in your baggage. You never know! And good luck to* Colonel Blimp*—the picture, not the man!*

What's Happening to the Movies?

W. SPEAKMAN/1945

SPEAKMAN: *Miss Powell, I'd like to—*
MICHAEL: Wait a moment—this is going to be confusing—two Powells, and no relation. You'd better call Miss Powell Dilys and me Michael.

SPEAKMAN: *Very well—if you both agree. It's the critic I want to talk to. I'm a film exhibitor. As you've just heard, I run a chain of cinemas in the North-West—Liverpool, and so on—and the facts I'm going to put now have been mentioned to me by scores of cinema managers. We take great exception to the type of remarks you newspaper and broadcast critics make about films. One critic reviewing films some time ago said, "If you're thinking of going to the cinema this week, don't!" Well, that week there happened to be a poor run of films in the West-end of London, but his criticism was intended for the whole country. What about the good films that were running that week in Wigan, or Manchester, or Glasgow? You critics take far too much notice of what's happening in London.*
DILYS: I certainly think that critic was going outside his province as a critic. But the thing cuts both ways. If you exclude him from saying, "Don't go and see this film," you must also exclude me from saying, "You must go and see this film—you will like it," because it's not my business to know whether the public will like a film or not!

SPEAKMAN: *Well, from what I see of the box-office returns the public certainly doesn't like what you like.*

Radio interview with Michael Powell and Dilys Powell, recorded January 26, 1945, Home Service, London. Transcript printed by permission of the BBC.

DILYS: In other words, you don't really want critics at all.

SPEAKMAN: *Well—I don't want to be rude. . . .*
DILYS: Come on!

SPEAKMAN: *I don't want to be rude, but I really don't know what useful function you fulfill. Luckily—and as exhibitors we're highly grateful—newspaper critics or BBC film critics don't materially affect public taste, or have much effect on the box-office.*
DILYS: What does "materially" mean?

SPEAKMAN: *Well, you will get the odd few patrons, who probably think themselves aloof from the other part of the house. . . .*
MICHAEL: Do you mean they're odd or few?

SPEAKMAN: *Both. Fortunately they are odd people and there are a few of them. They may think, well—Miss Powell or Mr. Norgate say so and so about this film on the wireless, so why should we come in and see it. But, as I say, fortunately they are the very great minority.*
MICHAEL: Well, what do the majority do?

SPEAKMAN: *The majority have their regular cinema. It's part of their life to go to the cinema once, twice or three times weekly, and if they have any complaints they invariably go to the managements—that is, in the suburban cinemas—and the cinemas I control are principally suburban. They know the manager and the manager can usually say "I know my Patrons."*
MICHAEL: But you know lots of husbands say "I know my wife."

SPEAKMAN: *That's a different topic! But I say that the films the public complain about aren't as a rule the ones film critics have damned.*
DILYS: Give us an example.

SPEAKMAN: *The film* A Guy Named Joe. *That was described by one critic—I can't remember which—as dream phantasy, stuff with no appeal today. Well, that film proved very good when it reached the provinces.*
MICHAEL: Do you mean just your cinemas or the provinces as a whole?

SPEAKMAN: *Generally—generally it was accepted as quite a good film.*
DILYS: I must make a stand here. I've got no business to criticize the work of my colleagues, but the critic who said that a film was "stuff with no appeal today" was not fulfilling the functions of a critic as I see them. I don't think it's my business to say, "Nobody will like this film." I think it's my business to say, "This is a good film—let them like it or not."

SPEAKMAN: *But what do you mean by saying "This is a good film," if it's a film the public won't come to see?*
DILYS: Well, I regard the cinema very much as an art. . . .
MICHAEL: Watch it, watch it. You've got Speakman on the other side of the fence and you don't want him on the other side of the fence.
DILYS: Surely he's there anyway. Well, in the other arts I think people accept the critic as having a double function, a function to his audience to say, "This I believe is doing something worth while in its own medium, this is an interesting or useless piece of work." He also has a function towards people who are working in that art. I think I have a very great duty towards Michael here—which I'm sure he thinks I fulfill very badly, but I have that duty—to say, "I think you're going wrong here, I think you're going right there—please go on doing this—this is really using the cinema in a way which exalts and excites and interests, which illuminates the whole business of living. . . .
MICHAEL: I think you've got something there. You're aiming at the way a film is made, the mind that's behind it and what they're driving at and what is film and what isn't. But Speakman's got something too. A film must make money or it isn't a good film. If it's technically perfect, well acted and directed, and nobody comes to see it, it can't possibly be a good film.
DILYS: I most strongly disagree. Why should we judge the cinema so differently from all other forms of expression? You don't say that "Paradise Lost" isn't a good poem because it was sold for £10 or whatever it was. To say a film isn't good because it doesn't make money seems to me absolutely extraordinary.
MICHAEL: If a film of mine doesn't make money, I'm very annoyed indeed. It hasn't happened yet. I'd be furious if it did.

SPEAKMAN: *I'd like to hear what you thought about your* Canterbury Tale.
MICHAEL: What do you mean? Didn't it go so well with you?

SPEAKMAN: *Unfortunately, no. Personally I thought the final scene in the Cathedral was worth the proverbial bob of anybody's money. I hate to say that it did bad business. I know it's quiet and slow moving but I still think it was a beautiful film—the ending in the cathedral sold it to me. And apart from the fact that I'm trading with that company I thought that was a film people* should *see. It was like a breath of fresh air—I thoroughly enjoyed it.*
MICHAEL: But if it didn't do well with your audiences it's evidently not what they want. Perhaps we made a mistake—
DILYS: You say it was a mistake. I think it was half a mistake. The background—the country stuff and the Canterbury stuff—was absolutely lovely, but the story was weak. I thought it was wrong in that background.

SPEAKMAN: *There's another point—about making money—you've heard of the fluke film, the film which all critics and we exhibitors would think a poor film. In quite a lot of instances it makes money. It just hits somewhere. Years ago A.B.C. produced very cheaply a film called* My Wife's Family *with Gene Gerrard. It wasn't expected to be a world-beater—we could judge that by the terms we were asked to pay for it—but when it came out to the public, it created an absolute furore.*
MICHAEL: The fact is, Speakman, you and I both need the critics. I want to make a film as good or as different as I can, but I also know that I have to spend a lot of money to make a film and I feel I am cheating somebody if my film doesn't make money. And *you* know that films have to make money, otherwise the theatre won't pay. But it's right to have Dilys caring only about the film and not caring whether it makes money.

SPEAKMAN: *But if you're putting so much emphasis on money, what do you want her for?*
MICHAEL: It's difficult to say without being high falutin'. From your point of view films are a business and I think you're quite right. And I have to make money because when I make a film I spend a lot, and I couldn't go on asking people to put up money if I didn't make it. But we both of us have something else going on in our minds at the same time. You'd like to see people coming out of your theatre and saying, "That was a fine film"—as well as take the money. That's what you're really batting for behind it all isn't it?

SPEAKMAN: *Absolutely.*
MICHAEL: Well, if I can please Dilys as well as the public, I'm tickled to

death—twice as tickled as if I'd just made the money. Naturally a lot of us quarrel with her. When she criticizes, *we* say, "Oh, she forgets how long it took to make," and *you* say, "She forgets it didn't take a penny at the box-office," but we both know, with one tenth of us, that she's all right. She's doing what we would like her to do. I've been in films for twenty years, and had a say in making them for ten years, but I haven't made one film as I would really like to make it. When it really pleases me, it will please you, Dilys—and it will please Speakman and his public too.

DILYS: Why haven't you made the film that pleases you?

MICHAEL: Too busy.

DILYS: Too busy making other films?

MICHAEL: Everybody's been too busy making films for fifty years. They've never had time to stop and think. What Hollywood company—producing company—has a chance to stop and think? Lots of books have been written about the film business, but it's no use a few very clever men outside films thinking about films; the thinking's got to be done by the people inside the craft—it's got to be done by the best men in the craft. That means in films the men who are earning the biggest money—men who order big stars about and say, "I want this. I want that." Well, these men have suddenly got to stop and say, "What is it all about?" We've got to realise what a craft we've got here—something which moves and can go anywhere in the world, can be heard and have colour, a wonderful thing. If it suddenly started from scratch now you wouldn't see films like the ones we're seeing now.

SPEAKMAN: *What do you mean? That they'd be much better?*

MICHAEL: They'd be different. What do you see now? You go in and see colour and sound added to the silent film. But you don't see a beautiful dramatic form of entertainment which starts from the fact that it is coloured and can be heard and which you, Speakman, can put up in town and show anywhere. Well, we're in entire sympathy with you; we *want* to reach those wide audiences. But you only reach those wide audiences, I'm sure, by making what's in your heart and not by saying, "I know what those wide audiences want, and I'll give it to them."

SPEAKMAN: *And do you consider that's why so many bad films are made? Because film makers are trying to give the public what they want?*

MICHAEL: Partly. But there's something else. Everybody who's been in films knows that a certain film has got a certain momentum at a certain time, and it just has to be made whether anybody wants to make it or not.

SPEAKMAN: *I don't understand that.*
MICHAEL: It's difficult to explain; but if, say, in Hollywood, they didn't announce that they were going to make 52 films in a year, or if they didn't sign up so many actors at so much salary a year, they wouldn't have to make these films, would they? They've got directors, actors, writers all signed up, and so they have achieved a momentum before they've even started to make a film.

SPEAKMAN: *You mean that films are made to keep the actors occupied and use up scripts that have been bought?*
MICHAEL: That does happen. And of course they have theatres to supply, and they've conditioned these theatres to expect one film a week, or two films a week, or six films a week, and they've all got to be new. So they've achieved a momentum, and God knows how they're going to stop it.

SPEAKMAN: *But why do you want to stop it?*
MICHAEL: Well, there's certainly a good side to it. It gives continuity. They say British movies don't build up stars. Well, how the dickens are we to build up stars if we haven't continuity?
DILYS: By continuity you mean . . . ?
MICHAEL: What we haven't had in England! Making a film in England has meant scraping together what you could get and then making it with people you knew were talented and at the end of it, everything you had collected was dissipated to the winds; the sets were all taken down and special props that had been built all vanished and the wardrobe vanished. Everything disintegrated into dust. We had no good experience of film here because no continuous production was going on.

SPEAKMAN: *And with continuous production you'll be able to build up stars?*
MICHAEL: Yes.

SPEAKMAN: *Well, there's no set rule about stars. If the story isn't known it does pay to have stars. But you'll get films going out with unknown stars that do very well.*

MICHAEL: But people never go to see *stories* in films, unless it's something that's either been sold beforehand by being a play or a book or unless it's been built up by publicity. People go to see stars—or they go to see titles.

SPEAKMAN: *Of course when you get a combination of the three you get something!*

DILYS: What they call a set up, isn't it?

MICHAEL: Yes. In every film we make we try to get a certain sort of set up. We say, "Well, that is a good film anyway," but what makes it into a big film is something more—a definite set up.

Take *49th Parallel*. That started as a film to be made about Canada. Pressburger and I set to work to make a story of the war coming to a country whose reactions the U.S.A. could understand. And we hit on this idea of having a U-boat crew ship-wrecked off Canada and taking them right across Canada from east to west and back again and seeing things through their eyes. Once that idea had been hit upon—well—that was the film—you could do it. But what made it a set up was that in each episode they met a new star. We said, that's all right, that's fine, but you can't do it unless in each episode you have a new big star coming in because you won't get the thing over, and you may or may not hold the interest. But if they're waiting for Howard or Olivier or Massey.

DILYS: That's what made it an ideal set up?

MICHAEL: Yes. It includes the combination of all the things you want. What made it a great film—I know it was a great film—was the sweep of the whole idea and the fact that it was perfectly timed. But what completed it as a great film was the idea of Massey and Olivier and Walbrook coming in at odd moments.

DILYS: Yet you say you haven't made a single film yet that has pleased you?

MICHAEL: No, I haven't. I keep coming back to what I said before. This particular craft of film-making has only been going for 20 or 25 years. And what's it done? Terrific things in the early days. Then sound came in. Well, that should have been a God-send. But what did it do? Put the brakes on! Colour came in. It should have been a God-send. But what did it do? Put the brakes on! I don't say the public don't want films in sound and colour. We all do. But it made the actual making of films more difficult for technicians. Things have happened too fast. So none of the new discoveries—colour or sound—are being used properly. We are still trying to create a naturalistic drama for the public and the whole soul of entertainment has nothing to do with naturalism and everything to do with illusion.

SPEAKMAN: *I'd like to know what you mean by naturalistic drama?*
DILYS: As I see it, naturalistic drama is the drama which takes the outward facts—which sees that the people charging in the Light Brigade are wearing the right hats and the right swords. But what does it matter? Drama is the emotion which makes the man face the gun and that's what I want out of film. What does it matter in the film of *Henry V* if the English archers are using the right kind of arrows or not? Producers spend thousands of pounds on details of this kind when all that matters is—does the audience believe in the film they're seeing? Charlie Chaplin didn't need to worry about elaborate sets. Take *The Gold Rush;* he just looked cold and you felt you were in the heart of Alaska.

SPEAKMAN: *Oh, I quite agree. Charles Laughton once said to me that the film actor shouldn't present the audience with his face showing an emotion, but should experience the emotion and that's enough. He shouldn't grimace, he should feel.*
MICHAEL: But we must be careful not to give the idea that we are drawing a line between the stage and films. It's nothing to do with that, Laughton on the stage is equally subtle.

SPEAKMAN: *Well, give us an example from a film of your own.*
MICHAEL: I don't think I can. Because I've only been thinking along these lines myself for a year or two. But I feel it's no longer enough to put on the screen exteriors and sets and process shots which all go to make up a modern film, which is occupied primarily in leaving nothing to the imagination. We should go deeper than that. We've a chance now to go straight to the man in the audience and not simply show him something, but speak to him.

SPEAKMAN: *Speak to him?*
MICHAEL: Yes. Not by re-creating the whole surroundings of somebody who's in a tremendous fix, but by getting to the heart of the fix and making the audience understand that.
DILYS: Don't you think that Orson Welles' film *Citizen Kane* did something there? That film said a great deal more to me than would have been conveyed by straight photography of the actual physical surroundings. It did convey

an extraordinary sense of mystery and loneliness and living in solitude surrounded by thousands of people and immense wealth—a feeling of a man living like a little mouse in a palace. Welles got that by making the palace unlike any real palace that ever existed. He gave the idea of colossal size and emptiness by the use of huge shadows and corridors you couldn't see the end of.

MICHAEL: Yes, Orson Welles is a genius. But I'd like to ask you, Dilys, if you'd been talking about it over the air, would you have advised the great British public to go and see it?

DILYS: I certainly advised them to go and see it. I didn't say whether they'd like it or not—because I really didn't know. But I'm told that a lot of people didn't like it.

SPEAKMAN: *They certainly did not.*

MICHAEL: I wouldn't think the public *would* like *Kane.*

SPEAKMAN: *But you thought it was a good film?*

MICHAEL: No. It's all brains and no heart. But I was excited when I first saw it because I'd seen people do all this in Russian and French and German and Italian, but I'd never seen it done in American.

DILYS: What?

MICHAEL: Well, I'd never seen a director having a good time in film in American. And I thought—"The next film Welles makes is going to be terrific."

DILYS: Is it the directors having a good time which makes French films so good? I'm always astonished by the excellence of French films on which no money worth speaking of has been spent compared with high-powered musicals which have cost thousands. But I don't expect Mr. Speakman will like my saying this. I had it put to me the other day that a critic had behaved extremely badly because he had condemned in a few sentences a film which had cost thousands of pounds to make.

SPEAKMAN: *I can answer that in a second. I think he was grossly unfair to the people who had financed and produced the film, and grossly unfair to the exhibitors who were going to show the film.*

DILYS: But surely a film is not to be judged by the amount that is spent on

it? Come back to these French films. I'm sure you, Mr. Speakman, like some of the inexpensive French films better than some of the expensive musicals?
MICHAEL: The only drawback to a French film is that it's in French.
DILYS: Yes, there is that.

SPEAKMAN: *And you know, French films don't do well in the provinces.*
DILYS: But that doesn't mean they aren't good.
MICHAEL: There's one thing that critics and professional writers on films often forget—that is, the advantage French films have because French stars don't talk English. Take a man like Raimu or Gabin. He can't all the time be saying "An American company will pay me so much, and unless you can pay me that I'll go and work for them. See?" There isn't this tremendous competition for them, and, anyway, they probably like France better and don't want to go. The French are sensible, you know. They don't have a star in a film unless the star wants to play the part and you don't get the money to make a film in France unless a star wants to play the part. So everybody, when they start work on a film, wants to make it and wants to make it fast. And they also want to live a good life at the same time. So they're willing to leave a little money in the film and live along. It's much easier to live along in France. That's why *I* like their films. And I think there is hope for England because our films are centralised in London which is a capital and has a heart.

SPEAKMAN: *But do you want film making to be centralised?*
DILYS: It's certainly extraordinary to think that this film business, which influences people's minds all over the world, alters their points of view about everything down to the clothes they wear and the way they do their hair, should be almost entirely controlled from one relatively small centre—a town in California.
MICHAEL: I think that sounds much more dangerous than it is. Anyway, the alternative is to split it up among a lot more people or have it controlled by one organisation—like the government. But if I don't like the government I'm much worse off than if the controls are with free business men—with one or two of whom I may have some say.
DILYS: Some people might still think that the power of the cinema in the hands of so few people is a frightening thing.
MICHAEL: It can only frighten you in a country where people think of

nothing but money. The cinema can't be controlled dangerously by one man, or any group of men, so long as the people who make the films care about films. If they only care about making money, then be frightened of it. I don't give a damn about money. If I couldn't make what I wanted to make here I would spit in anybody's eye. That's the only craftsman I respect.

SPEAKMAN: *But you admit that your films must make money.*
MICHAEL: Of course they must make money, otherwise I am wrong. But in the film business, speaking as a film maker, I don't have to make anything I don't want to make.
DILYS: Ultimately, then, you get back to the artist—the man who actually makes the film—the craftsman if you like. I firmly believe that in the long run the artist has the last word and the whole thing depends on him. The serious, conscientious artist or craftsman does ultimately get to the point, as you've done, when he doesn't have to make anything he doesn't want to make—or he perishes completely. And the good man doesn't perish.

SPEAKMAN: *I don't care who* you *say has the last word. For me it's the public. It's our business to give them entertainment. They're not interested in anything else. If your artistic films flop—the whole industry collapses.*
MICHAEL: I don't like the word art. My view is that the cinema is a craft and while it remains a craft, it's all right—no one need be frightened, but once it becomes an industry . . . .

SPEAKMAN: *What?*
MICHAEL: *Look Out!*

Artists at Work: Michael Powell and Leo Marks

BRITISH BROADCASTING CORPORATION/1959

ANNOUNCER: *Michael Powell's pictures are always strongly individual. It's almost impossible to tie neat labels on any of them. But there are one or two quite definite labels which fit* Peeping Tom. *To begin with it's a horror film with an X certificate, and it's a melodrama. It's nearly as melodramatic as* Pearl White. *And then it's about a very shocking subject: murder by a young man who's afflicted with the perversion called scoptophilia, the morbid obsession which makes people into peeping toms. And finally, much of the action takes place in back streets and sleazy joints including a photographic studio which manufactures more or less pornographic pin-ups and what are called 'art studies' for stealthy sale across the counter of a news agent's shop below. The story which binds these ingredients together is so extremely complicated and ingenious that one of the first questions I asked Michael Powell was how does a film begin?*

MICHAEL POWELL: Well they all start different ways. This one started by a meeting with Leo Marks. I'd read one or two of his scripts and I said to him, "Have you got an original idea for a film, one we can write a script from?" And he started to talk about scoptophilia. And so as he went on talking about this morbid urge to gaze, I'm not sure first if he didn't say, "Would you mind making an X certificate film?" And I said, "Not if it's the right kind of X certificate." Finally he said, "You know, what makes people into peeping toms?" And I said, "Well that's a good title!" And he was rather shocked, you know. He said, "Oh, it's not that kind of film. Won't that get all the wrong people in?" he said, "Well, let's get the wrong people in as well as the right

---

Transcript of BBC radio program. Printed by permission of the BBC.

ones." And he looked rather disapproving of this but then he started to tell me the idea of this film. And unlike all writers when they do tell you an idea—they say very quickly an idea and you say oh that sounds wonderful and then you find they haven't got an end, or something. He told me the beginning, the middle, and the end. And I said, "You're on! You're engaged! You're commissioned! Write it!"

ANNOUNCER: *How long ago?*
MICHAEL POWELL: Oh, a year ago now. And about nine months later—he was going to deliver it in four months, and then he was going to deliver it in six months, and always he had a new story or maybe a new idea—but in the end, nine months.

ANNOUNCER: *So then what do you do next? You've got your script.*
MICHAEL POWELL: Well I work with him all the time on the script and we gradually evolve. He was always worried in his script that as there was a film within the film, I would get too technical my end. I was worried he'd get too technical his end. Since he took a course in psychology and since he's got a chess player's mind, I haven't. And he thought the film end would get too technical, too. So we were also playing this against each other, and gradually the script emerged this way. Because the boy, as you know, is a cameraman, and, really, a peeping tom anyway—he's a film director.

ANNOUNCER: *Leo Marks, who wrote the script, was one of this country's finest code breakers during the war. And certainly his story could hardly have been conceived by any other kind of mind. It contains a black and white film within the main colour film and a second color film being shot inside the main film. And cameras taking pictures of each other's view finders until the world seems to consist of endless reflections and parallel mirrors. There's a reason for this. Mr. Marks feels that the sense of sight divorced from the sense of feeling has run riot in the modern world. This mad dance of cameras reflects our present state. He regarded the film as a challenge.*
LEO MARKS: The challenge of bringing to the screen the story of a man who wanted to commit murder through his camera—because fundamentally it was part of his character—'tis a case history. And in thinking up what could drive a man to the extreme lengths of this particular peeping tom, I had to create a case history complete in itself and got the concept of a scientist who

was interested in training a camera on a baby at all times in order to see how he grew up. I then wanted to show the result of that camera being trained upon him.

ANNOUNCER: *Do you connect scoptophilia with the diseases of our civilization?*

LEO MARKS: I think scoptophilia, or the urge to peep, is a very common, prevelant complaint. And that when it comes before the average magistrate today, the victim of this is usually summarily sent to prison without reference to psychiatric treatment because it's considered that the act of peeping is something which he can control. I wanted at some stage or other to do a study in scoptophilia. The idea of a young cameraman who uses his camera as a method of murder and as a symbol of murder came at the same time as thinking about doing a subject about peeping toms. I'd been introduced to Michael Powell because we wanted to do another subject altogether which was the life of Freud. But we very soon discovered that another producer had acquired the rights and Powell said have you anything else that might interest me? So I told him the whole theme of *Peeping Tom,* and he listened in silence—and he has a habit of looking into the middle distance when he's interested—I didn't know it at the time, I thought it meant that he was bored—but it always means he's concentrating, and he stared into the middle distance and then he said, "That's mine, go and write it." So I went away and wrote it and came back and read it to him. It took two and a half months to write from the moment of leaving Powell's office to delivering the script.

ANNOUNCER: *So the director is now fitted up with his first essential: an idea. And for an independent producer like Powell that idea will have to have more than simple box office possibilities. It will be have to be something he can play with as a producer. Not until he's sure that it's going to hold his attention and release his imagination does he go on to think of finance.*

MICHAEL POWELL: Well, an independent producer doesn't make a film unless he absolutely believes in it. Nobody wants to make a film just to make trouble for everybody else. And even though you may not expect to make a lot of money with it you must believe in it—in independent film production. You can go to private sources, your own sources, or you can go to the National Film Finances Corporation which was formed by the government for just that purpose. They're there to put up the end money for a proposition which seems a sound one. And they're pretty shrewd at guessing which are sound ones. They're there for that when you can't find the money anywhere else, and if they have pretty good reason to suspect that you can get the money somewhere else, then they're entitled to refuse.

ANNOUNCER: *Casting is a long slow process.*

MICHAEL POWELL: While the film is being written and while you're looking for the money, you're already thinking who will photograph it and who will be the right designer for it, and whether it will be in color or black and white and also, of course, who is going to play it. And you start keeping fingers on various actors, sometimes for small parts, sometimes for big ones. Because really, in a film, there's no such thing as a small or a big part. There are short and long parts. 'Cause what a lot of actors don't understand is that a part can be very short, but during that one time the whole audience are looking at you and only at you. You better be good. You're concentrated. It's a burning blast. You're on a diamond point. And that's the essence of film acting. It's the difference between stage acting, where you can diffuse the energy, and film acting, where you have to concentrate it all in a single moment. And, of course, you start thinking of the idea of the actors for each one of these parts. In *Peeping Tom,* I think, there were perhaps sixty or seventy parts which were personally cast. And maybe forty of them had little fingers put on them all over the place—where they were working on tour, or in radio or on television, or in other films or in plays, you know, and then you have to keep tab on that maybe they're going on tour, maybe you can't get them, maybe you get disappointed. So all that's going on all the time like a little spider's web.

In films, more or less, you can have who you want. So long as you don't want all stars. But you can have the best actors in the world and so you should cast every single part yourself. You shouldn't leave it to anybody else. There are so many good actors. We have wonderful actors in England and there are so many of them who want a chance. So whenever I cast a film I just throw my doors open, and I see everybody.

Mr. Michael Powell on Making Horror Films

THE TIMES/1960

WHEN *PEEPING TOM* OPENED a month or two back in the West End, *The Times* found in it finesse and that first essential of a thriller, the ability to thrill. Other critics were not so happy: "The nastiest film I have ever seen," wrote one, and another said, "It's a long time since a film disgusted me as much as *Peeping Tom*—beastly picture." Such reactions have been produced, to a greater or less extent, by several of the current cycle of British horror films, but what distinguished this one, apart from its being an unusually good example of its type, was that it was directed by one of Britain's few major directors, Mr. Michael Powell, whose past successes have ranged from *I Know Where I'm Going* to *The Red Shoes,* and *The Tales of Hoffmann* to *The Battle of the River Plate.* Why, at this juncture in the history of British films had he turned to a story of, in detail at least, quite gothic horror?

His answer, when we asked him, was simple. "As usual at the moment, I had two or three stories in preparation, and this was the one the companies wanted to finance, so I made it first." Was this, we wondered, because horror films accounted for many of the major box-office successes of the moment? "Quite possibly—I really don't know. Of course, I don't think of it as just a horror film at all—I tried to go beyond the ordinary horror film of unexplained monsters, and instead to show why one human being should behave in this extraordinary way—it's a story of a human being first and foremost. That's why I had my own son play the central character as a child" (and

---

played the child's sadistic father himself, we interposed?). "Yes, I felt it gave the whole thing greater truth than if we had a routine child actor. My son understood what we were doing—I explained it all to him—and enjoyed joining in." We suggested that one reason for the outraged response was the casting of a normal, handsome young man in the role of the murderer instead of a conventional fairy-tale devil. "I think that had something to do with it—he was a figure to disturb an audience by asking to be identified with, understood. My wife's criticism was that he was not in fact ordinary *enough* to achieve this; that's a criticism that makes sense to me. I think she may be right."

Themes of horror, we remarked, were not so novel in Mr. Powell's work as some critics had suggested—they occurred in *The Red Shoes* ballet, in *The Tales of Hoffmann,* and, perhaps particularly relevant to the present instance, in *A Canterbury Tale,* which featured Mr. Eric Portman as a magistrate who goes round pouring glue into girls' hair. Mr. Powell politely disagreed with the last instance: "That was really Emeric Pressburger's film. I'm a director; I hate writing. With *A Canterbury Tale* I had doubts, because the script had a wonderful idea—this man who cares so much about truth and beauty that he has to act for it, even on pain of being regarded as some sort of lunatic for what he does—but it was a Continental idea that did not fit into an English film. If I was going to make an English film with it at all, I should have done more with it, translated it more. But I didn't. I filmed it straight and the result was a tremendous flop. Since then I've never filmed anything I had reservations about, as I'm not conceited enough to think I'm so good I can get away with anything I'm not absolutely sure of.

"You're probably right about the horror themes in my work generally, though. I think they occur naturally in the work of any masterful director (by that, of course, I don't mean a director who makes masterpieces, but just a director who knows what he wants). Rex Ingram, with whom I served my apprenticeship, and who still remains for me a model of the real director, always had them—there were hunchbacks or monsters lurking on the fringes of all his films, and he made at least one thorough-going horror film, *Black Orchids*. Indeed, he liked it so much he made it twice."

Would his own next film be still on horror lines? "Oh no. It's a film in praise of the Brigade of Guards. I'm shooting background material now and casting the four main parts later. Of course it's not just an animated recruiting poster—in fact its irreverence will probably annoy the Army intensely when it's finished. Still, they were furious about *Colonel Blimp* at the time, and now they speak of it with the greatest affection. The English will always laugh at themselves eventually, even if it's not till 10 years after the event."

An Interview with Michael Powell

BERTRAND TAVERNIER/1968

MIDI-MINUIT FANTASTIQUE: *If you were asked to characterize* Peeping Tom *what would you say?*
MICHAEL POWELL: It is the most sincere of my films.

MMF: *That is rather disturbing isn't it? (Laughter)*
MP: No, not at all because *Peeping Tom* is a very tender film, a very nice one. Almost a romantic film. And I was immediately fascinated by the idea. I felt very close to the hero who is an "absolute" director, someone who approaches life like a director, who is conscious of and suffers from it. He is a technician of emotion. And I myself, who am thrilled by technique, always mentally cutting the scene unfolding in front of me in the street or in life, I was able to share his anguish.

MMF: *The film is very elaborate. Are there any sequences which posed problems for you?*
MP: No, now I think I have resolved all the technical pitfalls. Wait, there is one shot which was thought to be impossible to work out. It is the scene where you see some different colored pens falling from a bridge in the studio. Do you remember? I was told, "It's impossible, no one will see them. It's completely unshootable." I said to them, "It's extremely simple. I want some pens that are ten times larger and I'll film them falling at a slightly slower

---

From *Midi-Minuit Fantastique,* No. 20, October 1968, pp. 2–13. Translated by Gina Honigford. Reprinted by permission of Bertrand Tavernier.

speed than normal." This optical effect goes completely unnoticed. I don't like a too obvious panache. However, if you look at *Peeping Tom* you can see that the composition of the shots and the rhythm of the scenes are very elaborate. For instance, the last sequence was shot in a simple take of nearly eight minutes. And it was very difficult to do because of the décor and because of the progression of Karl Boehm's emotions through a series of different stages. Luckily he helped me very much. You know, he's the son of the conductor Karl Boehm and he has great artistic sensitivity. He hasn't got the mentality of an actor at all. I find him quite remarkable during that long scene. It was only afterwards that I added some shots of flashes and the reels. All the rest was filmed in continuity.

MMF: *How did you come to collaborate with Leo Marks, the scriptwriter of* Peeping Tom*?*
MP: I was familiar with Leo Marks because he had been involved in different projects of which I myself had some knowledge. I knew that he had worked for Foreign Affairs during and after the war, for the Civil Code Service; it's for this reason that the film *Triple Cross,* which was recently produced, was already in the planning stages at this time. When we met, I was first struck by his out-of-the-ordinary wit; then, I discovered that he was interested in psychology and I felt like producing a film on Freud; not exactly about the life of Freud but a film about his work. We had just finalized a project to do together when John Huston announced, the following week I think, that he was doing a film on Freud! It's then that Leo Marks came to propose an idea to me that he must have had in mind for a while, one of a man obsessed, not so much by the camera as by the lens of the camera, who lives his life through the lens of the camera, who is even obsessed sexually by the lens of the camera. I saw in this an extraordinary possibility, certainly because I was a director my whole life, and I hired Marks to write the story then the screenplay; but I must say that at this moment I didn't imagine that this would be as complex and as erotic as *Peeping Tom.*

MMF: *Did you work together on the screenplay?*
MP: Yes, in the same way that I have always worked with Pressburger. That is to say, we discussed a sequence together and at times, I would say to him that as a director, I didn't see things in the same way. As a matter of fact, sometimes we had a very precise idea of what we wanted to capture, but

sometimes only an image which we hoped to develop, like in a symphony. There was much more dialogue in the first screenplay than in the final version.

MMF: *Was the idea of the child terrorized by his father in the initial plan?*
MP: Yes, it was an original idea of Leo Marks. He envisaged a child whose father had always been accustomed to film emotions rather than images—to whom he has served as a guinea pig since his infancy.

MMF: *Who had the idea of the 16mm black and white?*
MP: I don't know for certain now; Marks had imagined the peeping tom making amateur films, possibly in black and white, possibly in color, and I naturally thought that since the story took place during the last twenty years he wouldn't have been able to allow himself to use color and that consequently he would have to use black and white. In any case, it works better in black and white because color is marvelous if you can choose what you photograph, but in the case of an amateur and of what he usually films, it is not always ideal. It is a question of style; black and white is a style and so can color be. But very often you get rather ugly color that is not at all natural. If you film everything you see in color the result has nothing to do with nature.

MMF: *More than color, black and white gives a documentary flavor, a realistic approach.*
MP: I thought that black and white would allow me to come closer to what the man in the street was doing. Certainly things have changed in the last ten years: color has become cheaper and amateurs use it more readily. When you have worked in the cinema for as long as I have, you don't think, you *feel* things. When I make a film, I take my decisions at the beginning and stick to them. As regards *Peeping Tom,* I *felt* at once that the film would be better balanced if the amateur sequences were in black and white. Moreover, I imagined that working in a studio, he would make use of the off cuts because on a film the assistant camerman sometimes collects 30, 40, 50, or even 200 feet of unused film which nobody wants, most often black and white. You see, I live in this milieu and I react to it. Take the film *Black Narcissus* which was supposed to take place in India; I decided not to go to India at all and to film it entirely in the studio and on location in England. That worked very well; in the same way, once the decision had been made that

the peeping tom made his films in black and white and that the rest was in color, there was no further problem. It is absolutely essential to make a clear decision at the beginning and to stick to it afterwards.

MMF: *Your own son plays the part of the child Karl Boehm and you play his father. Why?*
MP: First, because I thought that they ought to really look like amateurs and naturally, my son and I are amateur actors! For the rest, I understood the story so well that I would not have wanted to ask an actor and his son to play the role. I found it completely natural to do it myself. I thought that it could even bring something to the film. In any case, it was not for any other reason!

MMF: *You must have terrorized your son on the set?*
MP: Yes, but you see, he trusted me! For a man who has spent all his life shooting and directing films, the subject of *Peeping Tom* is rather delicate and I think it's better to keep it in the family as much as possible! (*Laughter*).

MMF: *Did you yourself film the black and white sequences?*
MP: Yes.

MMF: *And did you make some amateurish mistakes on purpose?*
MP: Yes, like everyone else.

MMF: Peeping Tom *is one of those rare modern horror films. Classical horror films draw upon the beliefs and superstitions of the nineteenth century. On the contrary, here, it is the modern elements which are terrifying: camera, tape, recorder, etc. It's very rare. What do you think?*
MP: I think that the camera is something very frightening. If you think that *Peeping Tom*'s camera acquires such a personality that it becomes a source of terror like the lens, I'm extremely pleased because that is exactly what I feel myself. Since H. G. Wells, Arthur Clarke and Ray Bradbury, they have all tried to think up frightening machines but it's very difficult to achieve. I don't think there is anything more frightening than a camera, a camera which is filming and which is watching you.

MMF: *Horror films rarely make you think of elements of real life in order to create anguish.*

MP: Really?

MMF: *No, they stick to conventional vampires, mad scientists. . . .*
MP: I suppose that certain directors are influenced by surrealism, but that's not the same thing, evidently.

MMF: *Mr. Powell, you are, let us say, a typically English director. You have made some very good films, some films with a high reputation, but none which comes up to* Peeping Tom. *This film even seems to run counter to the image one has of you. You make films about love, psychological films.* Peeping Tom *is very disconcerting in this respect.*
MP: It's very interesting for me to hear you talk like this because if I had held your views at that time I would never have made the film. I was only fascinated by the possibilities that the subject offered. You see, most directors of my generation have their own style, but I don't. Take Hitchcock, for example, or Renoir; these are directors who have found their own style in the cinema. I haven't. *I live cinema.* I chose the cinema when I was very young, sixteen years old, and from this time on, my memories almost coincide with the history of the cinema. I have been working actively for the cinema for the last 40 years and I live equally in the future because I am deeply dissatisfied with what I have made up to the present day. As I have already said to you, I am not a film director with a personal style, *I am the cinema.* I grew up with and through the cinema; if I interested myself in pictures, books or music, it is again thanks to the cinema. So, when I make a film like *Peeping Tom* I am the cinema. And only someone like me can do *Peeping Tom* because it is necessary to identify oneself with the cinema more than with a personal world.

MMF: *Have you already produced other fantasy films in some aspect, or films containing scenes of terror and of cruelty?*
MP: English critics have often told me they found evidence of extreme cruelty in my work; but you know the English critics! It's this kind of remark that makes a person want to be cruel! (*Laughter*). For a long time the English cinema—and I am myself English—was very removed from any realistic preoccupation and stuck to a poetic nature; poetic because it dealt with England, its climate and the character of its inhabitants. But this was in no way a creative cinema. Since the beginning I have always worked with Euro-

peans, not with the English: Pressburger, Korda, Ingram and the French and Italian technicians that we used at this time. Anyway, I'm not interested by *English* cinema, only by *the* cinema.

MMF: *You met Hitchcock under very special circumstances, I believe?*
MP: Yes, at the time I was looking for work as a set photographer. They told me, "Hitchcock is in the middle of filming a movie which he didn't believe in at all. Since he is furious, he takes out his anger on the photographers. He doesn't leave them the possibility to take photos. He turns off the spotlights after each take and if the photographer persists, someone knocks over his camera. If you have courage, go ahead." The film was named *Champagne.* I arrive on the set and the drama fuss begins. Hitchcock has the lights turned off. I decide then to play the director and I begin to adjust the spotlights in a manner different from Hitchcock's. I had already studied a lot about the cinema, in France, in Nice, with Rex Ingram, and as far as photos are concerned, the ideas were very different. Someone tries to knock over my camera, which was on a tripod, when Hitchcock comes over and asks me, "Why do you light the scene like that?" I have never seen this type of lighting." I answer, "It's the French way." He was very interested right away, questioned me for a long time, then let me work. We became very good friends and I admire him a lot. He's an extraordinary creator.

MMF: *Did you work on the screenplay of Hitchcock's* Blackmail *in 1929?*
MP: Yes, he had taken an idea from a Charles Bennett play *Blackmail.* Charles Bennett was one of these extremely talented writers who are capable of writing two acts of a play but not the third! And there are a lot of them like this! In a sense I was responsible for the sequence of the rest: he didn't have any ending for *Blackmail;* we therefore had to invent one, and this could only be a continuation. One day after I had discussed it with Hitchcock and had begun to have gathered enough ideas, I suggested to him to use the reading room of the British Museum; the blackmailer would be pursued by the police on the roof of the British Museum and would finish by falling from the dome into the area of all of the books. Hitchcock liked the idea and he held onto it; and this is a trick of directing—not really of style—that he will often use in the future, to know how to transform a very tense situation into a "bizarre" pursuit, in circumstances which no one would think of.

MMF: *You have told me that you really liked* Psycho?
MP: That's right, I love this film because it's full of humor.

MMF: *Didn't* Psycho *come out in London at the same time as* Peeping Tom?
MP: Yes, and I think that it was a much more successful horror film than mine because I took the thing too seriously while he put in an extraordinary amount of humor; for the public it's a wonderful film. I don't know what you think?

MMF: *We like it a lot as well. What was your first film?*
MP: A rather short film, four reels, since the Americans financed them a lot at that time in England. Since they didn't want to invest large sums of money, these films didn't exceed four or six reels; I was hired by an American for whom I worked several times afterward; the film told the story of a London taxi driver who found himself involved with, by accident, a group of gangsters and crooks, what provides for many humorous situations.

MMF: *Did you film in the street?*
MP: Yes, with the sound . . .

MMF: *This took place in what year?*
MP: 1932.

MMF: *The new wave?*
MP: Yes, except that the new wave doesn't benefit a lot from the capital of the old one!

MMF: *What was your first really long footage?*
MP: A film like what all young directors want to do, on the depopulation of the island of Scotland; a film comparable, in the history of French cinema to *Pêcheur d'Islande.*

MMF: *Was it a melodrama or a social documentary?*
MP: A melodrama. The entire population of a small island must decide if it is going to continue to live on the island or leave it; at the end everyone leaves and abandons the island.

MMF: *Was it a good film?*
MP: Yes, a good film 30 years ago! It obtained some prizes in America, but naturally none in England.

MMF: *The title?*
MP: *The Edge of the World.*

MMF: *What is, before your meeting with Pressburger, the film that you prefer among the ones you did by yourself? Your most personal film before 1941?*
MP: That one: *The Edge of the World.* Then, since no one offered me any work, I had decided to leave for Hollywood where I had a lot of good friends. Americans are very warm toward directors, and since I had worked with a few of them, I thought that America would provide me what I hadn't been able to find in England. I didn't go there because Korda saw the film and offered me a one-year contract. Naturally I wasn't aware that at the same moment when he offered me this contract, he didn't have the first dime for making a movie! This was typical of Korda: when he liked something, he risked everything for everything. The first film that we had to do together took place in Burma, with Conrad Veidt starring; I went on location, I took a few photos—this didn't cost me much—and upon my return he told me, "I'm sorry, but we cannot do this film, it's too expensive, you're going to do another one in northern England in the islands, still with Conrad Veidt, but in the role of the German underwater commander." This was *The Spy in Black* (*U-Boat 29* in the United States), a spy film.

"OK," I answered, "I'm going to go take a look!"

"Why?" cried the producer. Actually it wasn't Korda who was producing, he had only begun the project.

"Because I need to, I don't know these islands and it's necessary that I have an idea of how I'm going to tell the story!"

And the producer, who was American, was still not convinced; so Korda said to him: "Oh, don't be so stupid, let him go!" I left, and two days later I met Conrad Veidt. I developed a great admiration for him and his role in the German cinema; moreover I knew that he wasn't really thrilled with the idea of doing a film with a young director whom he never heard of.

"Mr. Veidt," I said, "I have the impression that we are going to be working together."

He looked at me while rubbing his monocle: "Yes?"

"I don't know if you've reflected on this role; for me it's one of a man who has a fanatical conception of his work and it's this way that I want to treat him."

He looked at me again and said in an icy tone: "Continue."

Then we became friends.

The script wasn't very good; one day, heading to a session of work, I found the producer waiting for Korda, and he said to me: "If I understand correctly, someone is supposed to rewrite the script; he has already messed everything up, transformed the masculine role into a feminine role, invented a few new characters . . ."

"Excuse me," said someone who was seated nearby, "I am Emeric Pressburger, the writer that you are talking about."

We went to find Korda; Pressburger unfolded his notes and began to read to us about a film that had nothing to do with the original script. I was absolutely delighted, everything seemed extraordinary to me. I took a look at the circular on Veidt and on the producer who was saying nothing; Korda began to speak: "This all looks really good to me, Emeric, what do you want to do the film?" And thus began our collaboration.

MMF: *Pressburger was the scriptwriter?*

MP: Yes, he did the writing, he never directed. We decided in forming our association that the credits would always read: a film written, produced and filmed by Emeric Pressburger and Michael Powell, in order to share entirely the responsibilities and so that no one else would take the title of producer.

MMF: *Did you collaborate on the scripts?*

MP: Yes, as a general rule, Emeric wrote the script and gave it to me to work on; I sent it back to him with modifications; in the beginning we really tried to discuss; but the discussion degenerated rapidly in a dispute! He always had the last word! Sometimes I changed entirely a scene, sometimes I approved what he had written without reservation.

MMF: *For* Peeping Tom *you worked alone?*

MP: Leo Marks wrote the script; I collaborated with him a little, but not as much as with Emeric.

MMF: *Did Pressburger not want to work with Leo Marks?*
MP: No, he was doing something else at that time; it had nothing to do with *Peeping Tom.*

MMF: *What was your role in* The Thief of Bagdad*?*
MP: The situation was very particular. It took place just after Munich and just before England declared war on Germany. We were all very conscious of the imminence of war; however we worked on the project of *The Thief of Bagdad,* this enormous fairy tale in color. One day Korda said to me: "Listen, Ludwig Berger is going to do the directing but I'm convinced that we will not have finished this summer before the war breaks out; do you want to join the team and produce the sequences that I ask of you?" I accepted. He proposed the same thing to Tim Whelan who was about to produce a sort of dramatic comedy for him. I took charge of almost all of the exteriors, all of the scenes with Conrad Veidt, all of the big scenes. Everything worked well. Sometimes Alex came to direct a few scenes. We worked in a very agreeable atmosphere. The Saturday when the war broke out, we were still in the middle of filming in order to try to finish—the film was only finished in America. And the next day, a Sunday, I was already in a bomber filming *The Lion Has Wings,* the first movie about the war. Tim Whelan, four other producers and myself, worked during the whole following week on this propaganda film. The filming of *The Thief of Bagdad* is a good example of a happy collaboration between several artists; Alex gave me a lesson. One day he arrived at the filming location. I had prepared three complicated, enormous shots: entry in the port, numerous action scenes, combat, etc. . . . we were suspended by the change of time which was never what was necessary. That is to say that it was perfect for England but not for Bagdad!! We were finally ready and I couldn't film.

"What's going on here?" asked Alex.

"Ah! We have a shot a little over a kilometer from here and another here as well."

"OK, very well, let's film them!"

"But Alex," I objected, "the time is not right!"

"Let's film them anyhow," he cried, "the time *will be* right!"

And we filmed them; in two hours the most important shots of the film were in the can because Alex had said: "Don't wait, go ahead!"

MMF: *What exactly did you film in* The Thief of Bagdad*?*
MP: A certain number of very visual and decorative scenes like the arrival of a boat, all of these wide-eyed shots. Tim Whelan especially specialized in action sequences. I don't know for sure who filmed what.

MMF: *What do you think of the film?*
MP: I think that it's a very beautiful fairy tale.

MMF: *Did you see Raoul Walsh's* The Thief of Bagdad *with Douglas Fairbanks?*
MP: Naturally, it's a fantastic film. I don't know how things are now, but Douglas Fairbanks had an enormous influence on all of us cinema people; he remains one of the greatest producers! He went from the stage to the screen to become a big star and he understood show-business. He also knew how to get the extraordinary people that he needed to come from the theater; that's how he always had the best costumers, the best decorators, etc. And when you film a movie like *The Red Shoes* or *Tales of Hoffman,* you are obliged to think about what a man like him would have said: You can allow yourself to take the best collaborators. This is what I finally did but I think he's the first producer who ever acted like that.

MMF: *Do you know that the French director Jean-Pierre Melville considers* Colonel Blimp *one of the best movies in the world?*
MP: Here's someone I'd like to meet!

MMF: *What does this film represent for you?*
MP: I must say that Emeric considers this the best film that we have done together.

MMF: *What's the idea at the base of the film?*
MP: The film was conceived on a purely emotional basis; it's the story of a marvelous old soldier who, at the time of the threat of German invasion, still has an order in England and who believes himself to be essential. He arranges some big maneuvers and decides that the war will begin at midnight. So a young officer at the head of a commando declares that if the war must be launched at midnight, he will begin it at 8:00, because this was a real war and not a gentlemen's war! The film should have been titled *The Gentlemen's War.* He launches his attack at 8:00 with some troops and captures the entire

military staff at the Turkish bath! And naturally this infuriates the old general and he has quite a scene with the young officer:

"But the war was to begin at midnight!!"

"How do you know when the war begins? Good God! It begins when I say it begins!"

And losing all restraint, the old man says: "Do you know how I was when I was your age? When I was your age I was even more rebellious than you!"

And they both fall into the pool. Then we go back 40 years in time, when he was a young man, during the war in South Africa. He was full of fire, full of fervor, meddling with everything, but they quickly made him toe the line; in Germany, where he had gone, he had some troubles. At the Ministry of the War, they said to him: "Say, do you want to have a career or not? So close it!"

Throughout, the film develops his love story with a girl he met in Germany and then lost; she will remain his feminine ideal for the rest of his life, an ideal that he finds again during the second war—1914–18—in the form of a nurse that he marries, precisely because she resembles the woman that he lost. But she dies; and during the third world war, 1939, the same girl becomes his chauffeur, because now he is an old man. In fact, he is the exact image of the traditional British soldier, with a single love in his life. Deborah Kerr played the role of the three girls: the girl from 1902, the one from 1916 and the one from 1942.

MMF: *Is it a bitter film?*

MP: No; but you pose an interesting question. Truthfully, in the beginning the role of Blimp was to have been played by Laurence Olivier. He had served in the Marines; and he was himself so full of bitterness for everything concerning the army and the way that they treat people and waste people's talents, that this would have made for the most bitter and most aggressive film ever done, and I don't think that it would have come out in England under these conditions. At the Ministry of Information, when they read the script, they told us: "Doing this film is out of the question!"

"But we're going to film it anyway, whether you like it or not!"

"Listen, we are about to lose the war"—this took place in 1941—"we cannot show a young officer saying to an old one: 'Leave your seat, you are about to lose the war!'"

"OK, we're sorry, but we're going to film it anyhow."

"Very well then, but in order to have Laurence Olivier, you need our permission because he is doing his military service, and we are not ready to let you have him!"

So I went to see Rank in person, who asked me what I was planning to do; I told him that I was going to take Roger Livesey, who I knew was another good actor; but being as he was a sentimental, the film became sentimental.

MMF: *The hero of* Peeping Tom *is a man who tries to be honest?*
MP: Do you mean the character portrayed by Karl Boehm? Yes, he is very honest.

MMF: *Until his death.*
MP: Right; what are you trying to say here?

MMF: *This struck me while listening to you talk about the character of Blimp.*
MP: You are right and I believe that it is precisely because he is honest that the film touches you.

MMF: *In addition, he has a sympathetic manner and has nothing in common with maniacs or traditional obsessives.*
MP: Oh! no, no; but no one of us ever has the appearance of it.

MMF: *Was it a good idea to choose Karl Boehm for the role?*
MP: I think so; I very much admired the way he interpreted it. I think I said to you that in the beginning, we were to have taken Laurence Harvey. He would have completely resembled what we call a "focus puller," the most important of the assistant cameramen, the man who controls the focus when you don't use the zoom; he must be able to follow the action, and in my opinion that is really an art. Laurence Harvey would have probably had more of the allure of one of the readers of "Films and Filming" or other magazines of the same style, neglected, half-dead from hunger, passionate, but I don't think that he would have been more sincere than Karl Boehm.

MMF: *Does a film like* Black Narcissus *present certain fantastical aspects?*
MP: Not so to speak. The success of the film surprised me; it's all based on a question of atmosphere; first the education of the girl, in Ireland, in a simple family, an almost religious education. The entire novel was built on the idea

that the house was full of painful things, wind, evil, etc. The fact that this made for a good movie, because this was a good movie, is rather surprising. This is the first film in which the music plays an integral role in the atmosphere; this was the first time that I worked with Brian Easdale, who did the music for *The Red Shoes* and a few other films. We prepared several sequences together with the themes already composed, not the music; therefore when I filmed a scene, I knew what was going on in his mind.

MMF: *The image was equally very interesting?*
MP: Marvelous! This was Jack Cardiff's second film, and one of his best.

MMF: *Completely unreal . . .*
MP: Yes; I think that the fact that the film was filmed entirely in studios, and in England, gave the film the style of a novel. When I read the book, I immediately thought that we were going to the Indies and that we would bring back some good shots to then try and match the others filmed in England. The result would not be brilliant. It worked better to film everything in England. This is what created the atmosphere of the film. As for *Tales of Hoffman,* this is what is called a compound film; someone had already produced a similar film that impressed me a lot: *The Robber Symphony* by Friedrich Feher, in 1935. He had composed the music and built the film upon it. I liked this idea. When Sir Thomas Beecham, who had directed the orchestra for *The Red Shoes* and had anticipated other possibilities, suggested *The Tales of Hoffman* to me, I have to say that I didn't know much about the opera, not less however than I was up on ballets when I had done *The Red Shoes!* I listened to the recording but I never went to a performance; after having worked a bit, I said to myself: I think that I can do it if we first record the music, the performance and then we do the film on top; otherwise I don't feel capable of succeeding.

MMF: *What was your visual approach to the subject?*
MP: This is a very difficult question. In truth, things happen in the following way: you take the best musicians, the best singers, the best cast that you can find and you record the most theatrical performance possible; then you must make numerous changes that are discussed in common: a new overture, a new curtain-raiser, etc. And, finally, you try to hire the most talented artists in the world to produce the costumes, the décors, the choreography.

Thus Frederick Ashton is responsible for the general choreography. L. Massine did his own choreography. Hein Heckroth the costumes and the designs. All of these people brought excellent ideas; it was my job to choose from them and to elaborate, little by little, the film that you saw.

MMF: *Did you give precise instructions for the color, which is unusual?*
MP: No, the idea came from Hein who wondered how I was going to be able to do the prologue, the epilogue, and even how I was going to edit the different reels. He suggested that the first act be completely yellow, the second Venetian red and the third Greek blue; I thought it was a good idea.

MMF: *The result pleased you?*
MP: I find the sequence in Venetian red by far the best; I also really like the immense yellow curtains, but I think that this was a bit of an arbitrary decision to make in the beginning. The best ideas in *Tales of Hoffman* are, as a matter of fact, those that we found as we went along. We proceeded a little bit like certain films from the beginning of German expressionism. We had so many great talents at our service that each minute saw a new idea born and realized.

MMF: *They have accused you of having used choreography in a very theatrical way and not film-style like Minnelli and Donen did? Do you think that that's true?*
MP: Not in *The Red Shoes,* but in *Tales of Hoffman,* yes and consciously!

MMF: *And in* Honeymoon?
MP: *Honeymoon* is kind of between two styles; what they call Spanish "dance" is not dance for me at all! It's as strange as bullfighting. I would not say in any case that Spanish dance is a true art . . . neither is film.

MMF: *What are your favorite films?*
MP: *49th Parallel,* where I had a wonderful cast and magnificent location shots. We filmed everything throughout Canada. It was sort of a race behind some Germans that had just landed. Another film that I equally love is *The Small Black Room.* It is very simple: a disabled genius tries to discover how the minuscule bombs launched by the Nazis on England work. They look like toys and numerous children kill each other in taking them. It's also the

story of a dying man who discovers a reason to live. I think that this is my best film.

MMF: *We aren't familiar with* Stairway to Heaven.
MP: That's the American title for *A Matter of Life and Death.* Do you know how this film was produced? At the beginning it was an order, an official order. They asked us to film a movie exalting Anglo-American relations. This was a diplomatic work. And little by little it became a film that headed toward fantasy. I wanted to treat it with a completely serious tone, but Pressburger added some elements of comedy. It was he who convinced me to mix the genres.

MMF: *We don't particularly like* Battle of River Plate.
MP: This was a film of classic prestige on the British marines. It's not very personal. There are some pretty shots of boats if my memory serves me correctly.

MMF: *And* Canterbury Tale?
MP: It doesn't have that much to do with Chaucer. It takes place at the end of the war. It's a love story, an exploration of two characters where the past and the present mix together. There were some good scenes, but something was missing in that film.

MMF: *We really like* Gone to Earth.
MP: Here's another film where the bizarre and the strange play an important role. I was always attracted by fantasy based on the atmosphere, on the historic or religious traditions more than on mythic creations. I really like certain short stories by Kipling like "Them." In *Gone to Earth,* the fantasy was created for the entire culture. It had a base in reality. The location shots and the color were magnificent. We made some attempts to somber, mortuary-like tones, what was very new at the time.

MMF: *The film was redone by Mamoulian.*
MP: Really, I didn't know that it was Mamoulian. Yes, Selznick is one of these producers who feels obliged to change something in all of the films that he produces. But it was only the American version that became a hit, not the one distributed in Europe.

MMF: *What do you think of eroticism?*
MP: In the past, the cinema wasted numerous occasions to be erotic. There is so much money, so much talent, and so much taste wasted by the cinema, which could have been so well used in the field of eroticism. Eroticism is not improvised: either you have the gift or you don't. At the time of the splendor of Hollywood, there was a pleiad of great directors, decorators, photographers who, visibly, were talented for eroticism, but they didn't let them do erotic films! And this is really a terrible waste! They did films proper enough to content the average American exactly like in Russia these days; now they're doing films that were produced in Hollywood in 1934. What a marvelous producer of erotic films von Sternberg would have been if only someone had encouraged him! Instead, he had to think about the "American middle class," amuse them with special effects, etc.

MMF: *You don't think that Fritz Lang is a more erotic director than von Sternberg?*
MP: Oh I think that Fritz Lang is capable of practically anything! He is truly a great man. You would have to do a real analysis of films made ordinarily in Hollywood to be able to discover some eroticism.

MMF: *Don't you think that the English are more talented?*
MP: I don't know, I wonder if the English are as advanced. But this is a subject for which I am not accustomed to giving opinions. I will have to reflect on it a little more. I would love to write a long novel on the world of cinema; I have belonged to it for such a long time. And I know why people do films, something few people know.

MMF: *And eroticism in your films?*
MP: They are, for the most part, fairy tales.

MMF: *That excludes nothing . . .*
MP: No, but there is a sort of literary eroticism that doesn't excite me much.

MMF: *In your next film, is there a big place left for eroticism?*
MP: My next film is the story of a painter who believes that he will no longer paint and of a girl who persuades him to begin again. It will be called *The Age of Consent*. He will probably end up painting her; but to see a painter sit down and paint a girl, this could be exciting, but I had the hardest time

explaining to my scriptwriter that this didn't excite me at all. What interested me was the problem of Creation and the fact that this creation in the case of the painter was very physical. He will have to struggle, to fight, even more strongly than he will move away from reality. It will be a slightly bitter comedy that I will produce with James Mason who will play the leading role.

MMF: *What do you think of directors like Whale and Browning?*
MP: I like Whale better than Tod Browning. He was a lot more talented with the actors and he really knew how to create atmospheres. He was also an excellent theater director, very original. I prefer Browning's silent films to his spoken films. I knew the film-makers of this time very well. There are many that I admire: people like Allan Dwan, Tay Garnett whom I met at Korda's. He had come to film a movie. Elmer Clifton who was a Jack London sort of director. Victor Saville who produced a large number of very interesting films before the war. I also met Karl Freund who was less an artist than a little survivor, a schemer who edged his way everywhere. One of my favorite directors remains Rex Ingram, whose work (and I'm thinking of *Mare Nostrum*) should be rediscovered.

MMF: *Have you seen the films produced by Val Lewton or works like* The Uninvited?
MP: Yes, I actually knew the person who wrote the novel that inspired *The Uninvited* very well. She wanted me to adapt another one of her works at any price, an enormous book mixing a ferocious Irish nationalism and a passion for divinatory practices or sorcery. But what especially struck me were the German films of Lang and Murnau, *Mabuse* or *Nosferatu.* I don't know Fisher or Corman.

MMF: *Since* Peeping Tom, *what have you done?*
MP: I produced a comedy in Australia with Walter Chiari, a little bit like *Ruggles of Red Gap,* the marvelous film by Leo McCarey. It's the story of an Italian who, called by a relative, lands in Australia and finds no one. He has to get by. I produced *Sebastian,* which was realized by David Greene, according to a story by Leo Marks. It's a magnificent subject, the story of a man who works for the codes service of the Intelligence Service. He directs a giant number of girls, possesses all of the secrets of the world and has no personal secrets until he meets Susannah York. He is Dirk Bogarde, and his boss John

Gielgud. The film is very amusing and Greene, a young man for whom this is the second film, shows proof of evident quality.

MMF: *Your films, and I'm thinking of the magnificent* I Know Where I'm Going, *often draw from current English problems?*
MP: You think they're funny, English problems? (*Laughter*). Neo-realism doesn't really interest me much.

Rediscovering Michael Powell

ROLAND LACOURBE AND DANIÈLE GRIVEL/1977

Part I

E79: *Michael Powell, your filmography covers almost all of the British talkies. What was your first encounter with the cinema?*

MP: Oh, it's a magazine. It was in 1921 in England. I read it and I was absolutely fascinated. From that moment on, I wanted to be a filmmaker. Three years later, my father went to Monte Carlo; he won at the casino and bought the lease of a hotel on the Côte. It's at this point that I explained to him that I absolutely wanted to be a filmmaker. And he told me: "It's easy because there are lots of people on the Côte who come to make movies. Mostly Americans." In Paris, he introduced me to Léonce Perret who was a great director of historic super-rubbishy films at the time. We talked. I think we were in Joinville. He gave me advice. And the following year, I went on vacation to Cap-Ferrat where Rex Ingram, the great American director, was making a film, *Mare Nostrum*. Rex introduced me to his entire team. I was lucky: he needed a young man who spoke English and French. He offered me a 100 francs a week. That's how everything started.

I was also very lucky to be with a great filmmaker, with great ideas, and who was making a great film! He adored perfection and the greatest artists in the world wanted to work with him. In those days, movie people in Europe, writers, theater people came to Nice and all went to la Victorine studio. Right

From *ECRAN* 79, January 1979, No. 76, pp. 37–48; and February 1979, No. 77, pp. 34–40. Interview conducted in London, September 1976 and November 1977. Translated by Dominique Duvert.

away I convinced myself that the cinema was a great art, made FOR and BY great artists. Not simply popular. . . . A Great Métier. That idea I had on the first day, I constantly kept in my mind. That's why I don't make many movies now. It's no longer fashionable. When one makes a film today, one does no longer feel like making something extraordinary.

E79: *You really started to produce at the beginning of the 30s, while shooting "Quota Quickies." Can you briefly tell us what these films were?*
MP: It was very simple: at the beginning of the talkies, Americans needed actors who spoke English but who were not necessarily American. They were looking for actors in all countries. They intended to make French movies, Italian movies, English movies, but shot in California! So naturally London was like private hunting grounds for them. And I met Alan Parker in London. Alan Parker was one of Douglas Fairbanks's great friends. And his director for *The Black Pirate* in 1926. Doug had sent him to London, telling him: "Make screen tests with all the great theater actors and send them back to me in California." Why make screen tests? Let's make small films that cost nothing. That way we'll see people who are really working in a film instead of actors who are undermined by stage fright in discontinued meaningless scenes! It will only cost 15 shillings a meter." And it was true. The Americans thought it to be an excellent idea and all the studios adopted it. It was a blessing for young writers, young directors. It was not always of an exceptional quality but we worked. We worked with actors, good actors. Previously, the British cinema was based on the London theater. Actors from the provinces were finally able to have access to the cinema. And actors who were just as good as the ones from London were discovered.

E79: *They were very quickly made movies then?*
MP: Oh yes. Seven, eight days . . . and sometimes, a great production: 10 days! (Laughs)

E79: *Copies of these movies have been preserved?*
MP: Unfortunately not. Except for a few. The first two movies I made like that were a big success. I was working with Jerome Jackson and a good team. We had very good scripts. But the first films did not last long: 40 minutes, 50 minutes maximum. American companies were paying us one pound per foot of film.

E79: *Your first important movie is* The Edge of the World. *Did you already have the idea of this film way before its production?*
MP: Yes. 4 or 5 years prior. And it was not an Englishman who gave it to me. It was an American. An old hand at the movies who had come to England and found it to be an Eldorado. His name was Joe Rock.

E79: *The same Joe Rock who had produced the Stan Laurel comedies in the mid-20s?*
MP: Yes, it was him. He had been famous in the United States where he formed a duo in the music hall: "Montgomery and Rock." Do you know that Joe Rock is still alive? He must be 90 years old. And he is still like a rubber ball. I saw him again 5 years ago.

E79: *At the time, what was your position on documentarism, the Grierson school, which was one of the great trends of the British cinema? Did it influence you?*
MP: No, no. Not at all. I don't like documentaries.

E79: *Then you never joined in this realistic trend?*
MP: I always had big ideas. On themes, images, men. *The Edge of the World* was not really an important film, but it helped me foresee making something impressive. And it worked since I won a prize in New York.

E79: *Your cinema is still very close to nature, folklore. Do you think it is incompatible with the research made by the "documentarists"? It seems that you stand apart from the Grierson school. Their concerns were not yours?*
MP: Quite different. I didn't find them sympathetic. We had sometimes very heated conversations on these matters. That's why Paul Rotha didn't like me very much. You see, I deeply like the content of great European films. The great German movies, the great French movies. Films made by White Russians. And actors of such caliber as Mosjoukine or Inkijinoff. Of course, at that time, the whole of Europe was influenced by Russian films, the films of the Revolution. So was I when I was a student. But we knew very well at the time that they were films made for people who did not know how to read. So, naturally, very strong images were needed, so everybody could understand. And intellectuals, here, thought it was for intellectuals. They did not understand these were films made for peasants! (Laughs)

E79: *Was your meeting with Korda decisive for the rest of your career?*
MP: Yes. He saw *The Edge of the World.* Most people in England had not seen it. And no one in film. But he saw it and he wanted to meet me. He offered me a contract. Yet he was having problems at the time. He had spent five or six million pounds[1] and he was looking for money everywhere. He even thought about getting some in America, even though he didn't like it very much. But he still made me that offer. It was the first contract. And with Korda, after *The Thief of Bagdad,* we were making films . . . and we signed contracts at the end of the film. (Laughs.)

E79: *It's at that time that you met Emeric Pressburger?*
MP: Yes. He was in Korda's entourage. He was a first-class writer and knew the cinema very well. A born writer. He came from Germany by way of Paris. Like Korda, who had shot *Marius* in France. And when Korda came to London, all the Hungarians followed him. When he left for Hollywood, lots of them followed him and stayed there. But Emeric preferred England. The first film we worked on together was *Spy in Black.* Korda had chosen us. But when the war started, we decided to make a film ourselves with the same actors: Conrad Veidt and Valerie Hobson. Emeric wrote a story in six days. A small story taking place in London during the black-out. It was called *Contraband.*

E79: *Yes, the publicity at the time had emphasized the fact that it was the first film showing the black-out in the British capital.*
MP: That's right. As a matter of fact, in America, they renamed it *Black Out.* I think that Selznick had bought it. In any case, it was really an idea: Pressburger wrote the script with me and I directed. It was new, rather well-done and very well photographed. Already at the time, we had adopted the usual "credits" of our films: Story and Screenplay: Emeric Pressburger; Produced and Directed: Michael Powell.

E79: *Your next film, 49th* Parallel, *was an official commission from the Canadian government, I believe?*
MP: Yes. First they asked me to do a movie in the English Channel. An ordi-

---

[1] When he built in 1936 the enormous studios of Denham. Moreover, *Rembrandt,* the first movie produced at Denham, had required important investments and had been a financial failure.

nary propaganda film with a pretext story. About minesweepers. And I said: "No, not at all. I want to make a film in Canada!" The minister asked: "Why Canada? What does Canada have to do with the war?" And I answered: "Because sooner or later, America will be at war. And we have to prepare the people over there for war. So, we are going to launch an attack on Canada with a submarine, so we'll be able to have the propaganda you like!"

E79: *There was a very beautiful poster.*
MP: That was Emeric's idea. I explained to him what I said at the meeting with the minister and he said: "Yes, it's a very good idea, but we must make a film with sketches like Julien Duvivier with *Carnet de Bal*. And in each episode, we'll meet a great star." I accepted the idea and immediately went on the lookout for stars.

E79: *And every time the character you met had his/her own idea about the proper attitude to adopt in an armed conflict?*
MP: Exactly. We had people like Leslie Howard, Laurence Olivier, Raymond Massey. And everybody was waiting for them to arrive. It was a rather long film, over two hours. So, you had to be expecting something in order to sustain interest.

E79: *It was a success?*
MP: Not at all. You must not know it in France?

E79: *It came out seven years after the war, in 1952 and went completely unnoticed. Your next film,* One of Our Aircraft Is Missing, *used exactly the same basic plot as the one before, but this time it took place in Holland, with Allies rescued from a plane shot down in flames.*
MP: Yes.

E79: *It's at that time that you created your first film studio. Is there a reason for the choice of the name: "Archers"?*
MP: It's rather complicated. The idea was: we always aim for the center but we sometimes miss it. But a good subject which is a failure is better than a bad subject which is a success.

E79: Colonel Blimp *is originally an Anglo-Saxon cartoon character?*
MP: Yes, it was a comic strip. Everybody knew him. It was the creation of a

great artist, a political caricaturist. This colonel Blimp was the true English "Conservative" . . . honorable . . . pretentious . . . impossible. So, we chose the name because it was as well-known as Astérix. And we used it to launch the film. But to tell you the truth, the caricature was really a caricature. In the movie, it was no longer so. On the contrary, there was a lot of sympathy for the character. Roger Livesey gave him a lot of emotion.

E79: *Originally, you had not planned the role for him.*
MP: No, for Laurence Olivier. If Olivier had played the role, for sure, he would have grated on the War Office.

E79: *Then you produced a small propaganda film that we don't know in France.*
MP: Yes, it's curious, when I went to Telluride, recently, they found a copy of *The Volunteer* and they showed it. But I didn't see it again myself. There were a lot of people eager to discover it. And they told me there were two charming things in it. I was very astonished. Because the story was not a story. It was a mere situation. We had begun to shoot scenes with Laurence Olivier, Ralph Richardson, Eric Portman, all the actors of that time. In the canteens of the Denham studios, Ralph Richardson, who was playing himself said: "I am an actor and all I can find to do is to dress into an Elizabethan costume and declaim Shakespeare's verse. But what are verses going to do against the Nazis?" Then there were scenes in the theatre and at the stage door. With Richardson and people who were waiting. He always made jokes like: "It's terrible for an actor to always find people waiting tirelessly for him to give autographs. But it's even more terrible not to find anybody!" (Laughs.) So there were quantities of short playlets and slowly, we reached the subject: Richardson had a dresser, a young man who wanted to enlist, and the actor asked him what he intended to do. And the young man said: "I spoke with my father and my mother. My father was on a ship and told me to choose the Navy. But my mother replied: 'At sea, you might drown. Choose the Army.' And my brother advised me to enlist in the Air Force like he did." And at the end, the young man decided: "I don't want to be any safer than the others. So I'm going to embark *in* the planes, *on* a ship!" (Laughs.) And the great story of this little film took place on a carrier in the Mediterranean. We went there with Ralph Richardson. We were on the *Indomitable* and we participated in the landing in Oran. Then we had to go back to England.

At that time, getting out of the Mediterranean was a problem, the skies were full of American planes. The Americans had everything they wanted. And us, we were stranded on a beach, near Oran, with our equipment. Then I met an American and we started to talk. He had seen *One of Our Aircraft Is Missing.* And he asked me: "Where do you want to go?" I answered: "Let's start with Gibraltar." Gibraltar was the way out. The next day, he embarked us in a big empty plane and in three hours, we are at the door of the Mediterranean. And by now, everybody was waiting to go back to England. It lasted for days. Among the people who were waiting were Leslie Howard, whom I knew well, with his lawyer. And he took the plane just ahead of us. And everybody disappeared. I think the reason was that his lawyer looked a lot like Churchill; and he liked to accentuate the resemblance: the hat, the cigar, the cane. Everybody was perplexed. Even the Germans. "Is it possible that Leslie Howard travels with Churchill?" We knew that Churchill was traveling in the area. The Nazis didn't want to miss such an opportunity. And the plane was shot down. Poor Leslie. And we followed him. As for Churchill, he came back another way. Another aerial route very high over France.

E79: *Then you made another film with sketches.*
MP: *A Canterbury Tale* did not have any success at all at the time. It was shown recently at the National Film Theatre and I saw it again with curiosity. I assure you that it is a magificent film. I was very astonished. Canterbury is my country. I was born in that region. I spent my childhood and my teenage years there. And that's the only time I returned, to make a film. I put lots of memories in the film. Emeric had imagined a rather complicated story, but very delicate and enthralling. The idea of the film at the beginning was to show Americans, who had entered the war, what England was. Where and with whom they were going to combat. And to explain to the English what the Americans were. That they were not all built the same; that there were many different types. Unfortunately, at the time the movie was done and released, it was too late: the introductions had been made! And at the time, we had not thought about that. It's the only time we were overtaken by events in a way. It was a bad combination of ideas. A film always requires between a year to eighteen months of work. And you have to be up-to-date *when the movie is released. Not before!* And we always succeeded in doing just that, except with *A Canterbury Tale.* It never had any success, and I didn't understand why at the time.

But it's a film to show again today. There were a lot of people at the National Film Theatre to see it because they knew it's a mysterious film, impossible to see. And I too, I was curious. I was filled with enthusiasm. It's extraordinary. With an exceptional photography. Sculptural. It was the first film I was making with Erwin Hillier as director of photography, and he did a marvelous job. I remembered that the last reel was very good. When the pilgrims arrive at the cathedral as in old times. I knew it was among my best. But I was afraid that the first part of the film was less well-made: too many dialogues, too many details; the story was too complicated. I was afraid it would be embarrassing. Not at all!

E79: *I only know the film through the English critiques of the time and the reactions were very enticing. They talked a lot about the character played by Eric Portman who scandalized all the film commentators.*
MP: Yes. He was playing a slightly bizarre human being. A man alone, always alone, so alone. I underlined this fact several times with books he loved, sports he practiced: climbing mountains, walking, always solitary. He met a young girl. But it was not a love story: simply a movement of sympathy, of understanding. But we knew that between them, it would never reach love.

E79: *What was the starting idea for* I Know Where I'm Going?
MP: After *A Canterbury Tale,* we came up with the idea to make *A Matter of Life and Death* and we had already finished the first stage of the script. But not the last! Except, it was impossible to get the Technicolor film. Because Technicolor films were requisitioned for aerial combat training. And it was impossible to make *A Matter of Life and Death* without it, because the entire basic idea was grounded in color: the earth in color and the sky, monochrome.

E79: *Yet, at that time, Laurence Olivier did* Henry V.
MP: He was the only one to get a dispensation. At the end of 1944, it was no longer possible. So we were stuck for six to eight months, in the best case scenario. And Emeric got worried: "What are we going to do now?" and I asked: "Don't you have an idea in your pocket we could use?" And he told me that he had been thinking for a long time about a film subject in which a girl wanted to go to an island. An island whose inhabitants you could see

from the opposite coast: but because of storms, of the raging sea, you could never reach it. It was an interesting idea. But why did she want to go to the island? And he answered: "That's precisely why I want to write the story: *to find out!*" (Laughs.) I thought it was possible to introduce things that were worth saying. On the war. It was the beginning of 1945 and we could maybe talk about the reasons why we had thrown ourselves in combat. Immaterial values? And Emeric told me: "I'm sure it's possible. Give me a few weeks." He left and I saw him six days later with the script! With the script, with the dialogues, ready to shoot!"

E79: *And the girl never gets to the island!*
MP: Never. I read it and I found the script extraordinary. And I left right away . . . to find the island!

E79: *It's a magnificent work. Very bewitching.*
MP: Yes. You never forget it. I'm often asked to come present the film.

E79: *Your next film was also a great success. And a success worldwide:* A Matter of Life and Death.
MP: And our biggest success in France, I believe.

E79: . . . *with* Gone to Earth.
MP: Yes, that's right. *A Matter of Life and Death* was shown after the war at the Cinémathèque Française and I received a lot of compliments. I was very moved.

E79: *The idea to use color and monochrome on a dramatic level was very new at the time.*
MP: Yes, and the idea of having the rose change color. To start with black and white and to go to color. And to see the color "come out" of the rose. It was impressive.

E79: *And remarkably well done on a techical level. But do you remember at the same time the movie that Jean Delannoy had produced on an original script by Jean-Paul Sartre,* Les Jeux Sont Faits? *Many ideas are similar to your movie.*
MP: I never thought of it!

E79: *Naturally, the treatment of the film was not the same. And the authors' ambitions either. But many visual ideas were directly inspired by* A Matter of Life and Death. *Charles Dullin's character, for example, is a direct reminiscence of the role played by Marius Goring.*
MP: Yes, I remember very well *Les Jeux Sont Faits*. Indeed. But our idea in fact, was not quite original. There had been other films before ours that made the most of that theme. I'm thinking of this American film. *Here Comes Mr. Jordan* for example.

E79: *For* Black Narcissus, *you adapted for the first time a novel which was already published.*
MP: Yes, in fact an actress who wanted a role in the film proposed the subject to me during the war. I had been seduced by the plot and I told her: "We should talk about it *after* the war." And it's very strange because after the war, Pressburger got married, and it was his wife who talked to us about it again after she read Rumer Godden's book.

E79: *What interested you in the story? The confrontation between the morals of the Western world and those of the Oriental world?*
MP: It was a very beautiful love story. In an unusual setting. But I didn't want to go shoot in India. Because this kind of film had always been done that way with studio scenes and link scenes on location, with real actors or sometimes stand-ins. I didn't like that at all. I was convinced that everything had to be done either in India or in the studio.

E79: *And you filmed it entirely in a studio?*
MP: Except for a few scenes. You know, you can find anything in England. And since we had an empire for a long time, there were always people bringing back things from all over the world: trees, flowers, rocks! Extraordinary things! I was able to find great gardens with rocks, and mountains at the edges; and all the colors in the world! And all the flowers from the Himalayas. The great vegetation and even the torrential rains! In Sussex! (Laughs.) And the rest was filmed in a studio.

E79: *The results in the change of scenery are astonishing.*
MP: We had built the great castle outside at Pinewood. It was Junge's idea. All around this enormous décor he had a big plaster background built at a 20

degree angle from the ground. That way, all day long, when the sun moved . . . there never was any shadow on the background! It was always well lit. And on the background we had painted the Himalayas: Everest, the great valleys, the forests. And all of it sunlit! And when a cloud went by it, it was magnificent! It was so simple! Alfred Junge: a great master.

E79: *We are now getting to the dance films.* The Red Shoes *was your first attempt in this field. What convinced you to embark in that project?*
MP: Oh, it was not truly a dance film. Originally it was a script that Alexander Korda had commissioned from Pressburger before the war. Korda wanted to make a great romantic film about a ballerina's loves. And I believe—I suspect—that it was for Merle Oberon. He probably was going to do it as it was done at the time: an actress would play the role of the ballerina and a real ballerina would dance in the ballets. With a cutting made in that perspective. It was probably Korda's idea. So Emeric wrote his story and liked it a lot. And he had always told me, as the project had never been made: "After the war, we must buy that back from Alex if he wants to sell." Korda had not paid Emeric a lot of money to write his script at the time. But when we asked him, he wanted a very high price, because he sensed it was an interesting idea. He sold it to us anyway: he regretted it later. Then I read the script and I told Emeric: "A dancer must play the role. And another thing: we have to create an original ballet. Today, we can no longer spend the entire film talking about creating a work of art . . . and not create it! We have to actually make it. And with the girl. Otherwise, needless to start the project." And Emeric who adored his story answered: "All right! Anything you want." After that, we had to find the art director. And the dancer. So I talked about the project to Alfred Junge. Before film, he came from the theatre, and he was a bit scared because he had never done that. And he told me: "Micky, you are going too far!" Me, I was disappointed because I needed a decorator who would say: "You have to go farther!" I looked and found Hein Heckroth who understood right away what I had in mind, and he went much further.

E79: *He also came from the theatre.*
MP: Yes, but he had also worked with Junge on *A Matter of Life and Death* and *Black Narcissus*. He deals mostly with "properties."[2] He was a great

2. Furniture and accessories.

painter too. And a great theatre man. Junge was rather a film man. And this time, I needed a theatre man. So, very simply, Junge left and I continued with Heckroth. We still had to find the dancer. And the actor Stewart Granger—a guy who knew all the girls—told me: "Micky, you're looking for a girl?" And I said: "Yes, a girl who knows how to talk and dance." "You know," he answered, "there is a Scottish girl in the Saddle Wales Ballet. She has a role in Robert Helpmann's new ballet. It's called *Miracles in the Garbals*.[3] She plays a prostitute. It's a character. She has red, very red hair. You have to see her!" So I made an appointment with her. She was very busy and so was I. We met. Five minutes at the Dorchester Hotel. And I saw right away that she would do: she was a ballerina. And she could act and talk too. You could tell. She was typically Scottish. Very proper, direct, energetic: "What exactly do you want to do, Mr. Powell?" "I don't quite understand, Mr. Powell. Are you proposing to photograph ballet?" So I offered her the role. And before she left, she said: "What are you going to pay me?" I had no idea: "I don't know, you are going to start with a 1000 pounds." She immediately found an agent and asked me for 5,000 pounds. (Laughs). At that time, Mme Valois was the ballet director and the great ballerina was Margot Fonteyn. And I think that Mme Valois was very disappointed we didn't offer the role to Margot Fonteyn. Moira Shearer was a nothing at the time. And she told her: "Girl, I can't prevent you from doing the film, but if you leave, I can't promise you can come back with us!" So Moira was very scared, because the ballet company meant everything to her. And during almost a year of preparation, she hesitated between dance and film. And it's only at the last moment, when I started to make tests with other ballerinas, that she accepted. She showed great courage. Because Mme Valois was powerful and influential as ballet director. A real female Diaghilev.

E79: *You are currently working on a book on* The Red Shoes, *in collaboration with Emeric Pressburger?*

MP: Yes. That's the idea of an American publishing company: Avon Books. A company born out of W. Randolph Hearst's empire. I talked about it with Emeric and he started to write notes: what happened to the young man in the film? Maybe with his parents? And the young girl's antecedents? We are talk-

---

3. The Garbals is a working-class area in Glasgow.

ing about it all. And we are beginning to write another story. Mostly the first half of the book. Because it's going to be rather thick: 300 pages in paperback.

E79: *But the book is going to include the story of the film? In some way, include it with other elements surrounding it? As though, in reverse, you had adapted a great novel for the cinema and you had cut out certain terms?*
MP: Exactly: we are trying to write a novel which was perhaps the one we adapted.

E79: *It's an enthralling experiment.*
MP: It's very interesting, because up till now, I knew the story only from the director's point of view. I worked with all the actors: Massine, Goring, Walbrook, Moira Shearer. But in fact, I know nobody! The characters are seen by my eyes through the actors. So in the book, I created all the characters: in fact, a blend of the mythic characters of the film and of the real character of the actor. Take Massine whom I know and adore: I know exactly how he talks, how he thinks; I really see his body; and I hear his voice. He worked for a long time with Diaghilev. So, when Emeric writes a sentence in a dialogue, I say: "No! Massine would never say that! Lubov maybe, but Lubov-Massine, no!" Because I know that all the people who like ballet and know it well will not be able, when they read the book, to abstract his true personality. And you have to take that into account because Massine has been in the Russian ballets for 60 years. He is now working in San Francisco. When I was in Colorado, for that festival in the summer of 1997, he sent me a telegram. He proposed to me to create a ballet, *The Red Shoes*. I refused and explained to him it was not the time to do that. And, at the same time, I was asked to do a musical on Broadway!

E79: *The conception of the ballet* The Red Shoes *is something revolutionary compared to everything that had been done in film in this genre.*
MP: Yes, even for the theatre. In fact, it was mostly a sketch for *The Tales of Hoffmann*. Because we had already composed the music. And after, we made the ballet. The second step was therefore to make an opera. To tape the score and then film the opera. There was no script in *The Tales of Hoffmann*. We simply followed the score.

E79: *And it was a success?*
MP: Considerable, and international too. Yes.

E79: *And very much appreciated by the professionals.*[4] *But did the public at large follow?*

MP: Yes, it made money. Not for us, because Korda went bankrupt at the same time and all the films went to other distributors. We never got a penny! But the film is still in syndication. By the way, I never told you that story about *The Tales of Hoffmann*. Hein Heckroth came to see me one day and told me: "We just finished the sketch for the décor. For the waltz sequences do you want Moira Shearer and her partner to climb the stairs to the top?" I agreed and Heckroth replied: "We prepared the model for you. It will cost 8,000 pounds." At that time, it was a lot of money. I asked why and he answered: "Because it's enormous! The music is very rapid and when they dance, they cover a lot of ground: we will need the whole set!" I asked: "Where is your camera?" He showed me a place by the décor. So I told him: "Put the camera in the flies and paint the stairs on the floor! . . ." Heckroth looked at me and said: "I will never understand anything about the cinema!" (Laughs.) I am sure that Alfred Junge would have reached my solution: stairs painted in perspective. Naturally, the dancers were dancing on a flat surface. But you can tell when an actor likes an idea like that and Helpmann who was dancing with Moira Shearer asked me: "Show me exactly where the stairs are from your point of view. Because we are going to go down the steps, even though they're flat." And to perfect it, Helpmann even pretended he slipped on the last step!" (Laughs.)

Part II

E79: *Between* The Red Shoes *and* The Tales of Hoffmann, *you directed three films, two of which have not been released in France. First,* The Small Back Room *about which Bertrand Tavernier spoke very highly.*

MP: A film that had no success. Because the thing did not work out at the time. Originally, it was a magnificent book, bitter, modern, enthralling, by Nigel Balchin. We had in mind to do it right after the war. I think in the end it was my fault to impose it on Pressburger after *The Red Shoes*. We were done with the war. We were already in another world. We no longer needed a film

---

4. Michael Powell carefully preserves two hand-written letters congratulating him for the plastic richness of his *Tales of Hoffmann*. The letters are signed Cecil B. De Mille and Joseph Von Sternberg.

full of psychology and reflections on this period which was over. In fact, it's the same story as *A Canterbury Tale* which was being repeated. Yet, it was a very forceful book, with perfectly portrayed characters. And I respected the atmosphere of the book with scrupulous fidelity. Toward the end, there was a long sequence—almost 25 minutes—almost without any dialogue. David Farrar found a mine on the beach. Several soldiers had already tried to clear other mines of that type, as it's done now in Ireland, and they had all failed. The hero was not a soldier, because he had lost a foot; he was a scientist. And everybody saw him a little bit like a pathetic individual, a "back room boy." A theoretician, not a man of action. He was there to give advice, and when he intervened, one last soldier had just been killed by a mine; there was nobody left. And suddenly he decided to do it himself. I studied this sequence a lot: each movement, each gesture he was making. Everything was combined in great detail. Truly an extraordinary suspense. And entirely shot on location on a beach I knew since my childhood. With kilometers of rocks of increasing size. On one side, very fine stones, on the other large round balls. All shot in perspective. With, at each step, stones that were rolling.

It was the first film I was making with a great actor, Cyril Cusack. I had always hoped I would direct him. For *I Know Where I'm Going* for example. Except it was impossible to have him come to England before the end of the war. He was Irish.

E79: *For the role played by Roger Livesey?*
MP: No, another character. A small role, but quite strong. In the foreground. A young soldier whose wife goes out with everybody while he is on duty. So, he is always unhappy. I really have a lot of admiration for Cyril Cusack.

E79: The Small Back Room *is also Bryan Forbes' first movie role?*
MP: Yes, as a dying man. He was very good. Except, he was completely covered with bandages, so he couldn't believe it! It's really impossible for an actor to think he is good if his face cannot be seen by the audience!

E79: *You also produced a new adaptation of* The Scarlet Pimpernel, *the tale by Baroness Orczy. You shot in France this time?*
MP: Yes. I shot in the Loire region.

E79: *And at Mont Saint-Michel. And surprisingly, the film is unknown in France!*
MP: I'm not surprised. I didn't want to do it because Korda had already

made a *Scarlet Pimpernel* in 1934. A great comedy with Leslie Howard, Merle Oberon. He had done everything that could be done with that, because it's a completely stupid story! But if you treat it as comédie de salon, it's charming. I had always refused to do it, and I ended up giving in to Korda because he found our color films exciting and he thought a remake in Technicolor would be extraordinary. After he insisted for several months, I finally believed him. But I had not been wrong when I refused: it was a mega-rubbishy film.

E79: *The color though was praised by the Anglo-Saxon critics.*
MP: That's true. There were indeed some interesting things. I made experiments with the costumes and their relationship with the back of the sets. They recently showed a few scenes in Telluride. I don't know where they found a copy, because I believe that in America, it was only released in black and white. Like an action film. But it was not an action film, mostly a film of manners. I don't like to remake a good film. Korda had made a film full of charm and elegance. And with idiotic situations, but everybody likes that. In fact, it's a very "pocket-size story."

E79: Gone to Earth *on the other hand is one of your masterpieces and had an enormous success in France.*
MP: But it didn't work in America. In fact, I've never seen the American version because David O. Selznick, who was the co-producer with Korda, did not like the version we delivered, and he had the right to modify it if he wanted to. He asked me whether I agreed to do "retakes" for the American version. "You have to change this, you have to cut that." I refused. So he asked King Vidor. Vidor also refused. As a last resort, he asked Rouben Mamoulian, and Mamoulian talked to me afterwards. He told me he liked the movie as it is a lot, but . . . Selznick paid great! Maumoulian was a very good director, and I told him I was sure he had done beautiful things. I didn't know his version. The film is often on American television.

E79: *And you were never tempted to see this version? They did alter your work.*
MP: No. Why? I have no curiosity of that type. I know the film was extraordinary. Jennifer Jones was charming.

E79: *Selznick imposed her on you?*
MP: But I liked her a lot. She was very nice at work. Enthusiastic. It was

practically the only film she made in Europe. She went back [to Europe] fifteen years later with Henry King, for a film adaptation by Scott Fitzgerald.[5] They filmed on the Côte. It's the last time I saw Jennifer. We all adored her: she had lots of charm, a strong character, she was young, very strong. A very good friend. The whole team was in love with her.

E79: *The film makes an interesting use of nature and of Hazel's character who becomes part of it.*
MP: The landscape was extraordinary. Originally it was a book and I tried to find the best environment to transcribe it.

E79: *It's a film that enjoys a considerable legend with French audiences. Everybody remembers it. A mythic film . . .*
MP: Is that true? I'm always very happy that France liked *Gone to Earth*. It's the kind of cinema that French film directors taught me: this way of looking at nature, of photographing it. And to make a character out of it. When I was young, I remember this "sympathy" between French directors and landscapes. I tried to get back to that in the film. And I was very aware of what I owed your country's precursors.

E79: *Where did you shoot the film?*
MP: In the region where Mary Webb set the book: Dropshire, near Shrewsbury. It's a strange area between Wales and England. But it's neither one. It's a little bit like an edge. The mountains are truly bizarre, not very high, with enormous valleys, cut in a very dramatic way.

E79: *There is not much to say about* Oh! Rosalinda!
MP: It's just a filmed operetta. Nothing more.

E79: *And* Luna de Miel*?*
MP: It was not a success. I made it because I was interested in Antonio, the Spanish dancer. He wanted to do ballet in a great film like *The Red Shoes*. It confirms the fact that you should never do the same thing twice. The music was interesting; it was "L'amour sorcier" by Manuel de Falla. In theory, it

---

5. *Tender Is the Night* in 1961, the last film Henry King directed.

was a film made by a visitor to Spain. And I did adore the country, but I didn't understand it.

E79: *In 1956 you shot two war movies back to back. For* The Battle *the documentation you gathered allowed you to write a book on the historical event you were covering.*
MP: Yes, we wrote a book after [the film] because we had learned a lot. Lots of elements we couldn't include in the film. It was a spectacular film. Sort of a maritime ballet.

E79: *Some critics accused you of describing war in an old-fashioned, almost too chivalrous way. A gentleman's war. Did all this really happen in that manner? With the beaux gestes of the German commander?*
MP: As far as we know, yes. We made a long enquiry. We asked all those who had witnessed the event. It's a simple film, but it has a lot of class.

E79: *And very beautiful on a pictorial level. The character played by Peter Finch was interesting, elegant, refined.*
MP: Peter Finch was very good, very seductive. He was a very great actor. Sometimes he would play a role he adored, and, in that case, he gave himself completely and he was superb. There was a lot of magic in his play. And the role of Langsdorff was for him. It's the only time we were able to shoot together, and we talked about it several times later on. And I always regretted not working with him. The role was what gave him his start.

E79: *The film you shot next in Crete also included a German general quite as chivalrous.*
MP: Yes. That was more difficult. It was Pressburger's idea to make *The Battle of the River Plate* and that film too. With the first one, I was able to make a well-constructed film, interesting and with a lot of success. A film that was true as much as possible. Thanks to memory, to remembrances, to descriptions. But for the other movie about the kidnapping of a German general in the mountains of Crete, during the war, by partisans, in this case we have to make it dramatic. We had to introduce women. We needed a romantic anecdote. And Pressburger, who was so enthusiastic about *The Rio de la Plata* and its success— it was really a great success—refused to invent a story. He told me: "No, The story is so fascinating. We have to follow it scrupulously." So I

went to Crete and spent a month in the mountains. I went on all the roads, all the paths, on foot. They're still talking about me over there. I was told later on: "After the war, a Scottish general arrived"—it was me: I was wearing a kilt—"who would ask all kinds of questions to the partisans, etc." But I learned many interesting stories, collected a lot of information, anecdotes. We had to build the story with all that. And I had discussions several times with Emeric. But he didn't want to hear it. And the result was not good, because I couldn't find a way to make a masterpiece with that material. I was always the prisoner of facts, of truth. I don't like the film. But some people liked the film, or at least some of its elements.

E79: *Personally, I like the use of music a lot. The first film participation by Mikis Theodorakis.*

MP: Yes, that was very good. It *was* actually his first film. I had convinced Emeric to find a Greek composer. An agent in London told me that there was a young Communist student in Paris who had won the Music Prize in Moscow. I sent a telegraph to see him. He arrived here with a few music tapes already made. He had done that for radio, television, cinema. We listened to them. I was very disappointed. So I asked him whether he had something else, a symphony, for example. He had one. And I told him: "Let us hear the symphony." And we hired him. It was very good. You're right, that part of the film was interesting. But besides that, I couldn't build scenes. I was tied by the weight of facts. So, out of desperation, I turned to other elements, music, the creation of an atmosphere. But it was not my area. As you know, I'm not fond of cinéma-vérité. It's not my voice, my trade.

It's the last film I made with Emeric.[6] And it might be because of that, because of our disagreement. I was not as enthusiastic for *The Battle of the River Plate,* and this last film was such a failure.

E79: *We are now getting to your most famous movie today. At least, the most talked about. Who is Leo Marks?*

MP: Leo Marks was naturally destined to become a writer since he was the son of Mr. Marks, who had a bookstore on Charing Cross Road, the Mecca of all bibliophiles. He and his wife were Orthodox Jews. During the war, Leo

6. Michael Powell and Emeric Pressburger nevertheless collaborated one last time in 1972, on an average length film, *The Boy Who Turned Yellow.*

Marks was an extraordinary cryptographer for the S.O.E.[7] He was always wanted by several governments. There is something astonishing in him. He was also a liar on the scale of Baron Munchausen. I met him and he pursued me, first for a film on Freud's life, then for *Peeping Tom*, that he imagined like a fisherman would create a fly to catch the king of salmons. I swallowed it. Then we created the script together. But he is the one who wrote it all word for word.

E79: *Originally, you hadn't thought of Karl-Heinz Boehm for the role?*
MP: No. Laurence Harvey was supposed to play Mark Lewis, and it was his success in *Room at the Top* that changed him into a big star. He was given offers he couldn't resist and I lost him. I gave the role to Karl-Heinz Boehm on our first meeting. I had already noticed him in the SISSI Austrian films and admired his father, the conductor, a lot. Karl had a sensitive character, full of suppressed emotions. You could tell.

E79: *Did you conceive the character played by Moira Shearer in a direct relationship with her character as a ballerina in* The Red Shoes*?*
MP: No. I needed a personality for this extra, and of a certain body type: capable of movement and talent in order to play a bit "amateur." Not an actress but a popular body. My first choice was Natasha Parry, Peter Brook's wife. Then it was Moira. She accepted the role right away without knowing the subject of the film at all. I took it as a compliment on her part. In any case, she created something very personal.

E79: *It's the second film in which you use both black and white and color. A new experimental attempt?*
MP: No. it comes from a realistic and non-aesthetic logic: it was natural that a scientist, a doctor, an observer with a camera shoot in black and white. On the other hand, it was a period in film when we shot in Eastman color. This being said, the mix of the two led to the creation of an aesthetics.

E79: *How was the film received in England? What were the reactions of the professionals, the audience, the critics?*

---

7. Special Operations Executive: the British Secret Services network which was coordinating, across the Channel, the actions of the French Résistance.

MP: The reception of the film? A disaster for me! It was the end of me with a generation of distributors and cinema owners. They said, "If Powell can't touch a film of horror and violence without making an artistic masterpiece, without even talking about "scoptophilia," without creating a human tragedy, without being full of compassion for the insane and the unhinged, there's nothing more to be done with him!"

I was very surprised. I was—I am—innocent and I thought my intentions were clear enough. When the critics reviled me, I didn't answer. All you have to do is read them: it was a frenzied attack. My colleagues were not interested in it. They already knew I was a loner. But they were following the crowd.

The film truly ruined me: after it, it was impossible to get funds for other projects. The fact that *Peeping Tom* is accepted today as "Doctor Powell's Testament" changes nothing.

E79: *About* Peeping Tom, *the notion of modern horror film was mentioned. How do you define it yourself?*

MP: Horror film? No! Film of compassion, of observation, of memory, yes! Film about the cinema, about the years between 1900 and 1960. A film to taste with delight in centuries to come. The opposite of a realistic film. It's a reverie.

E79: *Could you say a few words about your last films? Those you made after* Peeping Tom *and that we don't know in France?*

MP: *Queen's Guard* was not well made. I even forget how I got to collaborate with that writer. A very good writer for the theater but who had no ideas for the cinema. In any case, you didn't miss anything! *They're a Weird Mob,* my first Australian film, was quite simply to introduce myself to the country in the manner of the American primitives at the beginning of the talkies. As in the films of Leo McCarey for example. The kind of film-makers who worked with very simple people, crossed the country, lived with them, understood them, felt their way of thinking, and then put in their films everything they had felt. That's why I did it. It was a book I had read. I bought the rights. I went to Australia to see whether it was true. And I saw it *was* true. I had the impression of discovering a new world. It was enthralling! I was more independent than the Americans. It was a comedy that gained an enormous success in Australia. Because people recognized themselves.

E79: *It's a film that must have been very badly distributed in England?*
MP: Oh, nobody saw it outside of Australia. Rank did not release it.

E79: Age of Consent *is probably the most important film of that period?*
MP: It wasn't bad; it had charm and it was well-acted. But I was disappointed by the painter. I was unable to find a painter to interpret my ideas. They had to be transposed on canvas. To show what he saw through his eyes. I had found a painter of Australian origins who had done numerous exhibitions in New York. He told me that he didn't understand, that it was too difficult. So I was forced to treat it as a comedy. A sensual comedy. Not a big success, but interesting anyway.

E79: The Boy Who Turned Yellow *is an average length film for children for which you worked with Emeric Pressburger again?*
MP: Yes, he is the one who wrote the story. Because I've been one of the directors of the Children's Film Foundation for ten years. And I asked Emeric whether he had an idea for a children's film. So, he wrote something everybody loved. It was very simple, a very good idea, typical Pressburger.

E79: *Hollywood never tempted you? You had many offers. Did you always refuse them?*
MP: Yes, because I know Hollywood very well.

E79: *It's not your way of making films?*
MP: No. For me, there is nothing in Hollywood. It's not my life. In England we want to make *our* films—not producer's films. French film-makers share the same concerns.

E79: *In an interview, you said that you considered yourself more European than English.*
MP: It's true. Europe as a whole has an enormous influence. Look at the Americans: they have a new school. For example, a film like *One Flew over the Cuckoo's Nest.* It's a European film made in California! Had it been made in Europe it probably would have been made better, but they still worked miracles to finish it. We have no idea of the struggle they had. In my view, the new school in California is very promising. If it can survive against the giants in the profession. Because once success comes, it's quite difficult to stay inde-

pendent, but the new American generation has made beautiful things anyway. I hope it will know how to keep its place. It's a daily struggle. The audience has nothing to do with it. It's simply agents against producers. And now that agents *are* producers, it's worse! It's truly the end of art. Because it's no longer about anything besides investing an ever increasing number of millions. You get nowhere that way. For example, in France, with people who are as commercial as the Hakim brothers, you can make a masterpiece like *Belle de Jour.* At least there, the struggle leads to something. But in California, you get *Chinatown!* What's left of Polanski in *Chinatown*? That's probably why he's acting: because he no longer is behind the camera?

E79: *Michael Powell, your career has been a full one. You have no less than fifty films to your credit, nearly half of which are internationally renowned works. You have a very distinctive taste and you are hard on yourself. According to you, which of your films are the best ones?*
MP: *A Matter of Life and Death . . . One of Our Aircraft Is Missing . . . Colonel Blimp.* There is a film I like a lot, that we produced, but that I never directed: *The Silver Fleet.* We had worked on that film a lot, chosen the subject, planned the cutting.

E79: *Yes, that's a film not released in France. Directed by Vernon Sewell. A British critic wrote at the time that he found it so well made he thought you had directed it.*
MP: No, it was better made. He had a way of stressing the dialogue through movements of the camera that was very interesting.

E79: *And* Edge of the World, *do you think that it could be shown again today?*
MP: Yes, probably.

E79: Black Narcissus*?*
MP: I think that now it would be a bit "postcard." I'm thinking of all those beautiful landscapes painted on glass.

E79: *And naturally* Peeping Tom *remains one of your achievements.*
MP: Yes. This poor *Peeping Tom* who from now on bears the name of Powell!

Michael Powell: Zoetrope's "Senior Director in Residence"

TODD MCCARTHY / 1980

BY THE TIME THEY'RE 75, many film directors are writing their autobiographies. Veteran English director Michael Powell is doing that, but he's also been hired by Francis Coppola as "senior director in residence" at Zoetrope Studios, is developing a new project of his own, and is basking in an international critical re-awakening to the considerable merits of his 49-film career.

Just departed for New York to appear on opening night, Nov. 20, of a 34-pic Powell retrospective at the Museum of Modern Art (a program which will be repeated in Paris, Helsinki and possibly L.A.), the spry director returns here in a week's time to set up shop in Hollywood for the first time in his life.

Praising Powell to the skies in a letter to his staff, Coppola wrote: "I hope you will feel free to consult him, get to know him, go to him for advice and comfort, learn to expect no quarter from him and that best use of him will be to overwork him mercilessly."

With a broad smile, Powell himself commented, "I shall be residing at Coppola's studio and shall do whatever I'm told."

There's little doubt that Powell's 56 years of experience in feature films will prove of value to the many young talents being hired by Coppola, and also gratifying that, after 10 years of relative inactivity, he is once again gainfully employed.

As also happened with many other senior filmmakers, Powell found it increasingly difficult to navigate his career once the old-style studio system

From *Variety*, November 14, 1980. Reprinted by permission of *Variety*.

broke down, only to be re-discovered by film history-wise filmmakers such as Coppola and Martin Scorsese.

It was Scorsese, in fact, who effected a N.Y. Film Festival showing and subsequent reissue of Powell's controversial 1959 psycho study, *Peeping Tom,* the film which essentially cast his career upon the rocks. After Hitchcock left for Hollywood, Powell was by far the most visually sophisticated and adventurous director in England, and such pictures as *Black Narcissus, The Red Shoes* and *The Tales of Hoffman,* among the 13 films he made with Emeric Pressburger, did much to establish the international viability of the postwar English cinema.

Powell, who recalled that he was first interviewed by *Variety* in 1926, was raised largely in the south of France and entered the business as an assistant to Rex Ingram on three pictures the extravagant American director made at Nice's Victorine Studios: *Mare Nostrum, The Magician,* and *The Garden of Allah.*

"Victorine then was actually very similar to Coppola's studio here," he observed. "You were able to move around a lot, to get a lot of experience. I started out as a grip, and nine months later I was writing titles for *Mare Nostrum.*"

Moving back to England in the late 1920s, he put in three miserable weeks in Elstree's story department before becoming still photographer on a Hitchcock silent, *Champagne.*

"They had been filming for a month and they didn't have any stills yet. They would actually sit by and wait for me to relight the set for the purposes of the stills. Hitch didn't want to make that one, he hated British-International because they were always giving him stories he didn't like. The next one, *The Manxman,* on which I also shot the stills, was a little more agreeable to him because he at least got to go on location."

Powell takes credit for introducing the idea of the British Museum roof finale to Hitchcock's next—and highly successful—feature, *Blackmail.*

"The story was strong through two acts, but it didn't have a finish. I suggested a chase, and the climax at the British Museum. Being an East End boy, Hitch had never been there before, so I took him over to show him the reading room and the roof. He said, 'Very good, Michael.'"

Powell insists he "would never have got a chance to direct without the quota quickie films." An infrequently remembered—and generally vanished—aspect of film history, the quota films were generally four or five-reel cheapies introduced in 1931 and made to meet a British demand that roughly 20% of American product shown in the U.K. had to be made there.

"To offset the threat to the local industry posed by American films, they were obliged to distribute and exhibit a certain number of British films, so they commissioned eager beavers like me."

With the help of Yank attorney Jerry Jackson, Powell raised the approximately $20,000 necessary to produce the 45–55-minute pix, which they then sold to American companies for a flat one pound sterling per foot of film, thereby generating about $5000 profit.

Powell made 23 quota quickies, most of which are undoubtedly lost forever. One by-product of them was that Hollywood companies could use them to scout new English talent, at a cost cheaper than special screen tests.

"I spent five years trying to raise the money for my first 'real' picture," Powell said. Finally, Joe Rock, an American working in the U.K., agreed to bankroll *The Edge of the World,* about the depopulation of a distant Scottish island. Although a flop in England, the pic was favorably reviewed in New York and also caught the attention of Alexander Korda, who gave Powell a contract.

(Powell returned to the island two years ago to lens a prologue and epilogue showing how the North Sea oil boom has brought hordes of workers to the area. *Return to the Edge of the World* is being featured at the Powell retros.)

His first effort for Korda, and with Pressburger, *The Spy in Black* (*U-Boat 29* in the U.S.), was a hit and immediately vaulted the team into the front ranks of British helmers. Before continuing the association, however, Powell worked on the ever-popular *The Thief of Bagdad* and explained the film's unusual three-director credit by simply pointing to the start of World War II.

"I was working on *The Thief of Bagdad* on the Sunday when war was declared. On Monday I was working on a propaganda documentary, and Korda had already left for Hollywood."

Aside from making wartime dox, Powell, with Pressburger in their "The Archers" company, made such pix as *49th Parallel, One of our Aircraft Is Missing, The Life and Death of Colonel Blimp* and *A Matter of Life and Death* during the hostilities. "We had complete freedom to write about current issues, but we didn't believe we should make combat pictures. We felt they should be about questions of morale, and big themes."

Speaking of his longstanding partnership, Powell maintained that,

"Working with Emeric I learned a great deal. He was a born dramatist and writer, and he didn't learn as much from me as I did from him. It probably started me off wanting to do something that was more ambitious and unusual than the usual sensible dramas.

"I, or he, would suggest a theme or a plot, and he would write the first story. Then I would write it the way I saw it, then I'd send it back to him." While Pressburger would be present on the set, it was Powell who did the actual directing, although they shared credit. For his part, Pressburger went on to direct just one picture of his own.

Despite the international success of several of his films, Powell was never tempted to come to Hollywood before.

"I was determined to convert the English," he smiled. "But, you know, I always had my chances given me by Americans or Hungarians, not by English. When the English finally got to making films, they had this bug about being realistic. Everyone says that what the English can do best are documentaries, but you can make documentaries anywhere."

Addressing the current malaise of the British film industry, Powell opined that, "There are no showmen, or at least no showmen with a gambler's spirit, except for the Arabs, who are anxious to make films but are very cautious, which they probably should be. We need people with show business flair."

Interview with Michael Powell

OLIVIER ASSAYAS / 1981

CAHIERS: *Could you tell us about your current activities in the United States? The last few years, your work has been rediscovered by film-makers as well as by movie-enthusiasts. How did it happen?*

MICHAEL POWELL: Two or three years ago, I was invited to the Telluride festival in Colorado. I was asked to show some of the films I had made with Emeric Pressburger. I brought the best known with me and also *Peeping Tom* which unexpectedly became a sensation.

Martin Scorsese has always been an admirer of our film. He regularly referred to us as an important influence on his work. At the time, he was on the road with the terrible film he made with Liza Minnelli and he was in Los Angeles, two hours away by plane from Telluride. So, to surprise me, the organizers asked him to come present my films. We had already met in London. He came and that's when he saw *Peeping Tom,* and he was completely enthusiastic. At Telluride there were also two young boys who were in the process of founding a distribution house. They told Martin they were interested in the film. So far, in the US, it had only been presented on TV in a version that was cut by at least twenty-five minutes. Martin gave them 15,000 dollars to pay for the copies. Nobody told me any of that at the time. I went back to London. And a few months later, in mid-79, I get a telegram from Martin who tells me that the film was accepted at the New York Festival and that they were sending me a first-class round-trip ticket. In France all that

---

Translated by Dominique Duvert.

would have to be cleared by the Cinémathèque Française. I didn't quite know what this was about but I took the plane and went to New York. Everybody adored the film and it was presented at the Festival under very good conditions. It received excellent reviews. Basically what the New York critics liked is that they were seeing it eighteen years after it was made, knowing that at the time the English critics had hated it and had made it known, that they wrote such things that any other critic can do nothing but be mad at them, that they went too far. So the critics in New York had a good time. They said: "Here's a marvelous film . . . we heard that our London colleagues tore it apart . . ." (gesture of disdain.) As a result, the film acquired an excellent reputation. These young distributors started, not without a certain apprehension, to circulate it, with three copies. Today, eighteen months later, it's shown everywhere. People like it a lot and many people have mentioned it as one of the ten best movies of the year. So here it is happening now for this poor *Peeping Tom* who is now twenty years old . . .

At the same festival, they were showing *The Black Stallion,* a film produced by Francis Coppola. He was there, and one evening we were both guests of honor at a very elegant soirée organized by the New York distributors at the Plaza. We were introduced. But we were each at one end of the table and all we could do was communicate by signs. So I called him the next day to tell him we should meet. He said, "I'm dining tonight on the East Side on Second Avenue; there's a little restaurant that doesn't look like much but makes excellent food." We met there. His sister Talia Shire who plays in *Rocky* was there. A very nice girl and an excellent actress. Their father and two or three friends were also there. In other words, it was a family dinner. We talked about the problems in making an independent studio function in Hollywood, how to gather all the independent film-makers who might work well in it, the type of team you need to manage it. All the problems we had with Alexander Korda or Arthur Rank. I know all that very well. There are things I don't need to ask anymore. I know them instinctively. We talked about all that and Francis asked me why I wouldn't join him in his studio for a few months as an adviser, to see what we could do together. He needs people in charge. I asked him: "Francis, what are you going to be? The final arbiter? Are you going to be the one who says yes or no?" He said: "I'm not very good at saying yes or no, but sometimes I say maybe." I think he needs to keep the possibility of saying no open, but what's essential is that he surround himself with a group of people, producers, directors or authors who know on their own what they want to do and how. It was a doable task and I told him so. That's when I went to Dartmouth College in New England where I had a previous commitment to teaching during the first semester.

CAHIERS: *What were you teaching there exactly?*

POWELL: I was talking about the cinema and then we shot a short experimental film . . . It was a lot of fun. Apparently what they do usually is very theoretical. I taught them how to divide the work, to have a production director, a cameraman, etc. Each of them had a specific task and they did a good job. So we made a twelve minute film. It was very long to begin with, fifteen minutes, but we shortened it to twelve (laughs). We had excellent equipment for the electronic music. We were able to do very interesting things. During that time, I was constantly getting calls from one of Coppola's advisers, Tom Luddy, a very good film strategist, telling me that Francis wanted to see me, and that in his opinion, it was to offer me a job. I said very well. I am ready to listen to all the offers, and I went to Hollywood where they had just moved in the studios. It's not a large studio; there are eight sets, two of which devoted to special effects. Coppola asked me to be his adviser. I asked what kind of adviser? He told me that I would give him advice about what to do . . . that I would read scripts, that I would see rushes. And what would happen if I advised him not to make a film? He answered: "Well, it could be that we would even listen to you." He added that if I had a personal project, I should prepare it, and once the script was finished, we'd see . . ." I said very well. It's been twenty years since someone made me an offer like that in England. It seems to me it's a very good idea.

I always thought that film-makers should be independent and should have their own structure of production. Like in the days when the great theater men had their own theater. It's exactly the same principle. Things don't change. George Lucas also has a similar policy; he shot all the special effects for *Star Wars* in the EMI studios in Elstree near London, but during that time, he was building his own special effects laboratory. He invested in this installation—he calls it his *installation*—part of the fortune the film generated. So he can now plan to make the most enormous film in the world entirely under his control, financed with the *Star Wars* benefits. That's exactly what I recommend. Kubrick also does it. He produces. Warner pays for the production but also all of Kubrick's equipment, lighting, sound system, everything

. . . The whole thing "on rollers" so it is mobile and he can take it before Warner Brothers notices. I'm for it. Film-makers must be independent.

CAHIERS: *Have you already started work at the Zoetrope studios?*
POWELL: Two months ago. I've read many proposals. There are some very good things and others that are not good at all . . . Like anywhere else. Take someone who wants to make films and give him carte blanche, he will inevitably present an idea he's had on the backburner for years waiting for the opportunity and that he finds enthralling. But between the time he had that idea and the time opportunity knocks, the idea has lost any kind of interest. You have to make them understand that. I have to read everything we receive, talk to people, see them. What you need is to work only with film-makers who know how to make a decision, carry their project to the end. We do not want people who come to see us asking questions. We are looking for people with answers. That's our policy.

When you have a studio, you have to choose projects that can be adapted to the specific technique it requires. It is useless to accept a project that takes place entirely in China, unless it is conceived to be completely recreated in a studio like, for example, *The Thief of Bagdad.* Most of the films Emeric Pressburger and I made with Rank were studio films, like *Black Narcissus.* The first question you should ask when approaching a script is: is it possible to make it in a studio? Where you can control everything, people, conflicts, contracts, the organization of the shooting. And most of all, you should not tell yourself that you will shoot on outdoor locations and that it will cost fifteen million dollars and in the end it reaches thirty-five million as it recently happened to poor Michael Cimino. You probably heard about that scandal. The scandal is not what Cimino did, the scandal is the people who gave him the money . . . they must be deranged . . . Cimino may not be very smart but at least he is not crazy . . . so to give him such a sum of money . . . these people should have their heads examined.

At Zoetrope, Coppola has been rehearsing his comedy *One from the Heart* for six weeks . . . It's the story of five characters in a miniscule suburb in Las Vegas whose lives cross each other, mesh. On the one side, there is this buzzing city, its boulevards, neon lights; on the other, it's the desert, the mountains. The main character, played by Frederic Forrest, is co-owner of a wrecking company—a very amusing set with a lot of compressed cars—he lives with an adorable girl but they spend their time quarreling. He leaves her and takes off with the young Nastasia Kinski, thinking she is a lot older than she looks and it turns out that she is much under the legal age. The whole story happens during one day and one night. Sometimes the characters are in the peace of their home, or in the middle of the desert. Sometimes in the rush of the boulevards in Las Vegas. In one scene, they are even caught in the middle of the Fourth of July celebration. In another, Frederic Forrest's wife meets a man in the street whom she finds terribly romantic and who turns out to be a waiter. It produces a series of dialogues in the style of Fred Astaire-Ginger Rogers. At least, with a bit of distance, of course. But it works very well. He rehearsed using three video cameras and a new mobile central control room he's having built so he can shoot and edit at the same time. As of now he has already rehearsed the whole film, and he even has the integral editing on video. The actual shooting started Monday (February 2). The film will be for the most part shot with the camera at the shoulder; the cameraman is Vittorio Storaro and fortunately, he is not too meticulous. He will not be overly bothered if two of his cameras collide, which is a very high probability.

The entire studio is therefore covered with naturalistic decor at this point. The alternative would have been to shoot in Las Vegas, but it's no longer possible. In any case financially. And anyway to shoot a comedy in the streets of Las Vegas would be really looking for trouble. Because of the sound, the onlookers, the tourists. Anyhow, he's been shooting since Monday; I told him as I left, I'm sorry Francis but I have this retrospective in Paris. I have to give it a good opening. He just told me to try to get us a little bit of good publicity. (Laughs.)

CAHIERS: *Did you intervene on* Hammett?

POWELL: No. I was there in the spring when Wim was finishing the first version. Nobody was really pleased with it. First it was underwritten and then it was not long enough. The idea though was very good and the new script is excellent. To take Dashiell Hammett while he was still a detective and already a novelist leads to very good situations, but in the first version, all that was too confused. People come into and get out of his life who are the people he got his inspiration from for the characters in his novels but who at the same time resent him for being in his novels. It's really very good, but it has to be very cleverly and very clearly written. I think it's a movie that will be very successful.

CAHIERS: *Could you talk to us about your collaboration with Martin Scorsese?*
POWELL: We talked a lot while he was preparing and shooting *Raging Bull.* We had long conversations, often on the phone when I was in England, mostly when they were wondering how to get the effect of a character who is gaining weight. I was very opposed to Bob de Niro doing it physically. I was telling Martin to let him put on some weight, just to give the feeling of someone letting himself go, but mostly to simply have big clothes made. It's a bit going overboard to have him putting on fifteen or twenty kilos. And I think I'm right because when I see the film, well, . . . one shot, you notice. Yes, he is fat, he looks different. After that he continues and acts the same way during the entire film. Which is a mistake. I think a fat man acts different than a skinny man. This being said, I think the film is terrific. The most touching are the love scenes, the inarticulate desires of this man, his jealousies, his love. It's absolutely superb. But what would have been needed is that the tour de force to transform the character physically go with a moral transformation. De Niro thought that being an excellent actor and putting on weight would be enough. It's not what I think. He should have played it in the manner of Hitchcock. (He makes gestures.) To give the feeling of manoeuvering his weight, to control it. Not to be controlled by it. It's a question of choreography. It's the only criticism I have about the film. A small criticism. But even that, Martin wouldn't like. (Laughs.) Bob would take it very well. I talked to him about all that. About the danger it meant for his health, because the question is not to put on weight, but also to lose it. I advised him not to do it artificially but rather to take three weeks of vacation after the shooting, to take a big trip to the Sahara for example and try to get the normal rhythm back. I told him I was very worried that he'd damaged his health, his heart by doing something so crazy. But since he's nuts anyway, it didn't change anything.

Martin asked for my advice on this subject because in *The Life and Death of Colonel Blimp,* Roger Livesey was aging and putting on weight during the film and I had had to deal with a similar problem.

CAHIERS: *And where are you now for your own film project?*
POWELL: It's a subject that looks a little like the *Thief of Bagdad* but a bit more adult. It's called The Earthsea Trilogy, and is based on the novel of an American writer, Ursula Le Guin, and takes place in an imaginary land. There are legends and magic. It's exactly the type of thing I should be making now.

It requires a lot of experience, of technical ability. It's very funny and it has a pretty moral: you must deserve your happiness.

CAHIERS: *Is the script finished?*
POWELL: I just finished it in collaboration with Ursula Le Guin. We had a long correspondence and I ended up sending her my version of the first twelve sequences of the film. She liked it enormously.

CAHIERS: *Will it be a special effects shooting?*
POWELL: Yes, there will be many special effects, with magic, dragons. The dragons in the book are very original.

CAHIERS: *Would you have conceived a film in the same manner twenty years ago?*
POWELL: Yes. They made films of that type in Germany fifty years ago. The only problem is that they made them better. Fortunately they are in black and white. You will not see a more beautiful dragon than the one in the *Nibelungen*, right? My dragon is different. No matter, that one was superb.

CAHIERS: *What I wanted to know exactly, is whether you would be using special effects like George Lucas?*
POWELL: If it's OK with George. If he doesn't want to, too bad, I'll deal with it myself. At Rank, we had a special effects department that had been built for *The Thief of Bagdad.* Most of all we had one of the best (mattes) painters and special effects technicians in the world, Percy Day. If before the war, special effects were more advanced in the United States than in England, after the war it was the opposite, in particular thanks to our films and those of Korda. All the specialists were in England. That's why George Lucas went there to make *Star Wars.* Once they are set up, these departments survive. At least as long as there is work. But when people abandon these kinds of techniques and decide to shoot outdoors and to make it all "real," they disappear. I am of course fundamentally opposed to it.

Undeniably a film like *Red Shoes* owes a lot to the fact that I know the Cote d'Azur like the palm of my hand. I lived in Nice when Diaghilev was creating his ballets in Monte-Carlo. I lived in the Russian quarter. We went to see the ballets, eight to a taxi and we came back during the night. Also in the part of the film that takes place in France, I am on familiar ground. Just like my

Scottish films which are influenced by my familiarity with the natives. But it's mostly about impressions, not realism. I don't like documentaries, and have never liked them. I've always had disputes with English filmmakers because they are so proud to be great makers of documentaries. Just like the Canadians. They inaugurated Canadian cinematography while relying on documentaries. Where are they now? After twenty-five years spent making documentaries, they are still making documentaries and they are still incapable of telling a story. I am against that. Films are made to tell stories, not to make statistics.

There is nothing very exciting about the fact that a film is realistic. In fact, I am very opposed to naturalism. I love real trees to climb or to lean against but I don't see what they can bring that would be useful to a film.

Michael Powell Interviewed by William K. Everson

WILLIAM K. EVERSON/1981

WILLIAM K. EVERSON: *Michael, you've been saying at least once over this weekend, when you were discussing your autobiography, that you consider the early part of any director's career his most interesting. So could we perhaps start off with your explaining how and why you got into films, and particularly your association with Rex Ingram.*

POWELL: Well, I got into films, like every kid gets into films: the famous American method of sticking around. In fact, that was the actual advice given me by the Americans who were working in France. They were making a big MGM film in Nice, France.

EVERSON: *This was around 1925, wasn't it?*

POWELL: Yes. And my father, who had a hotel down there, expected me eventually to go into the hotel business, but he was very broadminded about it and perhaps he was quite happy not to have me breaking glasses in the bar or burning omelets in the kitchen because he introduced me to a number of the executives and took them out to a party. Next morning I went to the office and the first person I met was Howard Strickling who was the chief of publicity then. Later on he was chief of publicity for the whole of MGM. Lovely, lovely chap. Easy going, long, dark. He said to me, "You working here?" I said, "No, I hope to." He said, "Oh sure, you just stick around." I always remember that. So I stuck around and I've stuck around ever since.

Transcript of interview at Walker Art Center, Minneapolis, June 1981. Reprinted by permission of Karen Latham Everson.

EVERSON: *What was it about Ingram in particular that excited you so much?*
POWELL: Well, then he was *the* great director. He was for the Americans, too. One of my friends that year, 1925, was Walter Strohm who came from a Los Angeles family and would become chief of production for MGM all through the stormy years, you know, the Wallace Beery-Jean Harlow. And Walter just adored Rex. Rex was an Irishman, appeared quite quiet but actually rather wild, and very intolerant, very well educated, and very theatrical in his tastes. He had the grand manner, the grand theatre manner. In those days, his pictures like *The Four Horsemen of the Apocalypse* and *Scaramouche* were huge successes and I used to think of them only as films. But now when I look back, I realize the thing he had, which was extraordinary, was this sense of theatre, sense of timing, sense of staging. He brought this into films. Griffith was rather a sort of tumultuous, epic sort of man. His pictures *rolled.* Ingram's were carefully composed, and built up to climaxes, and all the young men and women in Hollywood just adored him. When he came to France to make this film *Mare Nostrum,* he decided to stay and make two more pictures. I stayed with him all that time. They missed him badly in Hollywood because he was a man who went his own way and said what he thought at a time when the whole picture business was being formed.

EVERSON: *Do you think he might have had a more successful or longer career had he stayed in Hollywood and been sort of subject to the dictates of the front office but had still made more films?*
POWELL: I think possibly, yes, because I don't think he ever would have been subject. But I think he'd have fought back. Of course, so long as he made box office pictures, they wouldn't mind.

EVERSON: *Was it your idea or his to put you in those two Ingram films as an English kind of comedy relief,* The Magician, *particularly?*
POWELL: Oh, it was just one of his ideas. I think Ingram's sense of humor was pretty rudimentary and my idea of being a comedian was equally rudimentary. But you know, as a young man with a big company and with famous people, you just did whatever they suggested.

EVERSON: *When one looks at your quite prolific output in Britain in the thirties, ranging from smaller quota quickies at the beginning on to the bigger films, like* The Edge of the World *and* The Spy in Black, *in that period were you setting*

your sights for the much more grandiose films like The Red Shoes, *or did you think you would pretty much stay on that level?*
POWELL: I never thought it as being any particular level. I just *loved* films. I loved this whole way of telling stories. When I was making these quota quickies, roughly £1 sterling per foot, which wasn't very much in those days, we usually made them for less than that because we had to turn them over for a profit. But I still looked on them as works of art. Took enormous trouble. Took them terribly seriously.

EVERSON: *That shows today. They're nice little films, most of them.*
POWELL: Hmm. Yes, some of the London West End actors didn't take it seriously. I used to get very annoyed. I regarded myself as the priest of an art. Somehow, the only film that I really had ambition to make at that time—I didn't think of it as an advance; it just was a subject I wanted to make—was *The Edge of the World* about the depopulation of a Scottish island. I wanted to do it because that was something I felt I could tell. No, I never really thought of making bigger and bigger films, and suddenly I was catapulted into making a film with Korda and then a big film like *Thief of Bagdad,* and I just took it all in my stride because I never for one moment had relaxed my general standards.

EVERSON: *Since the British industry has always been very cautious, not only financially but also in terms of creativity and imagination, it's been a source of amazement to me that, after having done successful but not particularly enormous films, like* 49th Parallel *and* One of Our Aircraft Is Missing, *you suddenly had this chance to make* The Life and Death of Colonel Blimp, *a very strange film to make in the war years and a very revolutionary film, by British standards certainly. What was the story behind the extraordinary faith they must have had in you to give you the go ahead on that film?*
POWELL: It was because it was backed by Arthur Rank, and Rank was forming, or hoping to form, his empire of distribution, owning of the theatres. He hoped to get the American market after the war. We had a disagreement with him about the films we should make. After *49th Parallel* (*The Invaders* here) we told him what we were going to make next, and he said his distributor wanted us to make something else. We said, "No, the producer knows what he wants to make and we'll get somebody else to finance it. Then when it's a success you can come and ask us what we're going to do next." And

that was the way it worked. So during the war we were making these—they weren't exactly propaganda films, but the agreement with Churchill and Brendan Bracken, who was the Minister of Information after Duff Cooper, was that if we made films, the theme and the plot had to be agreed with the Ministry of Information. This way they managed to keep the English film industry going and keep not a control of it, but a rough guidance of the films that were made. In the case of *Colonel Blimp,* we thought it was about time to make a film about the old stick-in-the-mud military mind. Very charming, very affectionate, but useless in total war. When the War Office caught on to what we were trying to do, since half of them were surrounded by people like this who'd been in the army for 40 years, they didn't take too kindly to the idea. That's where all this—they found these minutes from Churchill saying, "Should this film be made at all?" and then finally, "Stop it." And when it was made, "Don't sell it. Don't distribute it." None of that came to light at the time. But he certainly was trying to stop it. I remember we had an interview with the Minister and I said to him bluntly, "Are you going to forbid us to make the film?" and he said, "Oh my dear fellow, we can't possibly forbid you. That wouldn't do at all. But *don't* make it or you'll never get a knighthood." So we made it. And I haven't had a knighthood.

EVERSON: *There's time yet. It certainly is of interest today if one looks back at some of those little Ministry of Information propaganda shorts from instructional films made at the very beginning of the war; they all reflect exactly the kind of attitudes that you're attacking in* Colonel Blimp.

POWELL: Do they?

EVERSON: *There's one little short about putting out firebombs. It's all based on the assumption that, at most, about two firebombs will fall, and that everybody will join forces to put it out, and they'll call the fire brigade. I mean, it's completely unreal. One wonders how we survived at all on the basis of that kind of training film.*

POWELL: I remember in the Ralph Richardson semi-documentary, the only time I've been really associated with a semi-documentary film—

EVERSON: The Lion Has Wings?

POWELL: No, *The Volunteer.*

EVERSON: *Oh,* The Volunteer.
POWELL: He was an actor in the story and he opened it as a Beefeater and he said on the screen, "When the war started we all rushed into funny costumes and declaimed lines about the wooden walls of England." 'Cause that's all there were.

EVERSON: *You've mentioned before your basic dislike of documentary. I think one of the nicest things that happened to British films during the war was they learned lessons from documentary and absorbed them into narrower fiction films like* Millions Like Us. *So they did have this rather nice underplayed quality which is the best of documentary without the boredom that went with it.*
POWELL: They had some very good actors in them, you see.

EVERSON: *Yes. I often wondered whether you deliberately avoided that kind of style, because none of your films had that underplayed quality. They were all deliberately flamboyant. Were you deliberately rejecting that style or did it just not fit the kind of films you wanted to make?*
POWELL: No, deliberately rejecting it. I believe the purpose of films is to entertain and if you've got a propaganda theme or purpose in the film then first of all, you must entertain. Every film we made during the war period right up 'til *Black Narcissus* after the war, was discussed with the Ministry of Information. I mean, even a film like *Stairway to Heaven* came from a suggestion from the Ministry that we write a story and make a film to improve Anglo-American relations. As the film is still going around and making money, we must have improved them. When we made these films before the war and during the war, the life of a film was still considered to be about 3 or 4 years. We were all working on this marvelous medium but we never thought that our work would live for years and years and years afterward. Of course, they probably wouldn't have if it hadn't been for all of the various archive movements throughout the world.

EVERSON: *And television, unfortunately. It's no way to see films, but at least they've promoted them.*
POWELL: Well, it keeps their memory green, all right. That's quite true. Because really until I came here in the last years, I didn't realize how many of our films had been seen on television. Maybe sliced up and all that sort of thing, but the images were there in people's minds. This was quite a surprise.

EVERSON: *Just harking back to documentary for the last time, possibly. I suppose* The Small Back Room *was the closest you ever came to an underplayed semi-documentary feel. Is that perhaps one reason why in your view it didn't succeed as well as some of the others?*
POWELL: No, it was a question of timing. Just like when Rex Ingram made *Mare Nostrum* it was 5, 6 years after The Great War, the First World War, and people by that time were fed up with a sort of serious, tragic treatment of the war. So although they said it was a very fine film, they didn't go. And the same thing happened with *The Small Back Room,* although it was such a thriller with the dismantling of the bomb. By the way there's been a television series—

EVERSON: *A whole new series now, yes.*
POWELL: After seeing some of the shots, I think they've looked at that picture pretty closely. But it was two years after the war was over and full of atmosphere of London and the blackout and that kind of thing, and although England was still full of austerity and people standing in queues and no butter and all this sort of thing, they didn't want to know about that.

EVERSON: *It's a pity. It was certainly a very good film and holds up beautifully.*
POWELL: Well, now of course, it looks fine, very interesting for people.

EVERSON: *I remember it was very difficult to see even in Britain. I think it had a very short first run in London and then no circuit booking at all.*
POWELL: Right. The BBC, who were our greatest competitors in a way, are also our greatest philanthropists because it's they who've been piecing together the long version of *Colonel Blimp* which runs 2 hours and 50 minutes. You see, when we made it in 1942, it covered the 40 years from the turn of the century on. Now when you look back from 1980, it covers 80 years of the century because you're looking back at 1942 and then beyond that to the First World War and beyond that to the Boer War. It's a much more fascinating picture now. A bigger show, too, because we're all older and at the same time we're younger. This is extraordinary because who knew this medium would last, not forever, but last *already* 50, 60, 70 years. It's extraordinary. A perishable medium, as Martin Scorsese is continually telling us.

EVERSON: *Yet at the same time, these are such very, very personal films that you and Emeric Pressburger made together. You must have had some feeling that you weren't making films just for the moment but that you were hopefully making them for a permanent life. Or didn't you feel that at the time?*

POWELL: Not really. Just making them as well as we could. And Emeric had the same feeling about films. He'd been hunted from every capital of Europe by the Nazis and finally came through Paris to London. But when he was a young man, almost a kid, he was already writing stories for the Berlin newspapers and starving in cafés. You know, in Berlin you could order a cup of coffee and sit in the café all day and write short stories. This was Emeric's life. He's a very civilized man. When we decided to make these films together, and write our own stories, and find our own themes, we were bound to follow a fairly high level. These were times of great tension. The whole of Europe was waiting for England to fall. Of course, we never thought about falling in England, we were very busy.

EVERSON: *We were too smug, too. We'd just never* dreamed *it could possibly happen.*

POWELL: No. Quite impossible.

EVERSON: *Since we're talking about Mr. Pressburger—so many of the writer/director teams seem to be split in the sense that one member of the team is very dominant and usually it's the writer that's the less important of the two. And very often that's proven to be true when they split up and go their own ways and the writer becomes a director. He usually doesn't function too well. It seems to me that your particular set up of writing, producing, directing teamwork with Pressburger was quite unique in that it's much, much better integrated than most filmmaking teams ever were.*

POWELL: I guess it was because we had so many original ideas. Let's think, the big teams really were Brackett and Wilder, and of course, Ben Hecht and Charlie MacArthur.

EVERSON: *Although, they stayed with writing and only directed occasionally.*

POWELL: They produced in films. *The Front Page* they made, didn't they?

EVERSON: *But there again, they had a producer and director working with them. It was their script, but they didn't have the control of the film that you and Pressburger had.*

POWELL: You don't think they did?

EVERSON: *I would doubt it. Especially in those days, in the thirties in Hollywood. And especially working for Howard Hughes, I'm sure he had the control.*
POWELL: I think Hollywood already had this weird system of the producer and the director which nobody understands, least of all Hollywood. Even now they mix the whole thing up. Just because somebody has a lot of money, they call him a producer. We imagined that a producer was a man who was responsible for the whole thing: finds the story, finds the director, finds the actors, and makes up this wonderful team which then makes a film. We called ourselves producers in England not because we wanted to call ourselves producers, because Emeric's a writer and I'm a director, but we call ourselves producers to stop anybody else from calling themselves producers of our films. Now in Hollywood you couldn't do that. Somebody's bound to be there representing the finance or the front office who calls himself a producer. It's been a problem, I suppose, for 50 years ever since Rex Ingram, with whom I came into this business 55 years ago, was in a feud with Louis B. Mayer. As you know, so definite was the feud with Mayer that his films were never called Metro-Goldwyn-Mayer films, they were called Metro-Goldwyn. So evidently this producer business goes a long way back. When it works, of course, it's a marvelous relationship because, well, for instance, a man like Martin Scorsese who's thinking of every word, every phrase, every image, doesn't want to be bothered with administration or big decisions about whether you move tomorrow to Colorado to get the scene. The kind of decisions I made on the Graf Spee picture: shooting in the studio 7 weeks, then going out with a very small crew for nearly four months with the whole British Navy to play with and then going to Montevideo for 10 days to polish it off. These are all conscious decisions made just like that, and a producer makes that for a man like Martin Scorsese. He's like a delicate watch. The films that he makes best like *Alice Doesn't Live Here Anymore* or *Mean Streets* could only be made by a sensitive genius of that kind.

EVERSON: *Quite often when we've been talking casually about film, Michael, you tend to be a little, I should say, irked by the Hollywood regard for film, only of film, and with total disregard for the rest of the arts. And I know you've always been very concerned about film as a major art, but as just one of many majors arts and you've always tried to use film to bring in music and painting and as many other aspects as you can. Did you find opposition to this when you started making your bigger films or did you insist on that always? Or do you want to comment on that approach to film generally?*

POWELL: I guess I was just accustomed to that always because the wonderful thing about films is, first of all, you have the opportunity and the money to get the best talent in the world, and that an essential part of a film has always been the music and the color. Even in a black and white film there is color, you know, there is tone and shade—real black and white, of course, is nothing like monochrome. I've always regarded it as something where you could use all the arts and get the very best talent available. At one time I was so innocent. After *The Red Shoes* and *The Tales of Hoffmann* were so successful, I thought people were ready to take all this kind of thing, and I'm sure they were. So I got together a lot of talent, big names all over Europe and America, and made it up to about 20 hours of entertainment. Some of them were stories and some of them were scenes with a song. Stravinsky was going to do something for me with Dylan Thomas writing the libretto, that kind of thing.

EVERSON: *Picasso, too.*

POWELL: And Graham Sutherland was going to make a detective story in the south of France. I took all this to New York thinking that's where they'll love to have it. They didn't want it at all. I explained to them, here's 20 hours of top talent that you'll never get otherwise, you'll never see it on the screen, people like this. I mean, you don't get Graham Sutherland and Picasso and Stravinsky all the time. But I couldn't interest them in the idea at all.

EVERSON: *You said specifically 20 hours. Were you thinking of hour-long shows for television or supports for theatrical productions?*

POWELL: Well, it would have been an hour program, I suppose. Some of the ideas only lasted 5 minutes, but they were very clever. The Stravinsky thing would have run 23 minutes. Somebody else had an idea which would have taken 2 hours. I think there should be room for all this. Of course, probably now, there is. But maybe I was too early, as usual.

EVERSON: *And now it might well be too expensive, too.*

POWELL: Well, it certainly would be with the kind of talent I had, those who aren't dead. Certainly whenever we made films, I always made it my business to go out and get the best talent. Just as you know, I've been writing the script with Ursula Le Guin on *A Wizard of Earthsea,* The Earthsea Trilogy. And from the beginning, I've been having discussions with David Hockney about being the designer of the film. That's the sort of thing I mean. Go for the top. Go for the best people available. Otherwise, why spend so much money?

EVERSON: *Have you envisioned the kind of design for that film yet? Are you planning on spectacular décor or simple décor which is made to look spectacular by your treatment?*
POWELL: Yes. That's really it. It's big stuff because we have to create a completely imaginary country, an archipelago of islands, and then big adventures happen in there with an allegorical meaning, too. The kind of thing that people love. But it could equally well be done in black and white and would be equally spectacular. In fact, I might even do it in black and white. That's up to David a good deal. I don't know whether you ever saw his little edition of *Grimm's Fairy Tales* that he illustrated.

EVERSON: *Yes, I have.*
POWELL: Well, that's the kind of style I'm looking for. That kind of proportion. That kind of use of space. I don't think an enormous décor necessarily means an enormous picture. Sometimes you can make an enormous film with very small means.

EVERSON: *There's gradually an acceptance of black and white again, plus of course the safety that it will be preserved whereas color may not.*
POWELL: When I think about the film, I think always funnily enough of a black and white film which was Ingmar Bergman's first film, *The Seventh Seal,* do you remember it?

EVERSON: *Yes, very much.*
POWELL: Well, that had the sort of quality I'd like to get into the film. A slightly bigger sort of effect but that kind of quality. He had control over the images from beginning to end; consequence is, they had enormous importance on the screen. If you let control get away from you, you'd be surprised how even big things fall quite flat on the cinema.

EVERSON: *What are some of the major unrealized projects? I know you talked about at one time wanting to do a film with Tyrone Guthrie, and I know that you're*

here seeing, or have seen, The Tempest, *another film that you wanted to make at one time. What are some of these major unrealized projects, that you may still make, but certainly are still in your imagination rather than on the screen?*
POWELL: Well, *The Tempest* was certainly one, and long before Tony Richardson made *The Charge of the Light Brigade* I was working with John Whiting, who's dead now, the playwright, I don't know if you remember his name or work.

EVERSON: *I remember the name, I can't think of any titles at the moment.*
POWELL: Well, *The Devils* was his most successful play. He was a wonderful writer. But we were basing it on Cecil Woodham Smith's book, *The Reason Why*. It was a study of the military mind, again: the thirst for glory, the panoply of uniforms, the color, the foaming steeds, all this glorification of war which ended only in a complete disaster led by a fool. This was a very appealing subject to me. I never saw the Richardson film. When I failed to get something done, when somebody else does it, I don't want to see it! [laughs] You know, it might be a bit too bitter?

EVERSON: *I think you might have been happy with it. It's an interesting film and it seems to have the same approach that you had in mind.*
POWELL: Good. Good.

EVERSON: *And how about the Tyrone Guthrie project which you mentioned just in passing yesterday?*
POWELL: Oh, that was to make a life of Lillian Bayliss, who was really the father and mother and grandfather and grandmother of all the arts in England. She had a very interesting and amusing life. The first part of it in South Africa as a girl. She was really responsible for Tyrone Guthrie becoming a great producer, for Larry Olivier, for Robert Helpmann becoming a great choreographer and ballet director, and Margot Fonteyn, Ninette de Valois—all these people were all sponsored by this extraordinary woman. She was particularly good at one-liners. She was very proud of running The Old Vic, on very little money indeed, and then when she needed room for the ballet and for the opera, she took this unrentable theatre in the north of London, Sadler's Wells, and that's where the name Sadler's Wells Ballet comes from, you see. She was very proud of this second theatre. She was knocked down in a street accident one time, and while she was lying unconscious on the

pavement, they were getting the ambulance, somebody said, "Why, that's Lillian Bayliss of The Old Vic!" and she opened one eye and said, "and Sadler's Wells!" Real showman.

EVERSON: *Why was that project particularly difficult to get off the ground?*
POWELL: Well, because Tony Guthrie just wouldn't do it. He was very intrigued. He worked with us for quite a long while and then he decided he was too close to her and too close to the whole subject. He said, "One day, perhaps." Unfortunately "one day" comes and he's dead. Wonderful man. Very good actor himself, too.

EVERSON: *I know him mainly from the one big film he made with Charles Laughton; he was extremely good in that.*
POWELL: Well, he was difficult to cast because he was a monumentally tall man, as you know, and had this north of Ireland profile. He was a very strong and craggy character, not so easy to cast. But this is definitely one of his towns. This town built his theatre for him which he never got done in England. He always hoped he would have the ideal theatre built for him in England. No, he had to come to Minneapolis to get it.

EVERSON: *And to write a book about it, too.*
POWELL: And to write a book. A very good book, too.

EVERSON: *The other day I asked you about your work with art directors, and I think somebody in the class we were with asked you how much you'd been influenced, or by which art directors you had been influenced. I remember at the time you said that you thought they were much more influenced by you than vice versa, which led me to want to ask you about the design of* The Red Shoes. *I remember that you had said once that Alfred Junge, with whom you worked very closely and for a long time, didn't agree with your conception of* The Red Shoes, *and that led to a very amicable parting of the ways, and that brought in Hein Heckroth to work with you.*
POWELL: No, it was really an almost full circle with Alfred Junge. When I was very young, before I got into the film business, but still loving it, the great films in those days—where the original work was being done—were the early German films; and Alfred of course was trained by UFA and so he had all these grandiose images and marvelous effects in his head. When I asked

him to pull them out of his head for things like *Colonel Blimp* and *Stairway to Heaven*, he was delighted. I think his masterpiece was the film you're showing here, *Black Narcissus*. Extraordinary. You give Alfred a very difficult task, he would rise to it and make something marvelous out of it. In that case, to create an entirely imaginary place in the Himalayas. Always his imaginative things were dealing with naturalistic sets, if you follow me. I mean, even heaven in either monochrome or color in *Stairway to Heaven* is based upon naturalism. And when I wanted to go over completely to unnaturalism, to theatrical effects, he thought I was going too far on *The Red Shoes* and said so. We had just made a huge success with *Black Narcissus*, but there again, I say, it was a very imaginative film made from natural settings. He couldn't take that extra step right into the theatre which was necessary to create a ballet of "The Red Shoes." I said, it isn't enough to have a dancer play the part. If you're saying you're creating a ballet for her, then we've got to create a new ballet, and you've got to see her dance in it. It all follows logically. But it was too logical for Alfred. So I went to one of his assistants, Hein Heckroth, who was a theatre man, really. Very good painter. Most of his work had been done in the theatre. As you know, the German theatre is very experimental, spectacular, and they use painters a great deal. So I went to him, and I never made another film with Alfred. I was very sorry; he was marvelous. But I want always to go forward, not backward.

EVERSON: *Had there ever been any thought at all about doing* The Red Shoes *basically in black and white and just exploding into color for the ballet sequence and then back to black and white afterwards? Seeing it now it's not a good idea, but I just wonder had it perhaps been envisioned that way at one time?*
POWELL: No. No, we were *thirsting* to get back into color again after the war. For most of the time during the war, you see, Technicolor was being used for training films and spotting films and all kinds of uses in the war, and we couldn't get color at all. The first chance we had was in *A Matter of Life and Death* which was called *Stairway to Heaven* here. That was followed up with an explosion of Indian color in *Black Narcissus* and then the full firework display in *The Red Shoes*. No, we were working then almost exclusively in color, to see what could be done with it.

EVERSON: *It must have been the first ballet film that really made money in a popular sense. I'm sure smaller, less ambitious, ballet films made their costs back in smaller art house outings, but in view of the basic uncommercial aspect of the film, how on earth did you get the project sold at a time like that? Rank had just had these big, prestige failures with films like, particularly,* Caesar and Cleopatra. *It must have been a very tough project to sell at that time.*

POWELL: Well, *Stairway to Heaven* was a commercial success and so was *Black Narcissus,* you see. Although, when Rank and his accountant saw the film finished—*The Red Shoes,* I mean—they didn't understand it. They thought they really had lost all their money. But these things are a matter of having the right people between you and the public, and there was just one man in America who really was mainly responsible at that time for the *The Red Shoes* being successful. I've always remembered that. He was working for the distributors, and the distributors were very doubtful about the film. They said it's too highbrow for the American public, because nobody had ever treated the public seriously before and said, "You love art, don't you? Come on in and help make this with us." That's roughly the attitude of the film. You understand how everybody ticks. I was talking about that, you remember. I think the audience contributes an *awful* lot to *The Red Shoes.* This was quite new in those days. But this man and his family, Bill Heineman, his name was, and he had eight children and they used to go and sit solidly in a row and look at *The Red Shoes.* He said I'm determined that this film is going to be put into a theatre and run as long as it'll run, 'cause that was a bit new in those days. They took a little theatre off Broadway and after it had run there for a year, people began to take some notice. Up 'til then they hadn't distributed the film at all. When it had run two years, they decided they could make money with it and then it became the biggest box office we ever made. So, it's a matter of faith: faith in making it, faith in selling it.

EVERSON: *Well, it certainly introduced a lot of people to ballet, including myself. I went to my first ballet performance in London after I saw* The Red Shoes. *I must admit I didn't stay with ballet—I came back to film again and films like* The Red Shoes *and* Tales of Hoffmann. *I do know—certainly in that period in London—that people who had never* dreamed *of going to the ballet went and experimented because of that film.*

POWELL: Yes. Yes, I guess they did. I learned a lot from it but we were so wrapped up in the whole theory of getting a great group of artists together and making a work of art, that I'd forgotten, really, almost, what a single-minded affair it was. And when we ran it in Copenhagen about four or five months later, because of Hans Andersen, the Danes didn't like it very much because it wasn't what they expected from a Hans Andersen picture. I looked at this very intolerant work of art on the screen which practically said, "Art is all that matters, damn you,"—that's more or less what we said—I thought what a cheek we had to make this film. I still thought that when I saw it again last night.

EVERSON: *One thing I meant to ask you. I remember when the film came out in Britain and I know the critics were waiting to sort of snipe at you when they could, but there was kind of a universal dislike on the critics' part at that one shot at the end of Moira Shearer being taken off the railway track. Admittedly, it's very difficult to be run over by a train and still look unbesmirched. It occurred to me that in some of your films, which are tremendously attuned to popular taste—and certainly* The Red Shoes *was and I think* I Know Where I'm Going! *certainly is. You may not have designed it that way but it came out that way—there's often just one shot, almost as though you're tweaking the nose of the public and sort of giving them what they don't want in that kind of a film. There was the shot, of course, of the blood on Moira Shearer in* The Red Shoes *and then in* I Know Where I'm Going!*—which is such a lovely film in every sense of the word, and everybody loves it, I mean, there's nobody who really doesn't like that film—and then there's the one shot at the end of the eagle swooping down off the dead rabbit and pulling off a sliver of flesh. Which invariably, after people have sat for 90 minutes enthralled by this film, you get a shudder through the audience. I just wonder if that's a kind of perverse deliberate trick.*
POWELL: Oh yes. Of course it is.

EVERSON: *It has to be, otherwise it wouldn't be there.*
POWELL: It's delightful to make the audience shudder. Just like it's nice to make them laugh in *Stairway to Heaven*—when he comes down from the monochrome heaven to colored earth, and says, "One is starved for Technicolor up there."

EVERSON: *That's a line that always pays off, too, even today. Even though the line is so famous it always gets a laugh.*
POWELL: It's the same idea really. Of course, Moira Shearer on the railway tracks—I was quite uncompromising about it. In the fairytale she has her legs chopped off to stop the shoes dancing. Fairytales are quite brutal in their

way and it was quite a conscious thing that I was doing. I quite expected the critics to say why this brutal naturalism all of a sudden. Why? The answer is that sunlight is sunlight, and blood is blood, and when you shoot a shot like that, you should shoot it the way it would be. The fact that it *seems* to clash with the sort of almost fairytale angle of the magic red shoes is, I think, half the point.

EVERSON: *Oh, absolutely.*
POWELL: Oh good. You agree.

EVERSON: *I like it but then I've always liked the slightly quirky element in your films, too. Michael, I was wanting to have your views on a certain aspect of the forties because, in the 1940s, British films certainly were a peak of craftsmanship they probably never enjoyed before and they were turning out really first-class films. But there was a sort of lack of imagination, a lack of inventiveness there, and what the public and the critics seemed to want was the very polished, well-crafted films like* Oliver Twist *and* Odd Man Out *and they were fine films and they were well-received. But because your films deliberately weren't in that vein, the critics always seemed to feel they were sort of out of step with the times or a little eccentric and they wrote a great deal on that line. Sometimes even the filmmakers themselves tended to be very orthodox. I mean, when Humphrey Jennings started making his very lyrical documentaries, people like Paul Rotha felt that this was not what documentary should be. Do you recall how your contemporaries of that time, people like Carol Reed and David Lean, if you knew them personally and I'm sure you did, how did they react to your films? How did they compliment you, or otherwise, when they saw them?*
POWELL: No, it's rather an odd situation really. We formed this group of producers with Rank. At first, there was only Emeric and myself. We brought in a company called Cineguild which was David Lean, Ronald Neame, now a director, but then a cameraman/producer, Tony Havelock-Allan and John Bryan, who was the deisgner. Then it was decided that people would join us by invitation—Frank Launder and Sidney Gilliat, who were two brilliant makers of films, mostly of rather humorous comedies in London life and that kind of thing, but extremely skillful. Sidney Gilliat was a very good writer. And then Ian Dalrymple, who'd been one of the great producers during the war; films like *Desert Victory* and those kinds of big war documentaries, he'd got them together. All of us were working on our own projects and

we hardly ever had time to see each other's. If we did it was a rather sort of casual way of looking over David Lean's shoulder and saying, "Oh, you're doing *Oliver Twist* are you? Who's that, Alec Guinness? Oh good." It was more that kind of attitude. We would ask each other to each other's premieres and we'd sometimes even go, but we were so obsessed with the idea of running our own film producing center; we called it Independent Producers and we took Pinewood Studios in England as our studios. We'd all been trained, more or less, at Korda's Denham Studios but after the war we had to choose one or the other and Pinewood seemed to be the most practical studio, as it is today even. Wonderful studio, Pinewood. It's funny that you ask that. I wouldn't be at all surprised if half of us never saw the other half's films at the time. We saw them later, probably.

EVERSON: *In your case, it's almost an advantage because so many of those films then seemed slightly out of step, particularly, I think,* The Queen's Guards, *which I think is a lovely film, and of course* Peeping Tom. *They suddenly come into fashion and they're totally up to date even though they may be 20 or 30 years old. So it must be rather rewarding I should think for people like Lean, perhaps, to catch up with these films that they missed and find that they're completely modern, almost new, experiences for them. At least it is for me, because I hadn't seen* The Queen's Guards *until quite recently.*
POWELL: Nor have I.

EVERSON: *It seemed like a totally modern film today.*
POWELL: Really?

EVERSON: *A sad film, but a totally modern film.*
POWELL: Really? Well, it was one of the few films we made with an American company, in this case 20th Century Fox, and it wasn't a happy film because they didn't like the film at all.

EVERSON: *I'm sure they couldn't have understood it.*
POWELL: Perhaps that was it. It wasn't just they didn't like it; they didn't understand it.

EVERSON: *It's always difficult and perhaps unfair to read auteur characteristics into films, but there does seem to be a very loose, maybe not even loose, connecting*

theme within many of your films, that of a way of looking at life. Sometimes expressed visually. In The Thief of Bagdad *you have this giant eye on the prow of the ship;* Peeping Tom, *of course, is about a filmmaker seeing life in a sense through his camera; even* Age of Consent *starts off with somebody looking at something: James Mason looking at the fish bowl in the store window in New York which then pulls back and he's already in the Australian area which is represented by that fish bowl. It seemed to me there's a rather extraordinary series of images like that which link the art of seeing, seeing life, with the themes of your films. Does that come naturally or intentionally? Obviously, it must be intentional.*
POWELL: No. No, well, it's not intentional as any sort of theme. It's obviously a recurring image or a recurring idea. I guess that if you've started in this extraordinary art as early as I did in the silent days, you always look on it from the point of view of the camera lens and that's probably what makes *Peeping Tom* so disturbing to people because it seems to disturb them even more than Fritz Lang's *M* which it's often been compared to. Fritz Lang was a great director, too, of theatrical effects and when you come down to it *M*, with all it's wonderful photography, is seen theatrically, whereas *Peeping Tom* is really like being inside the camera. I suppose I can't get away from that. I've been swallowed up by this lens and I have to spit it out.

EVERSON: *It's interesting, even in* The Volunteer, *that little documentary you made, that when you do make your appearance in the film briefly at the end you're behind the camera lens shooting.*
POWELL: Yes, that's significant.

EVERSON: *Somebody, I've forgotten where it was, perhaps in Santa Fe, somebody recently told me they'd asked you for sort of instant advice on how to make a good film and without a moment's hesitation you jumped in and cited* M *by Lang and said, "Shoot it hard," in other words make every image count. And you had obviously no chance at that time to expand on that, but has Lang had that much of influence on your work and do you really—*
POWELL: Yes. Yes, big influence. And it was a very big thrill at the end of the war when Emeric and I first came together to America. We were looking for the girl for *Stairway to Heaven* which turned out in the end through Hitchcock, who found us Kim Hunter. On the train going west, because you went by train then—United Artists was looking after us for Rank, and they fussed about and got us on a drawing room on a train going west. You went to

Chicago and then you changed and then three days across the continent. A wonderful experience for us, but particularly when we found that, in the drawing room at the other end of the coach, Fritz Lang was traveling back to Hollywood. We spent the whole three and a half days with him, had a wonderful time. Emeric knew him from the UFA days; I'd met him once, I think, but we didn't know each other well and we had three and a half days to tear the whole film business to pieces! A wonderful man. Very funny.

EVERSON: *Yes. I knew him very slightly at the end of his life and* Peeping Tom *was a film he'd seen and was very fond of.*
POWELL: Really?! Oh, I didn't know that. Oh, Bill, thank you for telling me. Did he really?

EVERSON: *Yes, that and a film called* Now the Screaming Starts *which isn't as good but is in a very similar vein in a sense. So right to the end he was very fond of the subtle psychological thriller and he was very, very enthusiastic about* Peeping Tom.
POWELL: Well, I remember when I saw *Spione*, what's it called, *Spies? Spies.* I was very much influenced by that picture. Particularly by the cutting of the images, the way the images were used. And then in those great romantic pictures which are all inspired by Reinhardt's theatre like the *Siegfried* and *Die Nibelungen.* He was very directly connected—sometimes people mix him up with what they call German expressionism. He never was an expressionist. *Metropolis,* after all, is massive sort of neo-realistic sets. Nothing like *Caligari,* Robert Wiene. No, he was a great romantic director and enormous imagination. Yes, he's had a big influence on me.

EVERSON: *Talking about influences, I think one notices today at film schools the students tend to gravitate for models, I think, mainly to Hitchcock and Renoir, mainly because that's the way the teachers tend to gravitate unfortunately, not that there's—*
POWELL: —fortunately!

EVERSON: *—not that there's anything wrong with Hitchcock and Renoir, but they do tend to get into rather a rut and stay in it, so most students making films make either Hitchcock or Renoir films. In view of that I think it's rather interesting that so many of the young people actually making films today successfully in Holly-*

wood or New York, like Martin Scorsese, do gravitate so much to your films despite any training they may have had in their background in film school. Have you ever discussed with Martin why your films have such a tremendous effect on him?
POWELL: No, I must.

EVERSON: *Because he's often mentioned films like* The Small Back Room *exploding and echoing films like* New York, New York. *It's rather satisfying to think of your own influence from Rex Ingram, to think that it goes back to Ingram, and you'll find an Ingram scene perhaps emerging in your own* Elusive Pimpernel, *and then a scene from one of your films emerging in a Scorsese film. It's rather nice to think of this ongoing influence and interweaving. Of course, that's what film is all about or should be.*
POWELL: Oh, yes. Films, particularly, do suffer a chain reaction like that, that's quite true. I think that's probably what's helped to keep so many famous films alive. It is extraordinary, as you say. Over the 60 or 70 years, a lot of people have been carrying those images in their mind. Of course, it's never happened before.

EVERSON: *Looking back on your own films, I think you've often said that* Stairway to Heaven *is your personal favorite. Is that because of the opportunity it gave you for tricks and for playing with technique or do you really feel it's your best perhaps on a philosophical, literary level?*
POWELL: Not so much literary, although the jokes are very good ones, I think, and the miracles and magic in it look so easy. It's wonderful when you get big effects like that and magical effects and it all comes off with great ease. You don't even think how it's being done. The whole picture looks easy to make and that's what I like about it, I think; because it's a big conception and there are all sorts of philosophical jumps which all come off. Like Emeric's idea of the only way that his life can be saved is to kill the doctor who's trying to save his life. A wonderful paradox, so I didn't do it tactfully, I did it quite brutally, which is a terrible shock for the audience 'cause he's a very sympathetic character, the doctor, played by Roger Livesey. When he's killed, and practically before their eyes burned to death, it's a great shock for them, particularly when in the next scene they see him being greeted by Marius Goring in the other world. But it's all these things, when done directly like that, usually in straight cuts like at the end when the only thing that hasn't been tied up, the only clue left, that somebody might say, "Bah!

But what about . . . ?" was the chess book, you know the book about chess problems. Somebody said we hadn't cleared that up. And so we very hastily—I had the setting of the staircase—in darkness, out of the darkness the book comes flying right into the camera and as it hits the camera you zip open a case and the book's inside it to show that it's only in his imagination that it ever went to the other world at all. It's one of the best cuts I've done, that book flying through the air and coming out of the zipped fastener. All these sort of things were done with insolent ease, which I like.

EVERSON: *Certainly, that particular film plays beautifully. I've often wondered how this tremendous affinity between you and Roger Livesey built up because no other British director ever seems to have really cared about Livesey or used him as well as he obviously could have been used. He wasted so much time in the thirties in minor films, from* Lorna Doon *in 1934. Even the few films he made in the forties like* Vice Versa, *where he starred, don't seem to be at ease in the way they use him and later on he becomes a character actor when his best years are gone. Somehow only in your films—it was almost like the John Ford-John Wayne liaison—you seem to work so well together and to do such good things together.*
POWELL: Well, first of all he was a great personality and a great actor. He combined lightness, marvelous lightness either in drama or comedy, with a big frame, splendid appearance. Remarkable person. It's partly because in England, the theatre and films are so close together. I see far more theatre and far more theatre actors than I do films in England. I knew Roger very well from having seen him play Caliban in *The Tempest;* I think it was in the one in which Charles Laughton played Prospero. But anyway, it was the best Caliban I've ever seen. First of all, he was young and he had this extraordinary ease of movement. Very quick Roger could be for a big man, and he was a big, glorious-looking young man with gold, red hair. I don't think I ever saw any of the films you mentioned. I never saw him in a film until I put him in one because I followed his theatrical career, mainly. He was in the group which Laurence Olivier and Vivien Leigh were leading. I tried to get Michael Balcon to cast him as the leading man in one of my films, *The Phantom Light,* and I made some very good tests of him. He looked magnificent, but Michael Balcon was a bit suburban and he didn't like Roger's voice. Of course, his voice was one of the most interesting things about him. But you know Balcon was a very conventional man and he thought, "That husky voice. People aren't going to like it. *I* don't like it, so they're not going to like

it." That's where the dangerous thing comes in of a producer. I wanted him but I couldn't have him so I played Ian Hunter instead. A good comedian, but nothing like Roger.

EVERSON: *Not unique certainly.*
POWELL: When the war came, I still hadn't worked with Roger, but he had made one big film for Korda, *The Drum* with Sabu. A rather dull military part, do you remember it?

EVERSON: *I remember the film very well. Michael, I'd like to make a blanket statement and then have you jump in and make some comments. Although there is a tremendous amount of humor in your films, particularly in the fantasies, you haven't actually made an out-and-out comedy that I can think of. Apart from the early quickies, the early second features, there's never been any one deliberate film that you can categorize as a comedy.*
POWELL: No, it's a great loss.

EVERSON: *I think for me, because you're a very funny person, you have a nice sense of humor, even in the films which are not comedies. I'm just wondering if there's any reason why—perhaps you felt Launder and Gilliat were taking care of that while you were doing other things.*
POWELL: No, there was no particular comedy subject that I can remember that I particularly wanted to do. But I was always urging Emeric, the writer member of our team, I was always urging him to write a comedy because he was essentially a comic writer and was always making jokes the whole time, as Hungarians usually do. Being a very clever Hungarian writer and knowing all the famous Hungarians like Wiene and people like that, he should have been able to write a comedy but he never wanted to. I often said to him, "I wish to goodness you'd think of a good comic idea. I'd like to try my hand at a really good comedy."

EVERSON: *I remember thinking at the time what a pity that you and Pressburger hadn't done* Vice Versa, *which Peter Ustinov did, because it was a comedy with a great deal of fantasy; in fact, it was a fantasy. It's almost like a British equivalent, in some ways, of* The Italian Straw Hat. *It had Roger Livesey in the lead and James*

Robertson-Justice, and I thought you and Pressburger could have done a marvelous *job on that. And somehow with Ustinov doing it and doing everything in it, writing and directing—not playing—it was somehow just a little bit too heavy handed. I remember thinking at the time what a marvelous film that would have been for the Archers.*

POWELL: I did think once of making a comedy from a book and later on Bryan Forbes made it and that was *The Wrong Box.* He made it very much of a period comedy, and I don't think I would have done that. He got a lot of jokes from the period whereas I must say I would have preferred something more modern. I used to admire the Lubitsch comedies very much because they were beautifully scripted and beautifully shot, weren't they?

EVERSON: *Oh yes.*

POWELL: I'd like to have done a comedy like that. Emeric had written comedies in the early days. When he was in France, he wrote a very good comedy which was very successful and it was remade in America.

EVERSON: One Rainy Afternoon.

POWELL: That's right.

EVERSON: *With Francis Lederer and Ida Lupino. A very charming film.*

POWELL: Yes.

EVERSON: *Getting back to the fantasies, since we touched on that briefly with* Vice Versa, *an awful lot of your films—*Black Narcissus, *for example—which essentially deal with emotional themes and themes of sexual repression, still veer into elements of fantasy to express those themes. I think a lot of people, especially Martin Scorsese when he gets into very in-depth emotional situations, also tend to veer into fantasy to release them, which suggests more and more that Martin has studied your films, as we know he has.*

POWELL: Can you think of an example?

EVERSON: *There's an awful lot of semi-fantasy in the way the deaths are shot, for example, in the end of* Taxi Driver. *They're not real, they're choreographed, they're almost ballet-like killings.*

POWELL: Yes.

EVERSON: *And I suspect that he indirectly probably drew that—not that your films are full of ballet-like deaths, but I think that that kind of reversion to fantasy in a very real situation is a characteristic of yours which he has certainly followed through. I don't know whether you've ever thought about that or—*
POWELL: No.

EVERSON: *—or agree with that.*
POWELL: It's interesting.

EVERSON: *I know at one time you thought about doing a sequel to* The Thief of Bagdad. *Do you have any thoughts on how you would do fantasy today if you had the opportunity and the money?*
POWELL: I think it would be based upon natural phenomenon because the world is so much more miraculous today and science fiction has blunted, probably, people's appreciation of elaborate fantasy. But that's why I'm interested in the Earthsea Trilogy, because there's a lot of magic in it, but it has to come quite naturally. It's natural magic, straight out of the ground. Happens right before your eyes. Like the opening, I think I told you, where the eagle comes stooping down and as it hits the ground it changes into a man. That can be done so directly that people will entirely believe it.

EVERSON: *Will you do that literally, do you think?*
POWELL: Oh yeah.

EVERSON: *Or get around it via a cut of some way?*
POWELL: Well, of course there would be a cut but they will be convinced that it happened. And of course anything can happen. That's probably what disturbs people about my films because I believe that. I think anything can happen. Just create the right conditions. Perhaps that belief is implicit in the images that I put on the screen. Which might be disturbing for some people.

EVERSON: *Let's move from fantasy to women, which perhaps is fantasy extended.*
POWELL: I would hope so.

EVERSON: *I was always very impressed by the sensuality of the two leading women in* Black Narcissus. *The fact that Deborah Kerr and Kathleen Byron, in some sense, are almost like doubles and they have exactly the same kinds of faces. It's almost like two heads of the same coin. The erotic quality—*

POWELL: I don't see that, having been in love with both of them.

EVERSON: *Maybe that's why you were in love with both of them.*

POWELL: Could be.

EVERSON: *I can be wrong in saying this is two heads of the same coin, but it always struck me that looking at that film one can see Kathleen Byron's character almost going in the direction of the Kerr character and the Kerr character, with the right kind of pushing, going insane the way the other nun did.*

POWELL: Perhaps that's implicit in Rumer Godden's idea. 'Cause she's a wonderful novelist but when a woman starts to create such complex characters then they're bound to have certain aspects of her own character as well, like any great novelist. Perhaps unconsciously I cast the parts also with some physical resemblance. Now I must say, at the time I didn't do that consciously.

EVERSON: *It's a remarkable performance from Deborah Kerr. The warmth from just a single tremor in her voice when she's talking about the past gives you an incredibly sensual, not erotic, but a very warm feminine feeling, so you understand this whole woman's past just from the way she'll almost break down in the middle of a sentence. A beautiful performance.*

POWELL: Deborah is a wonderful woman. She came on the stage the other day when I went to England with Emeric to receive the British Academy Fellowship Award for long service; they always give it to you when you're either dead or dying.

EVERSON: *Well you're going to fool them, I'm sure.*

POWELL: I am going to fool them, yes. But Deborah appeared from nowhere and she's working in a new Peter Ustinov play—you were mentioning him just now—and she appeared from nowhere to give us the award. She looked absolutely wonderful and I fell in love with her all over again right in front of about 12 million viewers. Wonderful girl. And Kathleen was an extraordinary actress. I'd seen her do a picture we produced, but I didn't direct, called *The Silver Fleet.*

EVERSON: *With Ralph Richardson.*
POWELL: She played the school mistress in it, do you remember, and had quite a long speech about this mythical character who symbolized Dutch resistance. I was very impressed by this. I didn't cast her in the part, the director did. Later on, she married an American and then came back to England and that's how she got into *A Matter of Life and Death* (*Stairway to Heaven*) playing the Angel.

EVERSON: *But she's another actress who seems to have really utilized her full potential only in your films. I've seen her in other melodramas and other typical minor British films and there's not one where you can really right away say what she really added to that film, or did a great deal.*
POWELL: Perhaps no director fell in love with her again. It's very important for a director to fall in love with his leading lady.

EVERSON: *Well it must be rather fun, too. [no answer. Laughs] Looking back on this tremendous body of work that you've done, this is probably a clichéd question, but is there any one film that you look back on and think that you really wished now that you'd done it differently? I mean,* I *can't. I look back on them and they all seem in their own way either delightfully imperfect, or almost perfect in their own way, but is there any one film that you would really like to have done differently?*
POWELL: No. No, I've been very lucky. I've been allowed to make my own mistakes so I don't regret anything.

EVERSON: *Well, that's a perfect exit line. There's nothing you can do to top that.*
POWELL: No, it's a good capper.

EVERSON: *Well thank you very much. It's been delightful talking to you.*

Powell and Pressburger

IAN CHRISTIE / 1985

IAN CHRISTIE: *Good afternoon, ladies and gentlemen. We have quite a complicated structure ahead of us as you might expect from the virtuosos of flashback construction in film. I'm reminded of something that Lindsay Anderson once wrote; he said that, "The tendency is to treat films of one's own country like its prophets, with less than justice." Lindsay Anderson wrote that in 1947 as the opening sentence of an attack on the latest film by Powell and Pressburger. I think he might now feel himself part of that persecuted band of prophets. At any rate, it's a great pleasure to welcome two of the most distinguished members of the British cinema's "band of prophets": Michael Powell and Emeric Pressburger. Not on their first visit to the National Film Theatre, because as some of you may remember, we had a marvelous discussion here in 1978 when the full collection of films that they made together was shown together with many of the films that they made separately. This afternoon, we're going to be joined by one of their better known admirers, Martin Scorsese, who'll be joining us a little later in the proceedings. Since that time in 1978 which, I think, marked one of the important moments in re-discovering of the joys of Powell and Pressburger's films, there have been a number of honors showered upon them: they became two of the first Fellows of the British Film Institute when we celebrated our 50th anniversary some years ago; they've been honored by BAFTA and by cinématheques all around the world; there's been a dizzying progress of re-discovery. Now, we're in the middle of another chapter of re-discovery with* The Life and Death of Colonel Blimp *showing at the Electric Screen to a*

Transcript of Guardian Lecture at National Film Theatre, July 28, 1985. Reprinted by permission of Ian Christie and the National Film Theatre, London.

paying public at present. This is something which the British Film Institute feels very proud to have helped happen; it's been a long struggle over the years to find the money and to make all the necessary technical preparations to actually restore The Life and Death of Colonel Blimp *as it was intended to be seen. For us, it's a great pleasure that the film is now being re-discovered with such enthusiasm and we hope that it's got a long life ahead of it, 40 years on. It's amazing to think of that reference in the film to 1983, and the young fellow of enterprise. I want to begin this afternoon by asking its makers how they think* Blimp *has stood the test of time. They both saw it at the re-launch a week ago, and I wonder how they feel about it now, 40 years after its first appearance. Michael?*
MICHAEL POWELL: I think Emeric's really the best person to answer that question. [laughter]
EMERIC PRESSBURGER: Now, repeat the question.

CHRISTIE: *How did you feel about* Blimp *seeing it complete for the first time in so long?*
PRESSBURGER: You know that *Blimp* is my best film. But Michael has more to say about that, haven't you?
POWELL: About *Blimp?*
PRESSBURGER: Not about *Blimp* but about the films, all together.
POWELL: Well, *Blimp* is part of a series of films that Emeric and I made together and people are always asking us, first of all, how we got together and then how we managed to work together for so long, something like 18 years, making about 20 films. And the answer is: Love. You can't have a collaboration in anything without love. Any married men here? [laughter] We had complete love and confidence in each other and we were very lucky that just at that time we managed to prove to the man who had the money—that was Rank, Arthur Rank—we managed to prove to him that he should let the filmmakers decide what they want to make. And that was really how *Blimp* came about: from an understanding with Arthur Rank that we knew best what to do at this particular time in the middle of the war. Because the war really shaped a lot of our films. There's a bit of secret history maybe you don't know: about two weeks before the war broke out in 1939, August, I was working on *The Thief of Bagdad* at Denham for Alex Korda and there came a call to all of us on *The Thief of Bagdad*—I think I was doing something with the flying carpet—and we all knew desperately the war was coming and we were all trying to finish this enormous picture before the war came, and we

were all asked to come to Alex's room in the old house at Denham, do you remember Imre?

PRESSBURGER: Oh, yes.

POWELL: And I remember being there. One of the people I remember most was one of the most unjustly neglected men in the whole history of films, I think, and that's Ian Dalrymple. He was a remarkable producer, remarkable editor, and he was standing there scraping away at his cigarette. We were all there, about 40 or 50 people, all the leading technicians and people at Denham. And Alex spoke and said Churchill had asked him to make a propaganda film against the Nazis the moment war was declared, and he'd said that he was prepared to do this and that the moment war was declared he would turn over the whole of Denham, and all the people working in it, including all the people on *The Thief of Bagdad,* to make this propaganda film. In return, Churchill agreed that there should be in the Ministry of Information, which would have to be formed in wartime with its difficulties with propaganda and censorship, there should be a Films Division and that films should become a weapon of war. If you think about it, there couldn't have been a more important moment in the whole history of films, not just British films, because as I said the other day at the private showing of *Blimp,* this is a 100% British film but it's photographed by a Frenchman, it's written by a Hungarian, the musical score is by a German Jew, the director was English, the man who did the costumes was a Czech; in other words, it was the kind of film that I've always worked on with a mixed crew of every nationality, no frontiers of any kind. I'm sorry, I've drifted away from the main point, which was that Churchill promised there would be a Ministry of Information Films Division and, in time, there was. Meanwhile, as soon as the war was declared, we dropped everything and started to make *The Lion Has Wings* and within a month, Dalrymple had got the whole thing done and edited and it was out playing in the cinemas, I think, within 5 weeks and copies were going all over the world to all the embassies everywhere. Certainly, for that time—that period of the war—this really settled the fate of the British film industry because Alex and Churchill, curious combination but they were great friends, they were determined that the British film industry shouldn't vanish at this time. Of course, the only way that it should not vanish would be that it became an instrument of war. Funny though it is to think of that, *Colonel Blimp* is one of the first big films that came out of this idea because it took time to establish the Ministry of Information.

CHRISTIE: *You've effortlessly covered the background to* Blimp. *I think the thing that struck a lot of people when they had the chance to see* Blimp, *complete at last with all those cuts restored, is that the film is in many ways a fantasy. It's a film of great comedy, of great humor, and of great fantasy. It's full of wishes being made, prophecies coming true. It's a million miles removed from most people's conception of a solid, serious, propaganda film. Did you have the feeling when you were making it, when you were planning it, that it was going to be something very controversial because of that?*

PRESSBURGER: Of course not. We thought it was wonderful. [laughter] Suddenly, we realized that Mr. Churchill thought that we shouldn't touch such things as we wanted to introduce. When the enemy started such things as bombarding those cities which had absolutely nothing to do with the war except that they were in England or in Scotland or in Wales, everybody thought, well perhaps we are different—we are not going to bombard as the Germans are doing. But in the fourth year of the war, suddenly Dresden was bombarded, because with the Americans it was decided that the Germans only understand what hurts. So, what they had done, or what we had done, was that Dresden in Saxony has been bombarded by heaven knows how many hundred American and British bombers and 21,000 people have been killed which is not very well. For us, it couldn't have been done any other way, quite simply. So, *Blimp* could do exactly the same thing. Mr. Churchill never touched it but it was put away. If he wouldn't have been worried about it so much then, quite obviously, we wouldn't be sitting here. Strangely enough, it has enough interesting stuff in it; I can't see what it's missing; I'm really happy with it and I'm sure that Michael is happy with it, as well.

CHRISTIE: *In a way, Churchill's opposition did some initial good for the film. It gave it a certain notoriety, but it did great damage in that it probably led to the film being cut and virtually disappearing.*

POWELL: No, it wasn't cut because of Churchill.

CHRISTIE: *But the initial cuts were for reasons of length, weren't they?*

POWELL: Yes, it was because Technicolor was very difficult to get and prints even more difficult to get. In fact, the next two pictures we made had to be black and white because there wasn't a Technicolor camera available. We had to wait two years to make the final war picture which was *A Matter of Life and Death*.

CHRISTIE: *Something which you've mentioned, the Ministry of Information—and we may talk a bit more about that when we look at the next extract in a short while—but you've often said that you had a lot of support from the Ministry of Information, from the people in the Films Division, and that you had very regular discussions with them. Can you tell us something about what it was actually like planning and making pictures during that war period?*

POWELL: Well, maybe Emeric will bear me out on this. We would finish with the one thing, like *One of Our Aircraft Is Missing,* and we wanted to make a film that would be inspired from something in that film and then the next film would inspire something in the next film and so on. In the end, we did almost 9 films like this but this particular film . . . where were we, sorry?

CHRISTIE: *On* Blimp.

POWELL: On *Blimp* only?

CHRISTIE: *Well no, by all means.*

POWELL: Well, there was a scene in the film we'd just done, *One of Our Aircraft Is Missing,* between a young man and an old man. It was cut out of the film but it made Emeric think when he saw it that maybe this was a great theme for another film. About that time, Arthur Rank had come to us—no, *before* that—he came to us and said, "What are you going to do next?" He'd come into *49th Parallel* when we were about halfway through, and he realized the work we were doing, and he was very ambitious then to get control of the British film industry, which eventually of course he did. But he came to us and said, "What do you want to make next," and I said, "Well, Emeric and I have been talking about a film called *One of Our Aircraft Is Missing,*" and he said, "Can I read anything?" and we said, "Well, there's a 20-page outline which we made for ourselves but you can read it if you like." He took it home and about 3 days later he rung up and said, "My partner in distribution, C. M. Woolf doesn't think the film will be a success. It's downbeat." I remember quite clearly, I said, "Mr. Rank, we're going to make this film anyway, whether you finance it or not." In fact, we went to John Corfield and Lady Yule, at British National Films, and they financed it because of that. I said, "And when it's made and when it's a success, then you're going to come to us and say now what do you want to do next and you're going to finance it. Is that a deal?" [laughter]. So he jingled the money in his pocket, being a Yorkshireman he was always doing that, and a very fine chap, Arthur Rank, huge, monolithic, very fine man; the sole architect of the British film industry during the war. And he said, "That's a bet," and sure enough, after *One of Our Aircraft Is Missing* had been playing at the Odeon-Leicester Square for about 5 weeks or so, he came to see it, and he said, "Now what do you want to do next?" So we said—Emeric said to me the other day, "He probably expected that we would say *One of Our Submarines Is Missing*" [laughter] which is a lovely joke and typical of Emeric—but when we said it was going to be about Colonel Blimp, he said, "Colonel Blimp? The fellow that David Low, the cartoonist, writes about in Beaverbrook's paper" (I didn't know if he was a supporter of Beaverbrook or not). We said, "Yes, that's right, we want to make a film about him." So he gulped a bit and then said, "Well, go ahead and let's see how we get on." From then on, he was a real champion to work with. It was a fairly expensive picture in those days, about £208,000, the final budget was: twelve weeks shooting, and Technicolor, as well. It was quite a big job. And yet, when we just finished, in spite of all this trouble with—not with the Ministry of Information, they were wonderful all the way through, they liked it and they supported it, but what could they do against the old man? They said to us, "The old man doesn't like it!" We said, "Well, so what?" [laughter] He said, "Well, don't you fellows feel you should drop it?" We said, "No." "Well, what are you going to do?" and we said, "We're going to do it!" I remember saying to Emeric as we came out of the London University, which was taken over by the Ministry of Information at that time—

PRESSBURGER: Anyway, he didn't like it and several other people didn't like it.

POWELL: Who, Rank?

PRESSBURGER: Not Rank. Churchill and Churchill's important men. But they just couldn't stop it.

POWELL: No they couldn't stop it. They said, "Do stop it, please, you know. We can't say to you, stop it. You know that. We're a democracy. [laughter] But don't make it. Everybody will be very cross and you'll never get a knighthood." [laughter]

CHRISTIE: *Emeric, I remember, had the uncomfortable experience which he had on several occasions of actually fronting for the film when it was finished before Churchill.*

POWELL: Yes. I was down in the Mediterranean.

PRESSBURGER: Yes. Mr. Churchill, I was convinced, when he sees the film, he will be satisfied.
POWELL: In tears?
PRESSBURGER: In tears, but in the dark so nobody could see. But the moment came that we had finished the film and shown it to him at the Odeon-Leicester Square. He arrived—
POWELL: You alone showed him the film.
PRESSBURGER: Yes, I don't know what you were doing then. [laughter]
POWELL: Just on the North African landings.
PRESSBURGER: Yes. Anyway, I was sitting there at about 11:30—
POWELL: Oh, I know, I was with Ralph Richardson on *The Volunteer.*

CHRISTIE: *Yes, this was a special screening arranged after the normal screenings at the Odeon.*
PRESSBURGER: Mr. Churchill came around at 11:30 and he didn't look right or left—actually, I sat myself on the left. He never stopped to say something.
POWELL: How many people did he have with him?
PRESSBURGER: About 8. And suddenly, amid all this—
POWELL: When the film was on?
PRESSBURGER: When the film was on, I heard the women who did the cleaning every night putting the seats up with their hands.
POWELL: Flip them up?
PRESSBURGER: Yes, flick them up.
POWELL: They always do it when you're showing a film. Late at night, I mean.
PRESSBURGER: So I got up and found the director of the cinema and he went out for a moment, and then he came back and whispered into my ear, "That's not our ladies cleaning, that's some anti-aircraft guns." So I thought, "Well, I don't like this very much, and I do understand that Mr. Churchill doesn't like it either." But it ran to the end. He went away without saying a single word about it and that was that. But the strange thing to me, who was still a foreigner here—
POWELL: A foreigner?! You were an enemy! Enemy alien. [laughter]
PRESSBURGER: Yes I was. I was. But I had permits to travel during *49th Parallel,* heaven knows how many times, to Canada. But anyway, I was astonished that they just, that the Prime Minister doesn't or couldn't just say: now

these chaps here, they have absolutely no idea, and we are not going to let them do it. He just simply couldn't do it. He had to see us make the whole film. So in a way it wasn't very difficult to believe he just didn't like it. Michael was saying to me so often that we ought to do a big film, with families, and 200 years and so on, and the funny thing was, before that idea, we had made *49th Parallel*—and the Nazis had the most important parts in it, get less and less in number until they disappeared entirely because the film, of course, was about six Nazis of whom one was just simply arrested.

CHRISTIE: *I think we're going to break there for a moment because since Emeric has been talking about the difference between* The Life and Death of Colonel Blimp *and the film that came two years before it, that's* 49th Parallel, *we've got an extract from* 49th Parallel *that we want to show. Let's go back to beginnings because it wasn't your first film together, it was your third, but it was the first film in which you had that degree of control over your material to really take risks and show what you both were capable of. The scene from the film that we're going to show is, for those who may not know it, the story of what happens when a German U-Boat is destroyed just off the coast of Canada and six of its crew are stranded on the shore; they have to find their way to the port or somewhere where they can escape.*
POWELL: And they're all different kinds of Nazis.

CHRISTIE: *And in the course of moving across Canada, they meet all kinds of people who have their own reasons for opposing the Nazi philosophy. It's a kind of an extended discussion, debate about varieties of democracy and varieties of fascism.*
POWELL: You make it sound a bit *dull.* [laughter]

CHRISTIE: *It's got much more life in it than I'm making it sound. This is the scene at the Hutterite community where one of the girls, Glynis Johns, has heard Eric Portman do his big speech and Anton Walbrook as the leader of the Hutterite community do his equally big speech in defense. So, let's look at that.*
POWELL: Do we lie down? [since they're on the stage] [laughter]

CHRISTIE: *We should leave the stage where we can sit down.*

[excerpt from *49th Parallel*]

CHRISTIE: *Well, that film was made two years before* The Life and Death of Colonel Blimp.

POWELL: Yes, 1940.

CHRISTIE: *That brought you, Emeric, an Oscar for your script.*
PRESSBURGER: Yes.

CHRISTIE: *You may not consider it the best script you've ever written, but it obviously made a terrific impact at the time.*
PRESSBURGER: If the best film of ours came out of it then it must be all right.

CHRISTIE: *I wondered if we could take this opportunity to say something about the relationship between you two over this long series of films: the relationship between writer and the director. I think that it's quite a mystery to many people exactly how you worked, what the kind of relationship between you was. We're all very used to the notion of directors as the people who really put their signature on films but you chose, uniquely of all filmmakers, to sign your films "written, produced, and directed by." You bequeathed endless confusion to critics and people writing about films in doing this. You once said the reason you did it was to keep other people out of interfering with the films, which I can well understand. How did it actually work as a relationship? You weren't The Archers quite at the point you made* 49th Parallel *but you must have realized you were going to work together.*
POWELL: It came about organically, really. Anybody that thinks they can just solely make a film needs his head examined.
PRESSBURGER: I remember a little poem which we used at the very beginning. . . .
POWELL: It was a jingle that I think James Agate threw together. We liked it particularly at the time. He said:

> The arrow was pure gold
> but somehow missed the target.
> Still, as some golden arrow trippers know,
> 'tis better to miss Naples than hit Margate.

And that really inspired the Archers trademark. But the answer really is that I don't think any one man makes a film. I don't think any one man *should* make a film, unless it's a very simple one. If you want to make a personal film, any one of you can do that; it doesn't cost so much now to hire lights, hire this, hire that, or buy this and that and make your own film. But a big production like *49th Parallel,* which started as just a small idea and grew into a very big film, I don't think one man can do it. Two men—if one of them is a very remarkable one, because it's no good if you haven't got a good story and a good script—two men, as far as we were concerned, could put a film together. But of course, we couldn't do it by ourselves, we had to have the best technicians available and at that time, probably some of the best in the world. The cameraman on *49th Parallel* was Fred Young. We discussed before making the film how to make it very rough looking, as if it had been snatched, snatched in black and white, out of the war. Some of the compositions were a bit ragged. When we were shooting in the north of Canada, we were very near the minimum exposure level and the film came out very grainy; we were delighted. We thought we'd made the whole thing look much tougher and much more natural. We had the best technicians, I think, available probably in the world at that time. So what started as an idea of Emeric's we developed, partly by immediately going to Canada and partly as an ordinary screen story. It developed organically that way.

PRESSBURGER: I wanted to mention that I occasionally take out my old scripts, turn the pages, and I find strange things. For example, in *Blimp* there is a love story. There are three, three different girls and Blimp, the old one, like the young Blimp, is interested in the girls; but in the script I find these girls never know that. The first girl knows that she falls in love with the German, and becomes his wife; the second one marries Blimp, but she doesn't know that she is the same type as the first girl was.

POWELL: But the audience knows.

PRESSBURGER: But the audience knows—*only* the audience knows. And the third girl, who we know he has picked out of 700, again—

POWELL: She'll never know why.

PRESSBURGER: She never knows why, we never tell why, but—

POWELL: But *we* know—

PRESSBURGER: Only the audience understands. Now I think that without knowing it at that time when we were making the film—we realised we didn't have to have a number of scenes between these girls and our Blimp. And because of that, after 40 years people don't have to think about it—I'm sure that you, Michael, you know what I am trying to say—

POWELL: I think it gives something special to the film and other films, too, if the audience knows things that the people on the screen don't. As in *I Know Where I'm Going!* for instance.

PRESSBURGER: And we are going to run another part of a very, very sweet little film?

POWELL: Did you say weak?!

PRESSBURGER: [laughs] No. Sweet.

POWELL: Oh, sweet.

PRESSBURGER: Here, the most important part of the film is that the War is on and in three days he falls in love with her, and she is in love with him, but we never show the other man for whom she has come to these islands. I have never thought about this before, but what if we had shown something between those two?

POWELL: Instead of this deliberate reticence?

PRESSBURGER: Yes. She went to the islands to marry a rich man.

POWELL: Don't tell them the whole story!

PRESSBURGER: Why not? Why not? [laughter]

CHRISTIE: *Well, I think you've done my job perfectly for me. You now know what the film is about. Let's look at a short extract from it.*

POWELL: Oh really? Which part?

CHRISTIE: *You don't want me to tell the story again, do you?*

POWELL: Oh, all right.

CHRISTIE: *It's about Joan, that's the girl who knows where she's going, has arrived on the island, not the island she's going to but the island* near *where she's going to. And as Emeric said, she never does get to the island she set off for. Nor does she get to the man that she's due to marry. But she meets some interesting people along the way.*

PRESSBURGER: Three days, the whole thing takes, and the audience is satisfied. True?

CHRISTIE: *True.*

[excerpt from *I Know Where I'm Going!*]

CHRISTIE: *At this point, I'd like to call on our third guest this afternoon who's come specially from New York to be with us, that's Martin Scorsese. Martin, you've talked quite a lot over the years and you've even been present at occasions like this in the past introducing Michael and Emeric before their films in New York back in 1980. I think what's interesting for the people who know your work, is that you find so many points of contact between The Archers' films and the films you're actually making now.*

SCORSESE: Well, actually it's hard to say. I don't really know where the contact is. I was just very curious to find them. Back around 1971, '72, we just kept looking at these films, myself and my friends in New York: Jay Cocks, Brian De Palma, Spielberg; a number of people just kept watching these films over and over again. We wanted to know where they were—who were they, first of all? Why did they sign together—it said, "written, produced, directed by"—that was strange. We didn't know who did what and we were always asking the same questions: Who was the writer? Who was the director? But it was all together on the same card, and that was really quite honest and quite interesting. I first met Michael through a man named Michael Kaplan, who was working for Stanley Kubrick at the time. I think he designed the poster for *2001* and the triangle of *Clockwork Orange.* He was working with Michael in London, I believe on *The Tempest?* Michael, was that it?

POWELL: I think it was one of my many attempts to do *The Tempest.*

SCORSESE: And Michael, who was a friend of Jay Cocks, said, "Sure, you can meet Michael Powell" and we had a meeting. I talked about *Thief of Bagdad,* talked about *The Red Shoes,* and talked about a number of films of theirs.

POWELL: Was that after you did *Alice Doesn't Live Here Anymore*?

SCORSESE: Yes, right before I did *Taxi Driver.* And we were just very delighted because you see we had only come across one article, in a magazine called *Monogram,* on Michael and Emeric, and we had no idea beyond that. Also, we didn't know what the association was between the two, how they worked together and then how Michael later on did *Peeping Tom. Peeping Tom* is sort of a cult film in America. It opened, I believe, in 1962 in a black and white print at a theatre called The Charles on Avenue A and B and 12th Street. It's an avenue you usually don't go into unless you're armed heavily—it's a rather difficult area to see films in—but all my friends—my co-students—went to see it and out of that came *David Holzman's Diary* by Jim McBride which is a very, very important film.

POWELL: Really?

SCORSESE: Yes. Literally from *Peeping Tom.* And ever since then we had missed the print, we couldn't find it except there was a man named Phil

Chamberlain in Los Angeles who had a print of it. It was fading fast; the color was turning—because of that Eastman Color that they shot it in—it was fading—kind of purplish hues and that sort of thing—and we saw it a couple of times and we were amazed that it was the same people. Now, we didn't know. So what we tried to do was meet Michael and Emeric. What happened eventually was that Michael, you came to Los Angeles when I was doing *The Act,* a stage play, I believe to try to get *Pavlova* made, with Frixos Constantine, and so we all became kind of friendly over the years. It took me a long time to realize that there were any contacts in my films that would compare, or to say the inspiration is from a Powell and Pressburger picture. I think the article written in *Sight and Sound,* I forget who the gentleman was who wrote it, was the first article that I actually read that explained *to me* what my connection was to them. [laughs] At least that's what they say, now I don't know. It was something about characters who were anti-heroes being heroes.

POWELL: What I found exciting was that you showed me one or two of your films, and you would say "Did you notice it? Did you get the quote?" and I would say, "No!"

SCORSESE: You have to understand that, let's see, *Colonel Blimp* was made the year I was born, so when I saw *The Red Shoes,* it was one of the great events for me: I was eight years old, I guess. It was the first time I was aware of the logo—"A Film of the Archers"—in color. It was extremely vivid. As I mentioned to you earlier, the only other film that I remember from that period that was as vivid was Jean Renoir's *The River.* It was a beautiful film. But it also turns out that Brian DePalma, having seen *The Red Shoes,* decided to become a director.

You see, what I'm trying to get at, I guess, is that whenever I saw the logo, later on, I knew that there was something very special and magical about the film that I was to see. So much so that eventually, when I got to know Michael well—actually I only met Emeric a few times in 1978 or '79—I was very worried about seeing *I Know Where I'm Going!* Everybody was telling me, "Oh, you must see it. It's wonderful, it's wonderful and you must see it." Quite honestly, I was afraid to see it because I had become friendly with Michael and I felt, what if I didn't like it? Eventually, he's going to ask me, you see. So I tried to worm my way out of it. But about two weeks before I started shooting *Raging Bull,* I decided I'd better look at it. And I was very overwhelmed by the film. I guess I've seen a lot of films that have been made, and I was wondering if there was any picture that I'd missed in the past that really would be considered a masterpiece. In other words, a new film to enjoy. Seriously enjoy. I didn't think I'd ever see another one from the past. But this was it. This was it for me. I was fascinated by how romantic it was and how mystical. I think the most striking moment for me was at the Campbell's birthday party, when they're playing bagpipes, and she asks Roger Livesey to translate the Gaelic in the song, and it's a medium shot of him, and he begins to translate ending with the phrase, "You're the one for me," and the camera moves in quickly, and the sound of the bagpipes comes up, and it was absolutely frightening. It was frightening in the sense that, in a way, you understood they were in love with each other, you understood that they were about to go through something wonderful, and absolutely terrible and frightening at the same time. It was quite remarkable. I was very, very moved by the picture. And also the wonderful ending.

POWELL: It's the skirl of the pipes that does it.

SCORSESE: Really? I thought it was the camera move and, of course, Livesey and Wendy Hiller's face.

PRESSBURGER: I was flabbergasted the first time you invited me and you said, "You will find something which belonged to you." I didn't know what he meant, but for heaven's sake his home was full of our posters and a lot of other things. But Powell and Pressburger couldn't believe it! [laughter]

SCORSESE: I became obsessed with the films. *The Life and Death of Colonel Blimp,* for example. I do have the posters, I got mainly from here, from the Cinema Bookshop, Fred Zentner's place. I've been collecting as much as possible on their films since 1970—the posters, the production books, the book on *A Matter of Life and Death,* the actual hardcover. Those sort of things I keep. But, actually, he's right, I do live with them. They're on the walls—have become part of my daily life.

PRESSBURGER: Including *The Red Shoes.*

SCORSESE: Yes, *The Red Shoes,* the posters.

PRESSBURGER: Do you remember how long it ran in that small cinema? I went to New York and I almost got arrested, because at that time *The Red Shoes* had already been running for a year, and I asked somebody how I could talk to the owner of the cinema. So, he went in and came back again and said "Who are you?" And meanwhile they had already called the police! [laughter]

SCORSESE: This was in New York?

PRESSBURGER: Yes. Anyway, it was a strange thing. And the film ran, I think, more than two years.
POWELL: Two years and seven weeks. [laughter]

CHRISTIE: *Something else which you said once that I thought was very striking was that you always thought of Michael and Emeric as the two experimental filmmakers who got away with making experimental films inside the commercial framework.*
SCORSESE: Totally. They're the only ones, I feel, who really succeeded. Twenty films, I feel, all totally experimental. Even the moment in *The Elusive Pimpernel,* do you remember, when David Niven sneezes at the end in the scene with Cyril Cusack? When he sneezes, he cuts to fireworks on a black screen. Okay, so you can say, there was a kiss in *To Catch a Thief* where they cut to fireworks, but this was made before that. And there was just no reason to cut to fireworks here for the man sneezing, except for the image, and it worked. And I was literally amazed.
POWELL: Oh, you mean the snuff sequence?
SCORSESE: The snuff. I tried to form the type of films I make within the commercial system the way they did and it's very hard.

CHRISTIE: *It doesn't get any easier.*
SCORSESE: No, it gets worse. It gets harder and harder, and people don't understand that. It's a remarkable feat—what they've done.
POWELL: We always had the feeling that other people were making the experimental films, and we had our feet on the ground. [laughter]

CHRISTIE: *I think one of the most amazing things is that you managed to make your most experimental films for that solid, reliable, Yorkshireman Arthur Rank, and you didn't make any really experimental films for Alex Korda, the man who'd brought you together. For him you made a smaller number of films—*
POWELL: Oh, there was *The Tales of Hoffmann.*

CHRISTIE: *Yes, but that was after you'd caused the Rank Organisation to fear for their profits with* The Red Shoes.
POWELL: They were a bit slow on the uptake. [laughter] We really broke with Arthur Rank and John Davis over *The Red Shoes* because I was shooting

some of the last ballet scenes which went on for some time and they wanted to see the film, and Emeric saw it with them. Emeric, tell—

PRESSBURGER: What I wanted to say was that *The Red Shoes* surprised them all.

POWELL: You could say that. [laughter]

PRESSBURGER: I don't know what one should have done. The film was prepared and they almost fainted—although the New York people were enchanted by it.

POWELL: Yes, but I meant first of all, when the film was finished, you actually showed it to Arthur Rank and John Davis.

PRESSBURGER: Well that was a sad business. I walked out with them from the cinema—

POWELL: Mind you, they'd backed us for a long while and they had backed this particular film, but they just couldn't understand the frame of it. Right?

PRESSBURGER: Anyway, it was fine, good.

POWELL: It made good in the end, yes. But what happened was that Emeric ran the film for them and the lights went up and he expected them to say something. They had been muttering together, but they just stood up and walked out. Never said a word to him. So I said it was time to move.

CHRISTIE: *Then you went back to Alex Korda for—*

POWELL: Four films. *The Small Back Room, Pimpernel—*

CHRISTIE: Gone to Earth *and* Tales of Hoffman. *And so you ended that phase as you had begun it, under Korda's sponsorship. He had brought you together in the first place back in '39.*

POWELL: Well, we were just under contract to him like other contract people anywhere else. Two technicians: one a writer, and the other a director, hopeful director. I'm fascinated by Martin saying that he felt something similar was going on in our films to what was in his own mind, but was it some definite point of view, was it a personal point of view that you sensed? I've always thought it was a miracle how interested you were in our films. I'm a great believer in this because, naturally, I went into films very early in the silent days because of the films I'd seen. And when I was first in films, an insignificant beginner, but meeting a lot of famous people from Germany, France, all over Europe, as well as America, I was always asking them what it

was that made them tick. So I'm fascinated, what was it about The Archers' films that you felt was something like a Scorsese film?
SCORSESE: I'm not sure, but one thing I know is when I saw The Archers' films I always liked the people. I was fascinated by the characters. Supposedly an antagonist like Lermontov in *Red Shoes* was fascinating. I tried to—
POWELL: Is it part of the writing, do you think?
SCORSESE: Oh, I think so. Yes. The dialogue and the conflict and the whole concept of it. Then I was fascinated by the style of the shooting and the cutting of the film. Learned a lot about camera movements from *Tales of Hoffmann,* a great deal, which I utilized in *Taxi Driver*. Robert Helpmann's gestures or ballet moves, I don't know what really to call them, when he's on the gondola and during the sword fight when he sort of moves his hand across his face and his eyes go from left to right. You'll see that, I've said this a number of times—
POWELL: That's really controlled movement.
SCORSESE: Controlled movement. You'll see that in *Taxi Driver* in De Niro's face—
POWELL: Which is the most effective thing you can do in a film.
SCORSESE: —when his eyes go from left to right, constantly. And what I did, I slowed up the action, I mean I overcranked it like 32, 36 frames a second to give it that ballet feeling, in *my* mind. But I'm always fascinated by how the camera moved and the cuts and I always tried do that. For example in *Colonel Blimp*—
POWELL: Well, we're always using different speeds, all the time. I was trained very early in the idea that 16 pictures a second for silent films was merely a convention. Every shot that you make in a film has a speed of its own. And this 24 pictures a second is the most *awful* betrayal of all because it's no speed. It's an approximation of the speed of the camera with the speed of sound so the dialogue is roughly in sync. And you know how that means, "roughly" when you start to put the film together. This speed of the camera has been dogging me my whole life. It's very important. And probably that's one of the things you sensed, particularly in *Hoffmann,* where in one sequence I might be shooting at 5 different speeds.
SCORSESE: Absolutely. I think there's another thing: propelling the story forward in the cutting. Also the characters in your pictures: I never saw quite clearly the good guy and the bad guy. They were people. Except of course in *49th Parallel,* I think that it's quite clear Eric Portman is not to be dealt with

on that level. But in the films like *I Know Where I'm Going!, Red Shoes*—Well, *Red Shoes:* Marius Goring's attitude at the end, his helping in her destroying herself at that point, but all the way through you're sort of with him to have her, and to go off and then suddenly he becomes part of the thing that kills her. And it's like life.

POWELL: Well, in *Raging Bull,* you and Thelma were doing all the fighting like I've just described with altering the speed of the camera and in practically every cut.

SCORSESE: Every cut.

POWELL: And making what was a glancing blow into a stunning punch with part of a sound. Wonderful. That's proper film work.

SCORSESE: But one other thing about *Colonel Blimp* was that the duel sequence was one of the most remarkable things I've ever seen, in that the duel itself is no longer important. What's important is the rules: the rule book.

POWELL: Right.

SCORSESE: Of course, the duel itself is not important because the rules bring together these two men who are to be friends for 40 years. And the concentration on the rules in that sequence—I don't know if anyone here has seen it—but you anticipate, and I was going along with it. All these rules are magnificent and "Would you like your sleeve rolled up or should it be torn?" and he says, "Well, I think I should tear." He says, "Good choice" and he tears it. Ah! So that was a good choice! What would I have said? I don't know what I would have said. And this went on and on, until finally they're about to fence, they're about to go into their duel and the camera goes up in the air and outside into the street—it's amazing! And I said, "My God, the duel, the fight itself is not important." It was bringing the two men together through the rule book.

POWELL: Now this was all planned by Emeric. He went into the British Museum when—at that time, of course, it was difficult to get hold of anything, in the middle of the war—but the British Museum, thank God, was there, and he found this little book of the code of dueling in German. And he brought it home in triumph and showed it to me, and proposed how we could use it this way. And I was absolutely stunned. It was so exactly the way to go about such a thing, you know, to go to the sources first. It's one of our rules, really. Massine used to tell me that Diaghilev would always say, when a new idea came up, "Let us go first to the museums." This whole code of dueling came out of the British Museum Reading Room.

CHRISTIE: *Well, I think if we're going to leave space for anyone else to ask questions we should open this up to the audience. So I'd like to ask anyone who wants to ask questions to come in at this point.*

AUDIENCE: *How did Churchill know about the production of* Blimp? *How did he get to hear about it?*
PRESSBURGER: We had to take the script when it was finished to the War Office, quite simply, and they said, "No, we don't like this." So I thought, what are they going to do now? It turned out that they were not going to let us have all those actors whom we were asking for, such as Laurence Olivier.
POWELL: He was the original choice for Blimp. He felt having been in the Fleet Air Arm for two years that he knew a lot about the military mind. [laughter]
PRESSBURGER: This was really what flabbergasted me. You know I came from having been several years in Germany where it wouldn't ever have happened. They would have thought that it will damage the war effort; and they would have said, "Well, it's finished! We are going to keep the script here and you have to bring in all the scripts which exist," and that would be that. But the strange and wonderful thing, even now, is to think that the script was not theirs, and they just couldn't do anything except say, "Laurence Olivier is not going to help you."
POWELL: Mind you, we couldn't have done it without the money, and Rank was backing us in this big film. We went back to Rank and C. M. Woolf, his distributor, and told them, "The M. of I. won't let us have Laurence Olivier though they're not against the film." They said, "What should we do?" I said, "We'll play Roger Livesey." They said, "Who is he?" I said, "He's a very good actor." "Is he available?" We said, "He's working in an aircraft factory." So without further talk, they said, "Well, can you get him out?" and we said, "Yes." They didn't say we're not going to give you the money, or do you wonder whether we'll give you the money, they just said, "Good!" and we went on to make the picture. But in reply to the direct question, how did it start? We requested certain things from the War Office and gave them a script to read: trucks, uniforms, guns, all the equipment, you see. And this got in the hands of some adjutant, went up to the Secretary of State for War, James

Griff, and he got on the phone to Churchill and said, "My people say this is subversive. It's against the army." That's how it started. It started with the War Office. Later on I was asked by someone in the War Office, "How did you get all that equipment, uniforms and things like that. Trucks! Military weapons. Where did you get them? How *could* you get them?" And I said, "You don't know a film property man." [laughter]

AUDIENCE: *Michael Powell, could you say something about* Peeping Tom. *As you probably know, the film is considered to be a play on cinema itself, and many think it shows the clearest influence on Martin Scorsese's work. A friend of mine who couldn't be here today asked me to ask you if you consider* Peeping Tom *to be at all autobiographical. [laughter]*
POWELL: I think you should ask the author of *Peeping Tom,* Leo Marks, who's here. I've seen him tonight. Right? Leo, where are you?

LEO MARKS [from audience]: *No, Mr. Powell, it is* not *autobiographical [laughter]. It was perhaps "a matter of death and death."*
POWELL: Thank you, Mr. Marks.

AUDIENCE: *To go back to the relationship of script writer and director: how was that relationship actually on the shooting floor and how present was Emeric?*
POWELL: Omnipresent. But we sometimes worked in different ways on writing the script, didn't we?
PRESSBURGER: Well, usually when a script is finished then the script writer gets his money and goes on to another script or does what he likes. But, of course, where Michael's and my business was concerned, it was not so simple, because if I wanted to ask Michael about some better solution, it was very difficult. He was tired—
POWELL: I was never tired!
PRESSBURGER: When Michael went into the cutting room to see the rushes the next day, then of course I had to be there, and I was there. That's how it went on—on and on. [laughter]

AUDIENCE: *So actually during shooting, you had feedback into the—*
PRESSBURGER: Yes. Yes.
POWELL: He was in the lucky position of a writer who's able to follow

through his work to the end of the picture. And, of course, that's the ideal way to work.

AUDIENCE: *I wonder if you could add further details of your collaboration with Roger Livesey, particularly in* A Matter of Life and Death. *You made at least three films with him, and you've just told us now that he worked in an aircraft factory.*
POWELL: Well, that was in the wartime. He was probably called up and put in that kind of work for the time being, because he was over 30 at that time. But what do you want to know?

AUDIENCE: *I think in some respects he's an actor who's very much associated with those three films—*
POWELL: Well, we gave him great chances, but he was a very, very good actor. He had this curious, husky voice which personally I liked very much, but I made some tests of him for Micky Balcon about five years before, because I wanted to play him in a thriller I was making for Balcon, and Balcon turned him down *because* of his voice. Which shows how suburban Balcon was. [laughter]

AUDIENCE: *This is British Film Year,* and I'd like to ask Mr. Powell and Mr. Pressburger, if they were younger men, how they would set about revitalizing the British film industry now.*
POWELL: I'd like Martin Scorsese to come in on this because my answer would be to collaborate much more closely with America. We work for an English-speaking market; it doesn't matter whether it's American, or English, or Canadian. We make films that are understood in the English-speaking market and it's a very big one. Usually an English film starts out with the idea that we're either competing with America, or we're going to do better. That's ridiculous. We're going to make an English-speaking film in competition with some of the cleverest people in the world. We're far too inclined here to say we've got to create the British cinema. Why? God didn't ordain a British cinema. [laughter] And I'd like Martin to tell me what he thinks. Much closer cooperation between the two countries, for a start, would help.
SCORSESE: You mean there isn't already?
POWELL: I don't see anything coming out of competition because the

---

*A year devoted to the promotion of British cinema by many trade and cultural bodies.

Americans will always win. But in collaboration, then sometimes we might make a point. Tell me I'm wrong.

SCORSESE: No, I would tend to agree with you. My feeling about the British film in America is that I personally don't see that much of a difference. It's an English-speaking film: the English film, the Australian, the Canadian and it's all the same market. Although, I never think in terms of market, I just try to identify with the people in the films and enjoy the pictures, and I happen to be an English film buff, I happen to like the English cinema. There was a question here last time I was here, with De Niro, and they said what do I think about the new English cinema: do I think it was revitalizing the industry, and do I think it's important; a fading industry has now been revitalized. And I said for me there never has been a period of time when the English cinema was lagging. I always found it fascinating.

POWELL: Yes. Fascinating that's fine. A pat on the head. [laughter] But, first of all we don't pay our people enough. We don't pay our directors enough, and they're the people who've got to lead: the directors and writers. They've got to be paid—not as much as an American, nobody can be paid as much as that—but they should be well paid. Because when there's a slump or when there's a change of wind and different things to be done, it calls for research, it calls for resources. When we were making films together, it was all done on a gamble with Rank and Korda. We took very little cash until we joined Korda after the war. He had more cash at the time. Before that we took very little cash and a large percentage of the film. And Rank's idea was that this would start paying off within 3 or 4 years after the end of the war. It took 24 years. So during that considerable time, we were very hard up, weren't we? We're still hard up. But it was worth it.

AUDIENCE: *We've all seen the sequence [in* Blimp*] where Spud Wilson struggles with Candy and they fall into the water, and then Candy gets out of the water, by the end of a long tracking shot, I believe it is, 40 years younger. Can you tell us how it was done? Was it one shot or two?*

POWELL: It's two.

AUDIENCE: *Thank you. Was another actor used? A man much bigger than Roger Livesey?*

POWELL: Yeah, sure. There's no secret about that. Doubles we used all the way through. And I brought this up when Marty made *Raging Bull*. We had long conversations over the Atlantic telephone, do you remember, about how Bob De Niro was going to put on 30 or 40 pounds and not die of heart failure. Or having put it on, take it off. Do you remember all those?

SCORSESE: Yes. Yes. But he wanted—

POWELL: *Colonel Blimp* came into this in a big way.

SCORSESE: He liked it. He liked very much the make-up that you did.

POWELL: It was partly make-up, partly acting on Roger Livesey's part—rubber things in his nose. Actors adore this sort of stuff: rubber in here, you do this with your neck, you know. He was a big, powerful man, Roger, so he was fairly good already as far as Blimp was concerned. And then the first thing he said to me, when his wife was there, lovely Ursula Jeans, who was in the picture, she played the baroness, and he said, "I've been thinking about this part; let's shoot all the first part first and the second part, and I'll shave back my head a bit, and then for the third act we'll take it off entirely." Patting his beautiful gold hair. She screamed. [laughter] But she gave in because she's the wife of an actor, and she was an actress herself, and she knows what a kick it gives an actor to change his aspect. That's one of the things with Bob—he loves to change his aspect.

SCORSESE: He loves it, yeah. He likes it because then people don't recognize him in between films on the street. It's true. Then he can do what his job is, which is to observe people.

POWELL: But you did look at it several times, didn't you?

SCORSESE: He looked at it but he admired the make-up—

POWELL: Sometimes we did doubles, sometimes make-up, once we did try making a sort of carapace of Blimp's body. The make-up department were very proud of it. It was all built up. It was the usual dreadful stuff that things were built up. And then all the muscles and everything put on, and the whole thing anchored on Roger. And as soon as he made a step it all split apart. [laughter] We had a wonderful time.

AUDIENCE: *Could you say something about* A Canterbury Tale *and particularly about the American actor you used in it, who I thought was marvelous but I've never seen after this?*

POWELL: John Sweet.

AUDIENCE: *Yes. And also, could you mention something about the glue episode which baffles me still?*

POWELL: Well, Emeric had better speak about the glue.
PRESSBURGER: Why should glue be so terrible? Doesn't it even happen nowadays?

AUDIENCE: *When the women came into the town someone threw glue in their hair and you used that later in a pivotal point for the sort of local magistrate of the town who is found to be guilty of this. It seems to me to be a very strange item to use.*
POWELL: Well, anything odd in England immediately has a sexual connotation. [laughter] You know, they're always looking for a relationship. You don't get enough thrown at you. Obviously, somebody suspected there's something in this glue business . . . or jam. Something sticky!
PRESSBURGER: I don't understand the question. At that time, quite obviously it seemed to us that this was something which at any moment might happen. Strange things were happening in the world. Now this obviously didn't work, and I can't—some people don't have anything against it. I think some other idea would probably have been better, but I just couldn't think of one—quite simply that.

AUDIENCE: *What happened to John Sweet, the American serviceman who appears in the film?*
POWELL: He went back to America, of course, at the end of the war. And he'd made—not a hit, because the film wasn't widely released at that time—but because he was so good in *Canterbury Tale* and he was good enough to know he was good, he tried to start an acting career. He worked in one or two Broadway plays; I think one was a musical. But he didn't like it and he hadn't got the kind of personality. . . . If he'd perhaps had a Thornton Wilder to write something for him, his honesty and his freshness and his wonderful, wonderful personality would have come over. But he probably just tried to get on in the commercial theatre, he soon got tired of it, and he went back home and went into business, and lived happily ever after. When we had a retrospective in New York (remember Emeric?) a wonderful retrospective of all our films, he and his wife and his children and a whole flock of neighbors, all properly homespun characters, weren't they, came from up in New York state. And he just sat back and looked up and said, "Well, I never knew I was as good as that!"

AUDIENCE: *Of your own films, which do you prefer?*
PRESSBURGER: Of all of them? *Blimp.*

AUDIENCE: *Would you say* Les Enfants du Paradis *was a more anti-Nazi film than* The Life and Death of Colonel Blimp?
PRESSBURGER: Yes. [laughter]

CHRISTIE: *I think the question about favorite films was addressed to you as well.*
POWELL: Of our films? I think *A Matter of Life and Death.* [applause] Oh good! [begins to clap too] I've got friends.
PRESSBURGER: Mind you, it doesn't mean that I don't like the film. [laughter]

AUDIENCE: *What about* The Tales of Hoffmann?
PRESSBURGER: Entirely different.
POWELL: I must say, I think it's a wonderful film, *Tales of Hoffmann.* It's a pity it's so difficult to get to see it. Because it's an opera it loses out quite often, but it's a wonderful film whether it's an opera or not, I think.

AUDIENCE: *In* Tales of Hoffmann *what was your relationship to the ballet company?*
POWELL: The idea was to record, with Sir Thomas Beecham, a wonderful performance with singers of the opera, and then make a film of it with dancers. Simple as that. It probably never occurred to the public that it was as simple as all that. But that's how it happened.

AUDIENCE: *In* A Matter of Life and Death *why did you film the celestial sequences in black and white and why the earthbound sequences in color?*
POWELL: You can answer that Emeric. I asked you at the time, I think. [laughter]
PRESSBURGER: Would you repeat? [they laugh]
POWELL: Well, remember we couldn't get Technicolor for a long time and then finally we could get Technicolor and the Ministry of Information told us we could go ahead with a film which they described as a film to improve Anglo-American relations. So, Emeric produced a story in about a week and we then thought about it a good deal. And as we were going to make it in

color, I said to him, "Well in your idea of heaven and earth, which is color and which is black and white?"
PRESSBURGER: Ah, but I remember now. I think that 8 out of 10 would have thought that color was the right thing for . . .
POWELL: . . . another world?
PRESSBURGER: Another world. Yes. But I thought that just because it would be what people would expect, it would be much more interesting [to film it as they did] than to do the obvious. I'm quite certain that in reality, I know it's not so simple what I'm saying now, that something will happen that people didn't expect. They don't know everything about the world.
POWELL: May I remind you also that you said, "Look around you, well, you're in the ordinary world. What do you see? Color. So we know the ordinary world is colored because there it is in front of our noses. But who knows about the other world? Make it in black and white!" [laughter] Actually it isn't, of course, black and white. It's monochrome. We shot all the other-world sequences in 3-strip Technicolor and then didn't develop the dyes. So what you're seeing is a monochrome Technicolor print of the other world and a regular Technicolor print of this world.

CHRISTIE: *Which is what makes possible those magical transformations from one world to the next in the same shot. We should have a brief pause in memory of Technicolor at this point, I think.*

AUDIENCE: *I heard last year there were plans to re-make* A Matter of Life and Death *which rather alarmed me at the time. Is anything further happening about it?*
POWELL: No, some people wanted to have an option to re-make it and I think we gave them a limited option because we never thought they would make it. But we liked the option money. [laughter]

AUDIENCE: *It always seemed to me from a personal point of view, when something is done as well as it was done the first time, what would be the point of doing it again? But that's their problem, I suppose.*
PRESSBURGER: You're asking the wrong people.
POWELL: [to audience member] A rich man would agree with you.

AUDIENCE: *In the fifties two of your films,* Gone to Earth *and* The Elusive Pimpernel *were not too well received by the critics. But you gave a spirited defense*

of them in a copy of Picturegoer *which I still have. Subsequently in Ian Christie's book, you were rather more critical. Did you justify them at the time because you felt it, or for publicity purposes?*
POWELL: I doubt it.

AUDIENCE: *I thought they were much better than some critics, even present day critics—*
POWELL: It's a question of whether you want to make a film to please yourself or whether you want to make a film to please the audience. That's the question. And we were so full of ourselves at that time that I think we thought too much about ourselves and not enough about the audience. *Small Back Room* was a very good film but it was a war film, and the war was just over and people had had enough of the bloody war. Particularly in England where there was all sorts of hardship. So although it was a very good film about the wartime in London, it wasn't a success. And I'm sure the same sort of reason applies to the film with Jennifer Jones, who was a lovely actress and was very good in the film. It was a heavy melodrama, in a way, a sort of Edwardian melodrama. Beautiful performance by Cyril Cusack as a sort of saint. I'd known the book ever since I was a little boy because my parents came from Worcestershire and I knew all that country very well. Alex Korda had bought these rights and he asked us to do it. I was anxious to do it partly because I was so interested in the countryside and the idea of country magic. But, you see, I don't think I considered enough, or we considered enough, because Emeric loved the story, I don't think we considered enough the audience. The audience didn't want a Victorian melodrama; it wanted something a bit brighter.
PRESSBURGER: Let us put ourselves a little bit closer to that film. I remember we were driving about, Michael and myself, for days and days. It was terribly hot and one day we went into a pub and the pub was entirely empty, except of one shepherd leaning over the table sleeping. And Michael knows very well, you know, the history of the country. And among other things he told me that everybody wanted not to let people from the other side to come here.
POWELL: Other side of what?

CHRISTIE: *That's people coming from Wales?*
PRESSBURGER: Yes, from Wales. They came from Wales and people there

didn't want them to come in. And this man who was asleep looked up and said, "They didn't manage to do it." And it was so strange that he was so against the Welsh, and that all these things had been done to prevent them coming in.

CHRISTIE: *It's planned that* Gone to Earth *will be restored by the National Film Archive, with luck and rather a lot of money, over the next year or two and will be seen again. There's another question.*

AUDIENCE: *I was wondering what Emeric thought of* Peeping Tom.
POWELL: Have you seen it, old boy?
PRESSBURGER: What?
POWELL: *Peeping Tom.*
PRESSBURGER: No, I'm afraid I have never seen it. [laughter]
POWELL: I can always rely on you! [laughter]

AUDIENCE: *Can you explain your statement about* Peeping Tom *being a tender film?*
POWELL: Well it is a very compassionate film. What Leo Marks described and created was a character who was steered not by himself but by his father's very powerful, but twisted, mentality. We're all familiar with the effect of fathers on us, that's why we leave home. In this case, unfortunately, he didn't leave home. And this attracted me, the whole idea of the quietness and what was essentially a very violent and brutal idea. So I made it very simply and very innocently and with great compassion because I believed in this young man—that he couldn't help what he did. And what he did also was wonderful because it was connected with delicate things like developing negative and developing film. In my early days in films I was in the darkroom, in and out for years, and I know what it's like in a darkroom and the isolation that it brings. All this came over in the film, I thought, very well. I don't know why it shocked the critics. I will never understand, never understand that. I think they lead very sheltered lives—the critics, I mean.

CHRISTIE: *I think we've got to stop the questions now. I know there are a number of people who would like to ask further questions but it's already been a rather long session. Before we finish we have two further things to do. One, which is partly the reason we've kept you here on the stage, Martin, is something that Emeric and*

Michael have planned and not discussed with anyone else, and it's something they'd like to give you.

POWELL: Is that the script of *The Red Shoes?* Do we sign it?

PRESSBURGER: We are going to sign it.

POWELL: It's a good fat copy. At various times *The Red Shoes* script was in three different versions. Sometimes much longer and sometimes much shorter. [to Emeric] I think you ought to tell your story about many changes.

PRESSBURGER: Oh, that's only a story for people who know writers.

POWELL: May I tell it?

PRESSBURGER: Yes, of course.

POWELL: When Emeric was a young script writer with the UFA with one particular . . . producer? Do you remember his name? Who was it?

PRESSBURGER: I don't know.

POWELL: Some name like Rabinowitz or something. Splendid name. Emeric brought him a new script. He didn't look at it. He just took it and weighed it in his hands like this and said, "Many changements." I thought it was a perfect film story.

PRESSBURGER: You write something. You are the older.

POWELL: [laughs] You haven't signed it!

PRESSBURGER: Not yet.

POWELL: All right. I'll sign down here and you'll sign there. I'm writing "love to Martin" and I mean it. [to Emeric] Where did you find this? I don't think I've got a copy.

PRESSBURGER: I can't think of anything to write on *The Red Shoes.*

POWELL: Your name would add a bit of glitter, old boy.

PRESSBURGER: What, Emeric Pressburger, *The Red Shoes?*

CHRISTIE: *We thought after that you'd like to see part of the aforementioned* Red Shoes. *So we'd like to finish with the finale of* The Red Shoes.

Midnight Sun Film Festival

THELMA SCHOONMAKER, PETER VON BAGH, AND RAYMOND DURGNAT / 1987

[Powell describes how the red shoes appear on Moira Shearer's feet during the Red Shoes Ballet scene]

MICHAEL POWELL: We cut to another angle and Moira runs towards the shoes. She said, "Mr. Powell," she was very formal, ballerinas are like that. She said, "Mr. Powell, do I jump *over* the shoes, or on *this* side of the shoes?" [demonstrating] The camera's here, the shoes are here standing up like this, she is over here. I said, "You run toward the shoes and . . . let me think now . . . yes . . . you run towards the shoes and then you jump over them." So she did that. "Okay. Cut." Then we changed the angle again. I think we changed the angle four or five times, just for about that much of music . . . and then we changed to another angle, and she now had to tie the tapes.

So what do we do now? How does she tie the tapes of the *chaussons rouges*? I said, "Well, we do that by running the camera backwards." So we line up a very nice close shot, and we had a magazine loaded so that it would run backwards, and we put that on. So now she was standing in the shoes, the ones we'd nailed to the thing and we were concentrating on the tapes. We didn't tie them, we placed the tapes around her legs. A very nice job [laughter] and then instead of tying them, we just had a tiny bit of thread holding them there, and a piece of black thread to break that thread.

Transcript of interview with audience at Midnight Sun Film Festival, Sodankyla, Finland, June 1987. Reprinted by permission of Thelma Schoonmaker Powell, Peter Von Bagh, and Raymond Durgnat.

When I gave the word, they just pulled it. You see, the camera was running backwards and the tapes fell, slithered around her legs and fell on the floor. But when you saw the shot in the projection room, the tapes were on the floor and then they just went [up] round her legs. I think that actual shot of the tapes, coiling round her legs like serpents, would be about 8 frames . . . it's over. The whole operation of her jumping into the shoes, I think, isn't more than 1 foot and a half [of 35 mm film]. But you can do an awful lot with 1 foot and a half. [laughter].

Well, that's an example of a trick shot which is combined—everybody together contributed ideas for it. There's another very beautiful shot at the end of the film, when she runs away—or *she* doesn't run away—the *shoes* run away with her. She dashes out of her dressing room and I thought it's going to be very dull if she just rushes down the corridor and down the steps, so I invented a spiral staircase, the kind you have in an industrial building, a big iron staircase, about 20 feet high. And the art department just put it up in an empty stage and said, "Is that what you want?"

So I came with the camera department and we looked at it. Moira came too. They had the camera on an elevator except it was elevating down. So I said to Moira, "Run down the stairs, Moira, in the ballet shoes. Can you do it?" She said, "Yes." So I said, "How long will it take?" "I'll do it as fast as I can." So I said, "GO!" and the camera started to go down and Moira beat the camera by about, oh, 20 frames! [laughter] They looked very shamefaced. So we did it again, and this time they managed to keep with her. Then they got interested, and Chris Challis said to me—no the *operator,* not the lighting cameraman—but the operator said, "Of course, when she runs down the spiral staircase there's this iron center and I keep on losing her behind it. Now if it was only turning too—the stairway—then we could time it so that it turns with the same speed as Moira runs down the staircase." "Hmm, alright."

So next day, the art department says, "Can we show you the steps now?" Now they were mounted on an iron platform, a circular platform, with a motor attached with a resistance on it, and we could turn the spiral staircase at any speed we liked. It could go with her, or faster, if Moira was faster. So we said to Moira, "Now Moira, you can go down as fast as you like, because we should be able to follow, all the way down, because the staircase will be turning too." So they said, "GO!" She beat them again! [laughter] I think she did it in around 2 seconds and 2 tenths. It was like timing a really splendid athlete. I said, "I think this is going to work, but you've got to be able to control the speed of the turning of the staircase." And then we did that, and we saw it on the screen, and the editor now came into it—Reggie Mills, who was a wonderful editor and who cut the whole of the Red Shoes Ballet without a guide track.

THELMA SCHOONMAKER: *Can you explain that?*

MP: Well, normally when people shoot dance scenes they record the music first, like we did in *Tales of Hoffmann,* and then they run the playback on the set and you fill in the picture. On *The Red Shoes,* we shot to a playback in the music. Normally cutters, editors, or ordinary human beings want to have what they call a guide track, so when they see the shots of the scene, they like to see the music with them, even if they're in bits. Well, Reggie Mills didn't like this. He's very musical. He said, "I would prefer, Michael, not to have a guide track." He said, "Dancers are never in time, anyway." He repeated this on *Tales of Hoffmann.* And he said, "Moreover, singers are never in time either! I will put the whole thing in time on *Tales of Hoffman*—the dancing, the singing, everything. I much prefer to do it myself." They were never more than 1 frame out.

Anyway, we shot this scene with Moira and the staircase, and Reggie looked at it and said, "Micky, can't you make it longer?" I said, "No. No, Reggie, I'm not going to have another stairway made. That's it! What's the answer?" He said, "Well, I suppose the answer is I'll make two prints and stick them together. And then I'll have a long enough cut. Otherwise the cut's only about 4½ seconds and that includes 2 takes." And if you look very carefully when you see *The Red Shoes* next time—I hope you'll go on seeing it for another 50 years—when you see it, if you watch very carefully when she runs down this spiral staircase, you'll see where the splice is.

TS: *In other words, the shot is repeated twice but you don't notice it because of the way it's cut together.*

MP: Do you see what I mean? In other words, by cutting two exactly similar shots together—we lined up the camera and tied it off and we shot it—then it was amazing how the two things cut together. But when you start working with music, and with ballerinas who think always with the music, then you really are doing magical things. That's a very good example of the way we all worked. On every shot, practically, everybody had an opinion and it was up to me to say, "That's the way it's going to be!"

[Raymond Durgnat, the British film historian, compares the Red Shoes Ballet with the "Watusi" sequence from Martin Scorsese's *Who's That Knocking?*]

RAYMOND DURGNAT: *I was just thinking that the Red Shoes Ballet in its visual conception is in many ways a very classic Hollywood conception, a combination of classical languages. And in some ways, Martin Scorsese's approach to film is what you might call post-classical, post-French New-Wave. The shapes and forms in the Red Shoes Ballet are very solid, very complex, very real, with wonderful construction and depth. And a mental world takes on the phenomenology of the real kind of solidity. And in a way, Scorsese goes the other way. In this extract he starts from a subject which is not exactly neo-realist, but it's fairly much a story of everyday life, everyday nasty games, everyday larking about between young men, that may or may not suddenly turn nasty. In a way it's a kind of* temps mort, *you know the French word for a moment in which nothing is happening, and then suddenly it happens to become a moment where something does happen. But basically it's about the low points of life, the spaces of everyday living. But in the end it becomes unreal. In the way that certain intense mental experiences do seem to make a physicality in the world around them, so that in these two particular extracts, they're going in the opposite directions—one is endowing the mental world with all the qualities of the real world and the other is endowing the real world with all the qualities of a mental world suddenly erupting.*

And even in the visual style, the Red Shoes Ballet is a choreography of depth, of strong spaces, of changing directions, and the Scorsese extract is very much flatter, more two dimensional, more like a frieze or a fresco in which people seem to move like this. And a very strange thing about all Scorsese's worlds is that even when, in theory, there's a kind of depth on the screen, somehow the arrangement of things and the strong punching from the faces make it a sort of two-dimensional world of little surges of energy and push. People sticking little needles into each other and tightly wrestling around each other. So I guess really that's it. The extracts together make two fascinating examples of how films have a lot in common, but they're going in completely different directions.

[Michael Powell interviewed onstage regarding the *Southbank Show* on him (London Weekend Television) directed by David Hinton]

MP: In fact it was a perfect collaboration [working with David Hinton] and I would like to pay a tribute at the same time to Melvyn Bragg who runs the whole show there for London Weekend Television and who appears in it as the interviewer, and who gives a lovely undercut performance, I think. Don't you?

DAVID HINTON: *I certainly do. Yes.*

PETER VON BAGH: *You are just the right person to talk about cooperation, having worked so closely with Pressburger, and your book is full of fantastic detailed descriptions of what similar persons do when a film is made. So could you talk about filmmaking from the point of view of cooperation?*

MP: Yes, that's okay, but I'd also like to bring a message of hope to hopeful filmmakers here in the audience. Filmmaking is a matter not just of luck, but of continuity. To me, continuity is one of the most important things in life. Well, naturally it would be, because you have to after all continue to live. Not easy if you're an artist. And I had the luck to start in films almost with all the great filmmakers of the early days. I mean the filmmakers who were making silent films, and who had this sudden power over the moving image, this sudden power over the whole world. Chaplin, unknown perhaps a year before, in 18 months was known by hundreds of millions of people. That's an example of a personality and a great clown, but it was equally true of great ideas and great images. And I came in at that time, when films were silent and you naturally turned to the greatest things around you in art, and the substance of the material in which you were going to work.

In *The Red Shoes* and in *Tales of Hoffmann* there are dozens, maybe hundreds, of images which represent my life up to that time. Just think, I was born in 1905, Emeric Pressburger was born three years earlier. When he wrote the first draft of *The Red Shoes* script, that was before the war in 1937—50 years ago. He wrote the script for Alexander Korda, who was going to make a typical sort of big classy Korda production then, probably starring Merle Oberon, and with a famous ballerina dancing the dance scenes. This was quite common in those days. Common and vulgar. After the war, Emeric said to me—this was already 10 years later—"Do you remember that story I wrote for Alex before the war? Why don't we buy it back from him and make it ourselves?" That was one step towards making *The Red Shoes* in 1947.

When Emeric suggested we make *The Red Shoes,* it was in our power to do so. Early in my association with Arthur Rank, the British magnate—originally he'd been a flour miller—he was always a very strong Methodist, a very powerful industrial man who came into films because he started producing religious films—early we had a disagreement about what film I was going to make, and I told him, "I'm going to make the film anyway, whether you like it or not, and when it's made it'll be a success, and then unless you're an idiot, you'll come to me and say, 'What do *you* want to do next?' " This was a very rare occasion. It may have been the first time in the history of the British cinema that an artist said to the man who gave him the money, "I know better than you."

This may sound to some of you a little dull, but it's no good having good ideas unless you've got the money to carry it out, or else somebody else has the money to give to you. And in this case, we'd already made five films with Rank and one of them, *The Life and Death of Colonel Blimp,* from which you saw some scenes today, was a big success. Partly on its own quality, and partly because it had so much publicity from Churchill trying to ban it. That's still good publicity now. So I said to Emeric, when he suggested making *The Red Shoes,* I said, "Hmm. Let me read it." So I read it and I said to him, "I think it's great, but Emeric, we can't make it like that today, with doubles for the dancers and that kind of thing. There's been a war, Emeric, and we've got to find a dancer who can act the part." He turned . . . well he didn't turn pale because he was Hungarian . . . Hungarians are never daunted. He said to me, "Where do we find a girl like that?" I said, "That doesn't matter, Emeric. The thing is, if we're going to make the story of *The Red Shoes* the way you've written it, I have to make a ballet." He said, "You do?" I said, "Yes! She can't just dance *Swan Lake* for Christ's sake. If you talk about her being a great ballerina and all the people around her being great makers of ballet, you've got to *create* a ballet." He said, "Yes, I see that." "And so we've got to find a girl who can dance the part and open her mouth and speak the words." He said, "Where?" I said, "That doesn't matter. If we create the part, the opportunity for the girl, the girl will turn up." It's always like that. You've got to start with confidence, go on with confidence, and succeed with confidence.

My theme to you today is partly confidence and partly continuity. I'm talking now about making *The Red Shoes* just after the war in 1947. Emeric had written the story and the idea of the girl and the Red Shoes, which was, of course, based on the Hans Andersen story, in 1937. In 1927, ten years earlier, I was working with Rex Ingram in the south of France; he was making a great film, *The Magician,* with Paul Wegener, the German star. It was a very interesting film about witchcraft, and already I was getting familiar with all the cultures and the aspects of Europe that usually an Englishman with his bloody island never knows.

Already I was full of dreams of wonderful scenes and wonderful creations. It was only 1927, and I was only 22—so ten years later Emeric was writing the film. Ten years after that we were making it. And now, 50 years after Emeric wrote that original outline of the story, you're sitting here looking at scenes from it on the screen up there, and I'll bet you're just as thrilled now as I was in my mind back in '27, 50 years ago when I envisioned something like that, doing something like that with this wonderful medium of film—which hasn't changed a sprocket hole since I started in it.

So in 1947, I had the inspiration still with me which I had 20 years before, and Emeric had given me the chance to really put it into action. And as already told in the documentary [*Southbank Show* on Michael Powell, London Weekend Television], I don't have to tell it again, the people who put up the money didn't believe in it at all, and it wasn't until it got to the public—the public understood it at once. Our problem in making films is first of all to get the money to make the film, and then convince the people who put up the money that the public are the best judge, not they.

The distributor in America—this was just after the war when they were already loaded up with American films awaiting distribution because of the war—they just sat around in a circle with their lit cigars and they said, "God, the film's an art film! How are we going to sell it?" But there was one man—I know this for a fact—there was one man who said, "I think the film is going to be a terrific success and particularly with young people." And he went to a very small cinema off Broadway—the Bijou—about a 300 seater and he said to them, "Will you run this ballet film?" And they said, "Well, if it doesn't drop below a certain gross every day and every week, we'll run it as long as you like." He said, "Be careful what you say, because I think it's going to run forever."

They put it into this cinema, the Bijou, and it ran for a week, it ran for 10 weeks, it ran for a year. They said, "Can we renew the contract?" Our distributor said, "Sure." It ran for two years. They said, "Can we renew it again?" He said, "Sure." It ran for another 7 weeks. By this time, the whole world knew about *The Red Shoes*. But the Rank Organisation which had sponsored it, still regards *The Red Shoes* as an ordinary program picture. If you really want a really good print of *The Red Shoes,* don't go to the Rank Organisation first. See if you can find a good print somewhere else. We had quite a good print last night, when you ran *The Red Shoes,* but it wasn't good enough. Those bloody distributors, the Rank Organisation, were told 30 years ago that the film was an art film and couldn't be sold, and they still believe it.

PVB: *I remember that somebody from Technicolor—Dr. Kalmus—has stated that* Red Shoes *is the greatest color film that they ever produced.*
MP: I think Dr. Kalmus, who owned Technicolor, did say that, but he must have said it about practically every Technicolor film he ever made. He was a good salesman.

PVB: Black Narcissus, *as well as* A Matter of Life and Death, *these three together, they're mentioned like that.*
MP: Very probably because at that time the war had just finished. Not many color films had been made and we made in succession *A Matter of Life and Death, Black Narcissus* and *The Red Shoes,* the most astonishing row of extraordinary films ever made, I think. I can say that now. Couldn't have said it then. So my theme really in any speech, even a question and answer, has to have a shape to it. My theme is continuity. If I hadn't started in Europe, not in England, but in France, with a great American company, Metro-Goldwyn, with a great director, Rex Ingram, I wouldn't have had the high ideals and the vision in front of my eyes that I have had all my life. And you wouldn't have had *Black Narcissus* and *The Red Shoes* and *The Tales of Hoffmann,* which in many ways is even better than any of the others, I think. And I wouldn't have had in my old age such a tribute as David [David Hinton, director of *Southbank Show* on Michael Powell] has paid to me in this film. And I am as proud of that as I am of any of the films I made myself. [applause]

PVB: *What was your relation to other British filmmakers at the time that you made these films? Some other films were actually more favored in England by the critics, because the main line probably was more like documentary and realism.*
MP: You mean in the silent days?

PVB: *No, I mean in the forties.*

MP: Well in the forties the British films were entirely dominated by the success of American films. Americans—you may not have noticed it—but they're very enthusiastic people. And when they caught on to the idea of movies, and when they realized how much movies could make, how much money movies could make, the Americans moved in in large battalions. We might have one person who made films, where they had ten. And they discovered, by sheer energy, an immense lot of things about making films. But I'm not talking about the business as a whole and I'm not talking about the Americans. That's an entirely different thing, nothing to do with me. I'm talking about art. I'm talking to you as artists.

If you're prepared to spend your whole life fighting for your art with people who don't like you, don't understand you, don't help you, then you have my respect, and I regard you as a brother. And every now and then, something will happen that will take the whole art towards which you're working, one stride forward. Sometimes it's only one stride backward, but the time hasn't been lost, I assure you. Rudyard Kipling says, "If you can meet with triumph and disaster, and treat those two imposters just the same." And he was right.

AUDIENCE: *I'd like to ask about* The Red Shoes. *You talked about the inspiration from the south of France and then you have the story about the Red Shoes and then you talked about surrealism. I would like to know about locations shooting and shooting in the studio and still having the same unity of style. And I'd like to know how much did you shoot on location anywhere in* Red Shoes*? How much did you work in the south of France? Did you shoot on location and make it look as if it was in the studio?*

MP: Let's see, that's about 23 questions. [laughter]

AUDIENCE: *It's only one question, actually.*

MP: Well, it's a pretty obvious question, and my answer must be pretty obvious, too. Emeric had been to Monte Carlo and the South of France when he was working with the UFA, and whenever a German UFA director got an assignment to make a film which wasn't in Berlin, he always went through the script and very diligently changed all the references to Berlin or somewhere else, in the mountains in the winter—he changed it to Monte Carlo in the summer. [laughter] So, I remember when I was working with Ingram on the coast, constantly there were French teams, of course, but also a lot of German teams arriving to shoot the exteriors of the film and then go back to Berlin and do the interiors. I didn't, in the case of *The Red Shoes,* depart very much from the norm.

Of course, I knew the Riviera backwards because my father had bought a small hotel there from some winnings at—I think it was baccarat. You don't know about baccarat, and you don't want to know. Anyway, he won quite a lot of money and with it he bought the lease of a small hotel, so on my school holidays from England, I used to go and stay with my father on the Riviera, which certainly made for a change of character. So when Emeric played the main action of the second part of *The Red Shoes* in Monte Carlo and on the Riviera, of course I knew exactly what to shoot and how to shoot it. We went down with the principals like Marius Goring and Moira, particularly, Moira. The first day's shooting was on the terrace at Monte Carlo Casino, where she runs down in the Red Shoes and throws herself over the balustrade, and then is killed by the train. All that was shot before lunch. [laughter]

There was a terrific scene with the wardrobe mistress, a much bigger scene than any in the picture, because she said, "But how can she be wearing the Red Shoes when she runs out of the dressing room. It's only the beginning of the act and in the beginning of the act she's wearing ordinary satin slippers." Obviously, she changes to the Red Shoes when the sorcerer convinces her. I said, "Yes, I know all that. In *fact* she would not be wearing the Red Shoes. But in theory and the way I see it, she *is* wearing the Red Shoes, so shut up."

Then there was another scene backstage, probably with Emeric Pressburger, who was busy writing another scene. And they all came on in a body and said, "Michael, would you shoot it both ways—Moira rushing to her death in the Red Shoes, and Moira rushing to her death in the oyster-colored satin shoes?" And I said, "No I won't!" Because once you start shooting things two ways you find something else will land you in the ditch. It's a matter of emotion. When the shoes run away with her, they must be the Red Shoes. So what I will do when we're back in England, I'll have the dresser—played by Yvonne Andre, a very good little actress. She's the one who says, "*Il est moins dix!*" Very important. I said, "She's holding the oyster-colored shoes in her hands all through the scene, and Moira is breaking in a new pair of Red Shoes." Nobody notices that, but it satisfied me and for the moment it satisfied Emeric Pressburger and the others. So I was able to shoot her running down the steps and into the station and of course dying in the Red Shoes. When you see it on the screen no other possibility is possible. But at the time you get these things and you just have to—that's what the director's there for—to say: "Shut up and get on with it."

And we were on the coast about three weeks. I knew exactly where to go for the big staircase where she mounts, not only a tower in her own career, but in a way towards heaven. But I had known that enormous great staircase going up through the gardens with the cypress. I'd known them all my life, and I had arranged to go there on a particular day. And the day before, I suddenly said to my assistant, "God! Christ! Get my car quick!" And we got the car and we rushed up there, and I was just in time, because the gardener was already out there with his scythe. He was going to cut the weeds on the staircase. And I had already told Jacques Fath, who designed the clothes in Paris—wonderful designer, he's unfortunately dead young—and I told him about this wonderful staircase with the weeds growing on it because of the war and he said, "Oh, really? She should wear a long *eau de nil* gown—cloak—and wear a little crown. And I will make the cloak just long enough, so that when it brushes over the weeds, it brushes over the top and they all bend as she goes up." I said, "All right, sounds a good idea."

When I arrived, the gardener had already cut the weeds first from the first three steps, and I stopped him. And if you look very closely, you'll see that. But don't look closely. [laughter] So just that one little sequence of going up the stairs of course would take the whole of one morning, and the rest of the scene—in the same sequence when she arrives at the villa—was somewhere else, a different lighting, the sun in a different position, and that was probably taken the same afternoon. In the morning one place, and the afternoon another. I knew all the locations very well, since I was a school boy.

I'm sure you don't want to hear very much more. You've heard almost—

AUDIENCE: *Could you go a little more about freedom of style? How was it while shooting on location and in the studio and then going back and forth? Because I think* The Red Shoes *looks like a studio film even when it's obviously—*

MP: Well, because I had a great cameraman. You talk as if I did everything. I don't do anything! [laughter] I'm there to guide other people. I surrounded myself—more and more as I could afford it, of course—with all the people that I most admired: the greatest operator, the youngest color cameraman and the best color cameraman at that time in the world, Jack Cardiff. He'd been a technician with Technicolor and I'd seen a film he made for Technicolor for Dr. Kalmus, called *This Is Colour,* and in it he used all sorts of devices like pouring pots of yellow paint into pots of red paint and wonderfully photographed and lit. He first worked with me on *A Matter of Life and Death.* [Jack Cardiff did some 2nd Unit work on *The Life and Death of Colonel Blimp.*]

And Alfred Junge was one of the greatest of all German film designers, and there was Hein Heckroth, another German, but not a Berliner like Junge. He was a Hessian and a typical Hessian. But also a great artist and a lightening sketcher and painter and costume designer too—almost more brilliant than his sets were his costumes. I had one of the best editors in the world and certainly the best musical color. Since I stopped making films, he's edited all of Zefferelli's pictures, and you know how well they're edited. About the direction and the subject I say nothing—but about the editing they're very well edited.

So by the time we made *The Red Shoes,* I had the best team of technicians and artists, all capable of inspiring me and all capable of inspiration themselves. All I had to do was give the final decision. They seemed quite happy about it, and I was the luckiest man in the world. Filmmaking is not a solo occupation except for a particular subject. If you want to go out for a particular subject and make it with just you and the camera, of course you can. But generally a film is a big show, or a show of some kind—a story of some kind. And for this you need a wonderful team of enthusiasts. I've been lucky in that, so lucky. I always have been.

And the editor was Reggie Mills.

PVB: *Let's see now, even Sir Thomas Beecham was conducting the ballet.*
MP: One of the greater makers of music. To make a film is not to drag people down to earth, it's to make them take off!

PVB: *I would like to ask about one of your friends with whom you worked for a couple years . . . Alfred Hitchcock.*
MP: About Alfred Hitchcock? I met him first when I was a very young man and he was a very *fat* young man. [laughter] I arrived in England and managed to scrape a job—it was about £5 a week—at the British International Picture Studio and the only great director they had in England at that time was Alfred Hitchcock, who had made his name with a film called *The Lodger,*

and then followed it up with another film about boxing called *The Ring*. He was quite obviously a great talent. They signed him up for this new company in England, probably the first long term contract that any filmmaker had had in England. But he had forgotten to stipulate in the contract—because he was only 29 then—he'd forgotten to say that he should have final say about what he made, so they unloaded on him the most appalling scripts which he had to turn into films.

And the one he was making when I arrived at Elstree was *Champagne;* that's what it was called. Ghastly title and a most terrible film. And Hitchcock was so cross he just sat there in his chair, twiddling his thumbs, putting the picture together, and he refused to allow anyone to take a still picture on his set. [imitating Hitchcock] "I don't wish my name to be associated with this film. I think the film is shit." [laughter] So I thought this is a good opportunity for me, because I had come from France and he knew who I was, I hoped. In other words, two young hopefuls, I was 24 or 5 and he was 29. So I went to the head of the studio and said, "I'll get you some still pictures from Alfred Hitchcock's picture." He said, "You will?" I said, "Yes." "How will you do it?" I said, "Shut up—I've got my camera, I'll go and do it. If I get the stills, do I get the job of chief still photographer in this studio?" And he said, "You're on!"

So I turned up on the set next morning with a lot of clatter. I had my own camera and my own tripod, my own case. And still photography then was not a matter of going "gingk." You set up a camera, you set up a tripod, and you set up the camera, things clicked and banged—it was quite a show. But I did nothing. I just leant on the camera, on the tripod, all day. And Hitchcock, who was sitting there like this, he kept on [gestures]. Then finally he couldn't bear it any longer after lunch and said, "Mr. Stills Man," and I said, "Yes, Mr. Hitchcock?" "Don't you want to take a still?" "No, Mr. Hitchcock." "Oh."

The afternoon wore on, and presently I said, "Mr. Hitchcock?" "Yes, Mr. Powell?" He'd known who I was all the time. [laughs] That was Hitchcock all over. I said, "I'd like a still now. This scene's got a bit of action." "Very well, Mr. Powell." Up 'til then whenever anybody wanted a still, they'd turn the lights out and walk away. So I set up the camera and said, "Mr. Hitchcock, can I change the lights at all?" He said, "Mr. Cox"—that was his cameraman—"Mr. Cox, Mr. Powell wants to change your lighting, do you mind?" And Jack Cox said, "No! Not in the least. What do you want?" I said, "Well, kill those two deep back lights and put me up a front light here for Miss Balcon and put a silk on it"—that was the star of the film—she looked a bit grateful for having a silk.

So then I said to the cast there, "When I say action, act the scene and I'll tell you when to stop." So they went through the scene and I said, "Not good enough. Act. You want to overact when you do a still." So they ran through it again and I took the still and Hitchcock heaved himself out of his chair, which was a very difficult operation because he'd just fitted into it, and he said, "Mr. Powell?" "Yes, Mr. Hitchcock?" "Mr. Cox and I usually have a few beers after the shooting. Would you join us?" And we were friends ever afterwards. [laughter] Of course, I should have said just now that that story is in my book which has just been published. [laughter] Volume One. £16. [laughter]

[Michael Powell interviewed onstage after a screening of *A Matter of Life and Death*]

MP: During the war British films were encouraged but we had to discuss with the Ministry of Information the subject of the film and the way the films were made. And then they gave us help if we needed war-type things like uniforms, that kind of thing.

[Missing from videotape is Powell describing the Ministry of Information inviting Powell and Pressburger to lunch in order to discuss a proposed film, which would become *A Matter of Life and Death*]

MP: Yes but I said: "Well, where will you?" 'The Ministry, of course.' I said: 'Oh no! My partner who likes his food is never going to agree to a Ministry lunch. But we will come to a lunch at the best restaurant in Soho, London'—which is the district where the good restaurants are—'and the restaurant we like is the Etoile.' Although I was talking on the telephone I could hear him wince. He said: 'Are you very sure?' I said: 'Certainly. We'll pick the restaurant and you'll pay for the lunch.' These were the kind of relations we were developing by then with the Ministry.

[Michael Powell at dawn after a screening of Erich von Stroheim's silent film *Greed,* accompanied by a live score by a Finnish rock group]

[great applause and hoots]

PVB: *How did you see it now sixty years after your first view of the film?*
MP: Well it's a great film but I never thought it would sound quite like that! [laughter/applause] I wish I had.

Well apart from the music, how did it keep on for so long? [laughter] There's something magic about Finland. [laughter/applause] I think they played like gods. They must look like them. We're so happy to be here and see this great film again. Quite right what people said. I saw it on the beach in Monte Carlo in 1926. [applause] It was a great film then. Great film. But all that it needed was sound like this. [applause]

For me, film is a way of life. It is my whole life. It's my career. I've been educated entirely by and with and in the film business. I'm now 81 and the film business as a big business isn't very much older. We've grown old and we have grown young, together.

[Michael Powell interviewed onstage after a clip from *Edge of the World*]

MP: I don't think films have changed very much and I know that I haven't changed very much. I'm still the small boy that was determined to make films. I still think that the world as far as telling stories goes is very much the same. History . . . the reason why I wrote this fat book and then found that it wasn't fat enough. I'm now writing the second volume. Thank goodness, I don't think it could be quite so long. [laughs] That's a fat book. But I started out to make it about—I thought I could tell the story of what it means to give your whole life to what is really a piece of social history.

Making films and then the results of making them are social histories. But the main thing in any film and any play, too, is suspense. What is going to happen next? When the curtain comes down on the first act what is it going to go up on the second? This is where so often enthusiastic young directors and young writers, who know what they want to say, go wrong. They think it's enough that they know what it's all about. But it isn't. You've got to get the audience thirsting to know what it's all about.

[Michael Powell interviewed onstage after a clip from *The Red Shoes:* "Why do you want to dance?"]

MP: We had a very big dialogue scene in the middle of *The Red Shoes* on the terrace of Monte Carlo. It cost God knows how much. It took three days and nights to shoot, and it was telling the audience what was the idea of *The Red Shoes* and how an impresario manages to build up an idea into a ballet. This was all done with very clever inter-played dialogue. As soon as we had the film together, we looked at each other—out it went. This whole big sequence went right out because in making the film, I had made the composer of the music a composer of the music, and he *was* a composer of the music, and the painter was a painter, and the ballerina was a ballerina.

Everybody was completely the essence of the art which they embodied, so it didn't need any explanation because you could see it work, because Emeric had written a very ingenious pattern of association of people and ideas. It became the most authoritative statement on the creation of a work of art that has ever been done until they did this film of *Amadeus*—Milos Forman's film, *Amadeus*. I consider that a film equal to *The Red Shoes* and remarkable in the way it makes the audience not only understand, but feel that they have created the actual work of art.

[Michael Powell interviewed onstage after a clip from *The Red Shoes* in which Vicky dances *Swan Lake* as Lermontov watches]

MP: But when the people who finance you have opinions about film, this is the beginning of the end. Their business is to put up the money and then to sell the film and get the money back. *Black Narcissus* led to *The Red Shoes,* which was our most adventurous picture and which I directed with an autocracy which was rather frightening. I took everything for granted. I took for granted that the audience were just as clever, just as knowledgeable, as we were and this is true: audiences are always ahead of us. I've never yet made a film where the audience didn't know what was going to happen. So when Arthur Rank saw the finished film, he and his fellow company director didn't understand it at all. It was a complete statement about art, and they said to each other, "It's an art film, it won't make any money." They put it on the shelf and it wasn't seen for a long while. But in America they understood it at once.

I've always been nearly independent from the time when I was 22 or 23 years old. I was very lucky. I knew I wanted to be a film director when I was 16, and I'm sure there are a lot of potential film directors here now in this room and certainly in this town. It's full of potential film directors. They know what they want to say and what they want to do, but I've been extremely lucky that when I started to make films I had very little money to spend on the film. I myself got a very small fee, of course, but whenever there was extra money to spend out of my salary I always spent it, because I had an ideal of quality.

The career of a European film director is not very different from any other European artist, and just as in the *Cinquecento* in Italy you've had these studios where lots of sculptors, writers, designers—they didn't have cameras then, but they had already a camera eye—and they already had studios and workshops where they were creating all the details of all this, either beauty, or terror, or horror.

[Michael Powell interviewed onstage after a clip from *Gone to Earth*]

MP: A director has a lot to learn from a set designer, from a costume designer, and from a writer above all. I'm often asked by young people, what about making films, how did you start? I say first of all you buy somebody else's idea, or you have a good idea yourself. Perhaps you get an option on a book or an option on a play and then the first thing you should do after that is to find a writer to work with you. When the war came, I had been introduced to Emeric Pressburger by Alexander Korda and we made our first film because we were put together by him the way you put chess men together and the combination worked. And so then we had the chance of being our own bosses all through the war, with the agreement with the Ministry to make propaganda films.

The reason why our films are so strong during the war is because there was a reason for making them, and that the theme had to be a good theme, a good human theme and a strong one, not just an idea and not just a plot. I'm a very dreamy or imaginative person. Emeric is a typical Hungarian, from his birth, a dramatist. But I think the Hungarian, or the Central European dramatists—Czech, Hungarian, German—they tend not to experiment too much with plot. It's more technique they deal with. I noticed it at once with Emeric when we worked together. I would suggest an idea which was usually an imagination or a fancy. When he suggested an idea, it was always a twist in the story. He always added suspense to the story, never took it away, because as a story progresses, or as you make the film, you're absorbing all the time problems of suspense. And a good dramatist, of course, adds to the suspense with another twist, another way.

[Michael Powell interviewed onstage after a clip from the opening scene of *A Matter of Life and Death*]

PVB: *What's your own special favorite in your own production and why?*
MP: I think *A Matter of Life and Death* is my favorite film.

[Michael Powell interviewed onstage after a clip from *Amolad:* "One is starved for Technicolor . . ."]

MP: It was a very big trick film and I had a wonderful crew of people—we all knew each other. Some of them had just come back from the war, back into films again. The cameraman was a young Technicolor cameraman [Jack Cardiff] who had never shot a big film before.

PVB: *It's a beautiful color film.*
MP: And of course, the tricks were so good and they all came off, and they all looked easy. After all a film has to look easy. It's not enough to make fine tricks. You just do it, and you don't dwell on it either.

PVB: *I agree with you on that. The best trick is the trick you don't see while you're watching the film.*
MP: Right, that's it. And we had such wonderful tricks in there and, of course, going from color to black and white, and black and white to color. It was the end of the war and I was bursting with excitement and optimism, and my partner gave me the script, his final version of the script, to take to America. I was brought to America on the Queen Mary and there were 11,000 American troops on board, all going hell for leather across the Atlantic to Halifax. The whole ship was full of Americans talking, sleeping, eating—you know, being American.

I talked with them when I wasn't writing and rewriting the script. Our agreement was always that each one would contribute what he could, but if we discussed it we always lost our temper, so we found the best way was always, "Well, that's as far as I can take it, now see what you can do with it." I was adding a lot of outrageous lines and jokes like "One is starved for Technicolor up there," you know, and all this sort of thing. It was just bubbling out of me. Of course, that helps a lot when you're making a big film of that kind, and I had those wonderful actors.

[Michael Powell interviewed onstage after a clip from *Amolad:* "Prosecuting council hates your guts"]

MP: We were actually asked to make a film to prove to the Americans that they loved us, because naturally, when it was a question of the Marshall Plan and a few other plans, we weren't so popular with our allies as we had been.

[Michael Powell interviewed onstage after a clip from the opening of *Peeping Tom*]

MP: The English critics nearly killed me for making *Peeping Tom.* But then English critics, I think, lead very sheltered lives. They build a wall between themselves and the rest of the world, I think. I know they think that film should be really realistic and documentary. It's ingrained very much in the English character. There's no reason for a man to be an artist. "What does he want to be an artist for?" they say. [laughs] And I suppose somewhere, I didn't understand that. But when we made *Peeping Tom,* we were not trying to score off anybody or do anything new, even.

A writer named Leo Marks, who I'd heard of because he'd been in the code—he was very high in the code business in the war, so he knew a lot about secret history and codes. He did some writing for a film, I think it was called *Carve Her Name with Pride.* He wrote a little code poem in it which attracted attention and the producer on that rang me up and said, "You're looking for a new writing partner. I recommend this man. He's as crazy as you are." So he came to see me and he tried to tell me a double agent story which I wasn't interested in. And then a few weeks later he came back and said, "Mr. Powell, would it interest you to make a film about a young man who kills women with his camera?" I said, "Oh, yes, I like that idea very much. That just suits me. What are your ideas?"

So after that he came twice a week with what he had done, and we worked out the script together. He had studied psychology before he became a code breaker. He was a rather interesting and sinister man. He would always arrive in the evening with a large cigar which had just been lit. Rather disturbing. But together we worked on it and I said, "I like the script very much. I think I can get the money for it."

[Michael Powell interviewed onstage after a clip from *Peeping Tom:* "Do you know what the most frightening thing in the world is?"]

MP: People have been leveled all round, steamrollered almost out of existence by too much television, too much radio, too much of this, too much information. But once that information is absorbed, the whole general level of comprehension, the whole general level of understanding, is raised worldwide. And I think to this century films have been, of course, the great discovery. The great art. They won't be that in the next century but all that information has been, not learnt, but absorbed by the audiences. And I mean audiences everywhere, because when films started silent, Japan, Germany, Russia, Africa, Argentina, everybody understood films because films were silent. Stories were told boldly and the titles were just rewritten for whatever country you were in, so at once the audience started to imagine the people in the film were talking in Spanish or Japanese.

This was a wonderful thing in the silent days and we lost 20 or 30 years of possibility of communication when sound was invented. But sound had to be invented. It had to come. We couldn't go on forever having silent films, you had to come to talking films. And the first talking films, what did they do? They just talked. They didn't teach anything; they weren't very good. They were mostly musical shorts, and anything that could be thrown in, all the rubbish in the world and all the good stuff of the world, all thrown into the mixer. And out of it came the modern talking film. So you can't say it isn't an advance, it is an advance.

Then finance moved in and people started to make enormous sums of money out of these artists who were single-minded. There are still single-minded artists in the film business and I think it's wonderful that they still exist. I know several. I'm sure in every country there are some. That's going to lead us to something new. It isn't enough to say television will take the place of films or radio. Radio is always going to be with us and wonderful, wonderful radio is. I think radio is one of the most wonderful arts and one of the greatest gifts that's ever been given the human race.

But people get so much on television in some countries that they don't go to see films anymore. They're quite wrong. They'll come back to it. Because the whole idea of a film is that you throw up a big picture on the screen and you have an audience big enough to share what you learn with them. You can't share that way with a small screen and two or three people, one of whom is making the tea and the other one is playing with the dog, and two children are fighting. You need a big screen. You need a theatre.

I'm all for big screens, small theatres, and people getting together to see films. Like here. For us it's been a wonderful experience. I've been to many film festivals, many, in many countries. Some of them they just took advantage of the possibilities of meeting people and of art. But here I feel it's part of the whole feeling of the country—that you do share everything and you take it very seriously, and at the same time you're always making jokes about it. We've had such fun at this festival, I can't tell you. It hasn't been a festival. It's been sharing an art with you. Sharing our lives.

[Michael Powell interviewed onstage after a clip from *The Red Shoes*]

MP: It started with this statement by me that I didn't want to have her just dance *Swan Lake, Coppelia,* these other old yawns. I wanted to create something original—perhaps purely by pride, first of all. Because the sequences that I remember most from films in my long life, were sequences like the hornpipe danced by Ivan Mosjoukine in *Kean* directed by Alexandre Volkoff, a Russian emigré working in France. When they started to get drunk in a beer cellar in London, he went into what I think Ray [Durgnat] was talking about. Not exactly a montage, but a magnificent display of theatrical image, and it had an enormous effect on me. Still has.

And then, of course, there are famous examples like Charlie Chaplin's dance of the rolls,—we called it in France *les petits pains*—when he's left alone in the house and his beloved, the dancing girl, doesn't come and doesn't come, and then he realizes that she never will come. And he starts to compose a dance with two rolls in front of him on the table, which was all he had for the supper anyway. And he does the most perfect solo with these rolls, with glides and splits and everything, finishing with an enormous bravura jump and he leaps up and acknowledges the applause of the audience.

In both these cases, I saw them in the Théâtre du Vieux Colombier in Paris, when it was a cinema and a theatre. The sort of films it showed were *Kean* and *The Gold Rush.* I remember when Chaplin did this dance with the rolls none of us were expecting it. We only had chairs there, not benches, and they weren't screwed down, which sometimes led to terrific riots. As you can imagine, at the end of the Odessa steps in *Potemkin,* there would be a considerable play made with these chairs. On this occasion with Chaplin, it was a peaceful reaction, but we picked up our chairs and held them up in front of the projector, so they had to stop, and then we made them play it again. [laughter]

These are memories of tremendous theatrical experiences created by the silent cinema. So you can imagine what an excitement and a responsibility it was when Emeric Pressburger came to me and said, "You remember a script I wrote for Alexander Korda in 1937 or 1938, called *The Red Shoes?*" I said, "No, I don't think I ever read it." I read all the scripts that were available, because I was an ambitious director trying to get Korda to say, "Yes!" to something. I said, "I never read it, but is it the Hans Andersen story?" He said, "Yes," Emeric Pressburger said, "Yes." So I said, "Then I want to read it." When I read it I said, "Emeric, the way the script was written then, won't do now." "Then" was before the war. "Now" was 1947. I said, "Everything has moved on now. Even movies. And if we're going to make it, we're going to make it in color. If we're going to have a ballet, I want to create a ballet. If we're going to be at the ballet, I want a ballerina who can play the part, otherwise it won't work." Well he wanted his story made, so he agreed.

And of course, we found this wonderful girl, Moira Shearer, who I'm glad to tell you is still a wonderful girl. Then we see them start to work on the story, and bit by bit the story is coming together with the ballet. Then it's the first night of the ballet, which you've just seen—the whole performance—and the whole story is told again. And meanwhile the story outside the story is developing towards its inevitable, tragic end. You won't believe it when I tell you that even Emeric Pressburger, the author of the script, the author of the idea—when we came to the final shooting, the final cutting—he said to me once with doubt in his heart, "Michael, must she die?" I said, "Emeric, don't ask me such foolish questions. You know what Hans Andersen did with the girl? When she couldn't get the shoes off? She went to the woodcutter in the forest and he cut her feet off with his ax, and she danced to heaven on the stumps." I said, "Yes, she has to die." [laughter]

And what happened when I practically cut her feet off in front of the nose and eyes of the critics? They all jumped on me for making a tragic, bloody ending. But the whole point of the story is to tell it again and again and again, and build up a story within the story, and a story outside the story, continually coming back to the same theme and ending with the same tragic end. I can tell you Alexander Korda understood the film when he saw it, and he was furious that he had sold the film back to us.

The people who put up the money didn't understand the story and they never have to this day. They didn't like the film, they don't like it now. But Alex Korda, who was a very good diplomat, asked if he could borrow a print of the film and he showed it in his office to the future Queen of England, with her sister and their parents. Because Alex was an extremely astute social climber, as well as a very good producer. At the end of it, they went out in floods of tears and they said to him, [imitating girlish princesses talking through tears], "Oh thank you, Mr. Korda, for the most lovely picture we've ever seen in our lives!" [laughter] So I want Ray [Durgnat] to admit that in his analysis—which is brilliant, which I followed line by line though I looked as if I were asleep, [laughter]—the one thing he's left out is this wonderful discovery that a film must have a story and it must have a very simple story, because otherwise it leaves nothing for the cameraman and the director to do. That's all I can contribute. [applause]

[Raymond Durgnat doing an analysis of *The Red Shoes Ballet*]

RAYMOND DURGNAT: *Most familiar for serious, highbrow, film students is the montage tradition, especially associated with French and Russian cinema which liked to compose hard strong simple shots and then edit them so that each cut makes a little graphic shock or collision. The Russians in their early Bolshevik fervor even argued that a film without dynamic cuts isn't a true film. This kind of cutting was very congenial to the documentary boys, and highbrow film theory from 1930 to 1960 was really very dominated by Russian and documentary ideas. Certainly to the point of neglecting the opposite tradition, developed by Hollywood in particular, of continuity editing, also called invisible editing. For Hollywood, the paramount elements of film were a story and the face.*

And camera calligraphy perhaps because camera movements are an extension of the picture before you come to an edit. Well there's three traditions, but it's actually very difficult to combine the strengths of each—to edit dynamically and invisibly—yet also give a sensitive picture its time to work, while still maintaining the wonderful speed and dynamism of American plot and human interest. The Red Shoes Ballet *is a marvelous example, perhaps because it's not just a montage of shots, but it's also a montage of all the elements in the shot. You know, Eisenstein really understood that montage happens within the shot, that it's a montage of attractions, a montage of striking features. And really film theory didn't understand him, and thought that the montage could only be in the cutting, in the editing. This extract is not only a montage of shots and of attractions but also of separate art forms: music, dance, the dance of the body counterpointed by the dance of the camera and lit by the flash of the editor's scissors, aspects of theatre. Many of the shots are very painterly, so here is an art of all the arts, a* gesamtkunstwerk, *a non-realistic spectacle.*

And really this whole sequence is a unity of opposites, a montage of surprises in which theatre space collides against film space, but collides so smoothly and invisibly that it seems natural. There are some wonderful cuts here where Moira Shearer seems to dance off the stage which we've seen in the theatre, and dance onto another stage which is beside it, and finally she ends up in a kind of fantasia-land which could never exist in the theatre. But every now and again we're brought back to the theatre by the applause, by the way the theatre curtain moves, by going backstage. There's a wonderful shot of Moira Shearer running off stage in the interval, and I think somebody throws her a towel to start wiping herself, something like that. I always think of it as an underarm odor shot, you know, the sweat of ballet we begin to remember.

Ballet put back where it belongs—in the circus of the mind. And sometimes I think we would understand film more clearly if we forgot photography and began with cartoons. Even if, instead of beginning with the Odessa steps sequence, we began with these Red Shoes steps. But not that they rule each other—but they don't rule each other out.

Michael Powell Q & A

RICHARD JAMESON/1989

RICHARD JAMESON: *One of my prerogatives of being up here is to get to ask you about a unique credit that has distinguished some of the best loved films of our experience: "Written, Produced and Directed by Michael Powell and Emeric Pressburger." I don't know of another such dual credit and it is my understanding that Mr. Pressburger really didn't come down on the sound stage and discuss the calling of shots with you so that he really didn't direct and yet you chose to share the credit with him in this way.*

MICHAEL POWELL: Well, we thought it was a great compliment to the writer if the writer was willing to share the credit with the director. After we made two films together, Emeric said to me, "Well, why don't we form a company because Sir John Arthur Rank is backing us now and we know we have Winston Churchill on our trail so it was time we formed a company of our own." And I said, "All right, it's a good idea but how will we do the credit?" and he said, "Well, Michael, what do *you* suggest?" And I said, "Well, I don't see why we couldn't share credit. Could always get to be you who'll do the main thinking and writing and I carry it out; I put it on the screen up there." He thought about it a bit and he said, "Michael, you know I got my first Oscar for writing *49th Parallel* (it was called *The Invaders* here when it first came out but I think it's known now as *49th Parallel*) and for a writer that would be a very serious thing to share the credit." I said, "Well it would be for a director, too!" [laughter] "What order would we use." He said,

---

Transcribed from video at the Seattle Film Festival. Reprinted by permission of Richard Jameson and the Seattle Film Festival.

"Oh, Michael, I think you should come first but I don't think I could come second, either." [laughter] He was really underplaying. I said, "I think we should just share the credit, and what order do you want to do?" But he said, "Michael, if the writer doesn't write a good story and a good script then there's no point in directing and photographing the stuff." So I said, "Fine." So it came to be: "written" first, the most important thing in making a film, and "produced" because you have to find the money and nobody quite knows what a producer does except find the money, and then that leaves me, "directing." So it came out "written, produced and directed by Michael Powell and Emeric Pressburger." Then Emeric said, "Well, what about trademark, a logo?" I said, "Well, do you know James Agate, the critic? He wrote a little jingle the other day I like very much. It went like this 'The arrow was pure gold, but somehow missed the target, still as all Golden Arrow trippers know, it's better to miss Naples than hit Margate.'" And he liked that, so we adopted a target with our logo and you heard the sound of the arrow, you heard the whistle through the air, it hit the target and I don't know whether you ever noticed it, but it didn't always hit in the bull. We sometimes would be our own critic and inch it a bit off-center [laughter]. So watch very carefully next time you see an Archers' logo.

RJ: *Let's let some other people have—are there any questions here for Mr. Powell?*
MP: Oh, I hope so! [laughter]

AUDIENCE: *Where did you find the Sergeant in* Canterbury Tale? *Was he a real Sergeant?*
RJ *(clarifying): Was Sergeant John Sweet the American soldier in* A Canterbury Tale *real?*
MP: He was a real American soldier and when we had the idea of *Canterbury Tale* the idea was to make a film about the almost invisible values that people were fighting and dying for. Not just victory but other victories. And we wove this together with the idea of pilgrims on the road to Canterbury. And the main characters were an English sergeant who was going overseas quite soon, and an American sergeant who'd been in England some months in training, waiting for the big attack, and an English land girl who was working on the land while all the men were away, and a local squire who was a bit of a loony. And out of this we wove a story.

I said to Emeric, "We can't possibly have an Englishman or even a known star play this part because it's a very good part for an American boy and the things he has to say are right if you haven't seen him before." But from an established actor, they become in some ways just stylized lines. I spoke to the American entertainment section of the Army and they said, after listening "Well, I think the man you want is working for us now. He's not really an actor but he's turned out to be a very good actor and even a director and they're putting on a production of *Our Town,* Thornton Wilder's *Our Town.*" I suspect most of you know that, and the big part in that, of course, is the store keeper of the town who watches what goes on and comments on it and brings it to a beautiful, sad close. So it was about the middle of the war and everything was a bit worked up—it was touch and go which way it would go. I remember going to see it in a London theatre. It was all acted by American servicemen and John Sweet was wonderful. Towards the end of the play, I started crying and I went on crying to the end. [pause] He got the part. [laughter] Now, he came—I'm not sure if he actually came from Oregon—but Emeric liked very much the sequence where they discuss timber and the way to treat wood, you're a carpenter or you're a man who handles wood, so I thought, well, I better get, best not say in New York. [laughter] Obviously, he probably comes from the northwest so I picked on Oregon because there was a scene where the British constable says something about, "We don't say that kind of thing, not like you do in Chicago." And John Sweet has to answer, "Who said anything about Chicago? I come from Oregon!" When we showed the film many years later in the retrospective in New York, I asked them to hunt down John Sweet and he reappeared, but he's very much the same, 20 years older, with a family already grown up and he got a tremendous hand and he's exactly the same. Easy, tolerant, interesting man who is such a success in the film. One of our happiest collaborations.

AUDIENCE: *Did you ever meet Churchill during the making of* Colonel Blimp?
MP: No. He was very friendly with [Alexander] Korda. They both had a taste for long cigars and glasses of brandy. The only reason why the British film industry didn't die when the war was declared as it did in the First World War was that Korda said to Churchill, "I've got this enormous studio in Denham only just being built. We've made wonderful pictures there already. I promise you, if war is declared, I promise you, Prime Minister, that I'll talk the whole studio into making a big, feature, propaganda film." And Churchill said, "What we'll do is we'll make a department of the Ministry of Infor-

mation and then this department will be called the Film Department and we'll have a Deputy Minister in charge. The subjects you choose to make will be left to you, but they'll have to be discussed in part by this department of the Ministry of Information." This was all discussed while we were making at that time *The Thief of Bagdad.* I remember just the week before war was declared, we had a meeting in Korda's office with all the principal directors, producer, and we were told that when the second war was declared we'd all leave *The Thief of Bagdad,* drop the carpet, the flying carpet, and go into making a big propaganda film which had to be delivered within one month. It was full of stuff about all the things we've got, you know, including radar. It was all a lot of lies, of course, and propaganda nearly always is. But it was quite a big job and this was actually done that way.

RJ: *Was this* The Lion Has Wings? *The propaganda film?*
MP: Yes. So this is the way we went on. Emeric said to me, "Well, Korda has had to take *The Thief of Bagdad* to America to be finished. Everybody here has shut up shop; they all think that the film business is finished." At that time quite a lot of films were being done in London, thanks to Korda. So Emeric said to me, "Why don't we write a story and make another film with Conrad Veidt and Valerie Hobson?" And I said, "Why not?" Because nobody knew what to do. We found somebody almost immediately who would put up the money and we made a second film quite quickly in six weeks which was called *Contraband* in England. I think it was called *Blackout* here. There's some mystery about this film. It seems to have disappeared. It hasn't disappeared entirely. We have the negative and a print in London. Maybe because the title was changed. They often were.

AUDIENCE: *You mentioned Churchill and the Ministry of Information. A number of your war films, like* The Small Back Room, *or the* 49th Parallel, *and* A Canterbury Tale, *focused on rural people leading intense rural lives. Did you feel pressure to make movies in that mold or was that something you wanted to do?*
MP: It's entirely our own. The deal with Churchill and later on with Duff Cooper, Kenneth Clark, while the Department of the Ministry of Information got together pretty quickly—the deal was that we would make, we would think up or write a short précis in 10 pages of what we wanted to do. This would be discussed with the Ministry and if it was agreed they would say anything you wanted. They would go ahead and get it for us in wartime.

But when we were going to make *Colonel Blimp,* for instance, the idea was to make a film about the young and the old soldier; each one has a little bit of the other in him. I think most of you have seen *Colonel Blimp.*

RJ: *It was shown at this festival several years ago. It was the restored version.*
MP: That's the complete one?

RJ: *Yes. It will be back. It wasn't possible to include a clip from* Blimp *in tonight's program because the shipping schedule was so close to the screening that it's coming up later in this festival.*
MP: Yes. So we applied to the war office for all sorts of trucks, uniforms, guns, all sorts of things, and this memo went up to somebody who showed it to the head of the Army, Secretary of State of War, and he said, "Well, they can't make a film about laughing and making fun of the Army and about losing the war when we *are* losing the war!" [laughter] He rang up Churchill and said, "Winston! Powell and Pressburger, you know, they're rather suspicious characters. I believe Pressburger's probably a German." [laughter] He was a Hungarian. "And I think it ought to be stopped. They're making fun of the army." So Churchill, without bothering very much, reached for the telephone, spoke to his Minister, I think it was Brendan Bracken, and said, "They're planning a film, quite a big film, making fun of the army. Tell them to stop it." And the Minister may have said to Churchill, "But Prime Minister, we've already agreed to this script and we've promised them help and they're going to have Larry Olivier from the Fleet Air Arm to play Colonel Blimp." He said, "Well, I don't know why—I don't know about it—anyway, stop it. They can't make it." Churchill thought he was rather a dictator at that time. So we had a meeting with the Ministry and after hearing what the Minister had to say I said, "Minister, do you forbid us to make the film?" He said, "Oh, my dear sir! Don't say things like that! [laughter] This is a democracy! [laughter] But don't make the film! [laughter] Because the old man will be very cross." And so we went outside and went down into the street, outside of the University of London, occupied by the Ministry of Information. And Emeric said to me—Emeric is a very tough, rather beautiful-looking, small Hungarian, a heart of gold and very brave because, after all, he was an enemy alien in London at that time—and he said, "Michael, what should we do about our dear little picture if they won't give us Laurence Olivier?" And I said, "Emeric, we'll find another actor to play the part." He said, "What

about the film?" I said, "We'll make it." He said, "Right?" I said, "Yes. Right." "Good!" So we went back to Rank, who was waiting for us to come back, and I said, "They don't want us to make the film; they won't give us Laurence Olivier to play Colonel Blimp." And Rank said, "What will you do?" I said, "We'll play Roger Livesey." "Who is he?" I said, "Well, he's a very good actor. Very well known in the West End but he's not well known in film. He's only been under contract to Korda. He was in *The Drum.*" Did any of you see *The Drum?*

RJ: *They call it* Drums *for some reason in this country.*
MP: "And he can do it on his head." So I said, "Shall we go ahead?" "Where is he?" I said, "He's working in a munitions factory, I know I can get him out of it." He said, "Fine! Let's go ahead then." Those were the days! We went ahead and made the film that way with Roger Livesey as Colonel Blimp. And many months later, after all the arguing because they were furious that we went ahead with it, Churchill had to have a private view, and many months later, Grigg said to me, "Powell, where did you get all those military trucks and uniforms, guns and things that you had in the film? We didn't give them to you." I said, "Minister, haven't you ever worked with a studio property man? We stole them!" [laughter]

RJ: *It's astounding to see* Colonel Blimp *and to imagine why anybody was ever afraid of it because it can't be represented as an anti-war film or anti-establishment or anything, it's just redolent of love for everything that—*
MP: Yes, but they were touchy about it in the war. [laughter]

RJ: *We have some clips tonight in the scenes from* I Know Where I'm Going *and Roger Livesey's work in Mr. Powell's films is indeed magical in a way that none of his other performances, that* I'm *aware of, are. You will see him later tonight in my very favorite of all their films,* A Matter of Life and Death. *Let's take a question from the back, people have been getting shorted. Does anybody in the back have a question? Then we'll take one from the right.*

AUDIENCE: *I'm very much interested in the dancers in* The Red Shoes *and what it was like to work with Leonide Massine, the shoemaker. Did he do the choreography?*
MP: No, he did his own choreography. Massine was a Russian, a wonderful

actor, and a very great dancer. By this time he'd also been a great choreographer and it was great piece of luck that he fell into my hands.

AUDIENCE: *How did that happen?*
MP: It just happened that he left America and came to Europe to see if he could find if any of his property was left in Europe because he'd been in America all through the war. I knew that he was around. I kept in touch with that kind of thing. You see, in art, generally, most people know what's going on. They may not know exactly, but they do know that so and so might be there, different plans are being made for a different program, different ideas. There are currents of information that go to and fro and I knew Massine was somewhere in London, although I didn't even know he had arrived. He was exactly the man I needed. But when I spoke to him about it, he said, "Who will do the choreography, Mr. Powell?" I said, "Well, Robert Helpmann will do it." "Ah. Robert Helpmann." "Yes." [laughter] "Uh, I think I will have to do my own choreography." [laughter]

AUDIENCE: *Why didn't you want Massine to do the choreography?*
MP: Because I'd already got an agreement with Bobby Helpmann. And he was to dance the part, play the part, act it, you see. Dance the part, play the part, *and* do the choreography of the whole picture. And to do all Moira's, too. Massine said, "Yes, I quite understand that, but what I would like, Mr. Powell, is—Mr. Helpmann will, of course, be the choreographer, but *I* will do my own choreography." [laughter] That's the way it was done.

RJ: *Did this relationship of theirs inspire all the writing about the bitchy relationship between their characters and in the movie? [laughter]*
MP: No, they were naturally bitchy. But I expected that. If there hadn't been so much temperament bottled up—I had four or five of the biggest European names in art in the picture, and the more they knew about what the other fellow was doing the better. Made 'em work harder. [laughter]

AUDIENCE: *Because it's so difficult to see so many of your movies in this country, this particular film I saw on public television when I was a kid in San Francisco and maybe 16, 17 years ago at the American Film Institute in D.C., but not since. Do you know if there's any move to have any of these released on video? I know a few are but most particularly some of your lesser known works are not available, that I'm aware of.*

RJ: Name some that you don't—

AUDIENCE: A Matter of Life and Death, Stairway to Heaven, I Know Where I'm Going!

MP: You mean why aren't they on video?

RJ: *I think most of the films included in this festival are in fact available on video. I've certainly got them on video because I tape them off American Movie Classics and Cinemax. I encourage everybody to do the same. Quite a few of them,* The Spy in Black, *for instance, the very first film that Powell and Pressburger worked on together, you can get on video.*

MP: Emeric and I met and fell in love with each other just one year before the war, and at that time, Korda was the great man in movies in England and he built this huge studio and he was making big pictures for the world. Things like *The Four Feathers, The Thief of Bagdad.* When he had to leave to go back to America and when all the other American producers went back to America, there was left a skeleton of a great film producing group which gradually put on pledge as the war went on, so that we were all doing training films, or recruiting films or anything we were asked to do as well as making feature films. We circulated this information between ourselves and those of us who were called up to tell us when they would be released and would be available. So that there was a tremendous amount of first class knowledge and first class material available immediately after the war finished. I have written about this in my book, *A Life in Movies,* and the second volume, which I'm writing now, tells how this went on after the war, after a certain point, and then disintegrated because of the leaders, partly, and also the intransigence of filmmakers like me. It's interesting because in my opinion this century is the century of the film. We're so lucky, all of us, to be born in this century with film. When you think about the entertainment, the information, the beauty, the motion, and in my opinion it's *all* got to be done *all over again.* Because we've now come to a complete stop where money is all that matters and that just isn't true. The whole making of film is put into sort of one pine box. Then obviously you've got a situation like today, where in Hollywood you've got an excellent filmmaker; they make one successful film and they're all immediately bought out and from then on bribed to go on making other films—not the films they intended to make in the first place, but films that other people think may make a fortune, as many do. It's a big subject, but I hope the second volume of my book, if I live to finish it next year, will make my point. I'm writing for young people, I'm not writing for old people. I think that we all can make very much better films than most people are making today. Except my friend Scorsese.

RJ: *You give me an opportune moment to say that Mr. Powell is accompanied this evening by Mrs. Powell, who is Thelma Schoonmaker, the Academy Award–winning editor for* Raging Bull.
MP: Stand up!

RJ: *She did stand up.*
MP: Oh. [laughter] You never win!

AUDIENCE: *What prompted you to make* Peeping Tom? *What attracted you to the story? Did you think while you were filming it that it was going to cause any kind of commotion at all?*
MP: No, I was very innocent, as you see. [laughter] When I was looking for another writer to work with after Emeric and I split up—he went off to India with David Lean. They were writing a story there for about two years and then came back again. But meanwhile another producer, who made very popular films, rang me up and said, "Mickey, I want you to see Leo Marks, he's just as crazy as you are. But I think you might find he's the kind of writer you like to work for—like to work with—like Emeric." This chap came along, and he was dark and mysterious looking, Jewish, and obviously had an enormous sense of humor. Very powerful looking man, very quiet. After some talk it transpired he'd been working in code all through the war. And he was trying to sell me, first of all, a story about double agents, people working on both sides, 'cause he knew all the facts of these sorts of things. I said I wasn't interested. Then we thought of an idea and I said, "Would you be interested in making a film about Freud?" We both thought this might be a good idea, but then John Huston announced that *he* was going to make a life of Freud, and as John's a better director than I am, I thought I better let him have it! Then Leo Marks came to me—as usual when I opened the door, he was always smoking a new cigar—and he said, "Mr. Powell, how would you like

to make a film about a young man who kills the women that he photographs?" I said, "Oh yes, I'd like to do that very much." How could I miss? Over two or three months, he came twice a week with two pages. We would discuss it. I never touched his script, just listened to it and suggested things. He made notes, then he'd come next Thursday, and next Monday. And in about two months time we had the script and I liked it very much. So I rang up one or two people and one very much the [Wall] Street man. He said he would put the money into it and he thought he could find most of the rest of it. So I really became interested then. And thought, "I will go ahead and make it." You don't want to hear about casting, that was the normal way. But everybody was very enthusiastic with the script, not just me. You know, the cameraman, Otto Heller, was a very old timer, he worked in silent films. To show you how far back he went, he used to work with Anny Ondra, a Czech actress who was the leading lady in Hitchcock's *Blackmail.* They had a company together before Hitchcock made *Blackmail,* that was way back in 1924. I'd always wanted to work with Otto Heller; I thought his work as a cameraman was wonderful. He came in, and Brian Easdale did the music, mostly piano music. Everybody was very enthusiastic. There was a 30-day shooting schedule. It cost £125,000, or maybe £130,000. And we were all rather pleased, you know, saying, "It is a rather good film, isn't it?" "Yes." "You want blood here?" "No, we don't want blood there. Don't need blood." He said, "Well, it was thrown on the wall." And Karl Boehm, who was the son of Karl Boehm the great conductor, always wanted to be a conductor but had to settle for being an actor. I met him by chance. He was exactly the right mixture of innocence and completely loony. Very touching. Very moving. And it was really for me a very compassionate and interesting film about a man. My own son, Columba, who was about 8 then, had quite an important part in the picture as the young man when he was a young boy. His father used to wake him in the night and drop lizards on him. That's Leo Marks, but I went along with the idea. Then they showed it to the critics and booked to go and needed to go into a big cinema, and such a scream went up that hasn't happened since Sodom and Gomorra. [laughter] They ruined it, they made me take it off the cinema, take if off the circuit, the distribution was canceled, and the producer sold the rights, or television rights, to America. Somebody almost immediately went bankrupt, and the film disappeared for nearly 20 years.

RJ: *One of the ways you went along with the lizard dropping father was that you played him, didn't you?*
MP: Yes, now that you mention it.

RJ: *Your mentioning Otto Heller cues me to mention that one of the remarkable qualities in your work, especially in the largely visually dull British cinema of that period, was the extraordinary richness of the canvases that you painted and many of them in a kind of Technicolor that we had not seen before and we've seen precious little of since. You were under some restrictions about being able to use color, were you not, during the war?*
MP: After *Blimp.* That was the last color film until the war was nearly won. Yes, well, you see luckily I'd worked on *The Thief of Bagdad* with Georges Périnal and all the Technicolor crew in England. Those boys were born into making films and color films for the war, and they were all people who'd been right through the Technicolor mill and knew all about the new exposures and the new way to handle dyes, and then they'd all been trained by the Technicolor plant. America was particularly good at that kind of thing. They set up this plant in England to train technicians for Technicolor in Europe. Well, Europe was gone during wartime, but England was still there. So all these boys were available to me as soon as the war was over. We had some of the finest technical color teams in the world at the time. Quite a lot of painters and modelers and designers, people like that, costume designers. They were all either available or they'd been interred all through the war and were now released. So there was a tremendous pent up amount of talent. As we were in entire control of the films we made, we didn't have some idiot saying, "That won't work" or "you can't put that green cushion on a red set." So things went ahead pretty quickly. And our work, the color work, was stupendous, I quite agree with you. Right up through *Tales of Hoffmann.*

AUDIENCE: *I had a question about* Tales of Hoffmann. *At the very end of the picture, a hand that looks like it must have been Sir Thomas Beecham's but I'm not sure, stamps "MADE IN ENGLAND" on the conductor's score as it closes. And I wondered who's idea was it to have that done?*
MP: Mine. When we were shooting, I said to Emeric, "I don't want to have a banal sort of finish, a big finish or an ordinary finish. Just finish up Tommy conducting." After all he conducted the whole score, he found all the singers, it was his idea originally. So we rigged up bit of wood, a sort of lectern,

and he got into this wonderful suit which he always conducted in, white tie and tails, the whole lot, and looking splendid he did the last 8 bars. Finish, boom. And he started to put down the baton and I said, "Hold on a moment. We'll do that again and just reach your hand out." "If you wish." So he did it that way. Then I said, "Now come in with the close-up." And we came in with the camera, took the close-up putting down the baton and picking up the stamp. Then I had a third shot with a piece of cardboard with the MADE IN ENGLAND stamp on it and put it on the paper. Am I right? Then we did the MADE IN ENGLAND. It was purely an inspiration of the moment. What I was talking about, I think I got a little mixed, because when Moira, for instance, dances into the shoes [in *The Red Shoes*], there are 3 or 4 different shots there, but the whole thing takes place in about 10 frames. I shot it on pure theory that way and Reggie Mills, the cutter, cut it. Next morning I said, "Put it in already and don't wait for the feet to hit the ground." When we were shooting, it was a question of putting the shoes on the ground by Massine. That was one shot. Then *nailing* the shoes to the ground and leaving them standing on their points. Then undoing the tabs of the ribbons of the slippers. That was done by a thread attached to it and we just had to give it a pull and the ribbon fell down her leg on to the floor. That was shot with the camera running backwards so that you didn't have the tape coming off; it had to be coming on. Then the new shot, the fourth shot, she had to jump and the shoes were still on the floor, and I said, "Just run towards them, Moira, and then jump and come down." She said, "Do I come down *behind* the red shoes, Mr. Powell, or *in front* of the red shoes?" That was a tough one. I thought about it and I said, "Jump over them." So she came from behind and jumped over the shoes which meant she was just coming past the shoes right in front of them. So the shoes are here, she jumps over them and came down and the camera was here. So that was 4 or maybe 5 different cuts. None of them much more than 2½, 3, 4 frames. The other thing with Sir Thomas Beecham and MADE IN ENGLAND was made the same way. I wasn't meaning anything particular by it; it was just a piece of cheek.

AUDIENCE: *In* I Know Where I'm Going! *I was impressed by the strong sense of place and I wondered whether you might have had the idea of making a film in the Hebrides before you chose the story, but as I see more of your films it seems to me that each of them has a strong sense of place, and I'm curious about that in your creating approach to the ideas that come to you.*

MP: Well, the first film I really wanted to make after I had already made 20—they were all cheap films, you know, learning the trade. But the film I had wanted to make for the last year or two was the evacuation of St. Kilda and I wanted to shoot it in the Hebrides. About the depopulation of one of the islands there. A love story which ends with the old population leaving the island. I did make it eventually, *The Edge of the World,* and it's still around. I nearly lost it altogether but then they found the negative and put it back together. Then almost immediately after Korda signed me to a contract to make a film in Burma, so naturally the film that I did make was in the Orkney islands, and this was *The Spy in Black.* It had a lot of the same atmosphere, information, pictorial sense of the specificity or complications, of the island. That was followed by *I Know Where I'm Going!* So I had already a tremendous love of the lore of the sea, and ships, the northern islands, western islands. During the war we were nearly always getting involved in something that had to do with the coast or the sea, like in *Contraband,* and I think it just came naturally out of that.

RJ: *On the other hand, one that came completely unnaturally and yet is one of your most triumphal realizations of place is* Black Narcissus, *which wasn't anywhere except in your studio's imagination.*
MP: True.

RJ: *It's utterly persuasive.*
MP: Well, that was somebody else's book.

RJ: *I'm thinking of its sense of place.*
MP: Yes, wonderful writer. Actually I had come to Emeric with the idea of making a film in Peru—this was when the war was over and we all felt we needed a real scream with lots of color and sex. When he produced this book of Rumer Godden, I knew it already, and although I didn't particularly want to make it, I just gave in. I said, "Yes, it's a wonderful subject, a wonderful part. All right I'd like to do it. Only I don't want to go to India to make it. I've been to India and I know the Himalayas *are there.* What I'd like to do is to make a film about the book that has nothing to do with the book but has a great deal to do with what's in the book." Oh, I'm sure you've had enough. [applause]

A Modest Magician

HARLAN KENNEDY/1990

SEE THE INDIAN BOY CLIMB the giant spider's web to steal the jewel! Gasp at the moving stairway that ferries the immortals to Heaven! Goggle at the sex-starved nuns teetering above the Himalayan abyss! Gape at the magic-shoed ballerina spinning to death and glory!

Michael Powell was the Scheherazade of cinema. *The Red Shoes, Black Narcissus, Stairway to Heaven, The Thief of Bagdad*—over five decades and 54 films, made everywhere from Los Angeles to the Great Barrier Reef (but mostly in Britain)—Powell spun enchanted yarns as if his life depended on it. But the life he truly saved was that of British cinema. Wheezing from lack of oxygen in the late 1930s, the country's creative lungs could take in little but squeeky musicals, somber thrillers and smoke-gray documentaries. Britain needed a miracle and got one. Cometh the hour, cometh the chap. From 1939 to 1960, Michael Powell was the most brilliant wild card in the whole pack of British cinema.

After 1960 (such is show biz), goeth the hour, goeth the chap. After two decades of pumping life into Anglo-Saxon celluloid, the mad doctor of English cinema (who got better results than any sane doctor) was all but struck off the register. He made a little horror film called *Peeping Tom,* about a photographer who kills women with a sharpened tripod leg, and people screamed, Eek! Terrible! Disgusting! (Just as they did the same year over Hitchcock's *Psycho.*)

From *American Film,* July 1990, Volume XV, Number 10, pp. 32–37.

Powell was shaken, but not stirred to contrition. He went on working fitfully, unappreciatedly, on large screen and small. But it was another 20 years before fans caught up with him and dragged him back into the limelight.

Michael Powell was the only filmmaker I ever met who gloried in self-deprecation. No doubt, in his Indian summer of celebrity, he felt that someone had to do the job. From 1980 onward, Powell-neglect turned to Powell-mania across movieland. The man who had been slung out on his ear by the British movie establishment after *Peeping Tom* (today considered a classic) was the darling of retrospectives, tributes and invitations to work in—yes—Hollywood. Under Francis Ford Coppola, no less, in the days when Zoetrope Studios was a bright beacon rather than a gleam in the eye of the bailiffs. (Almost a half-century before, Powell had worked on those very same sound-stages on *The Thief of Bagdad.*)

Before all this, we met, and met again over ensuing years. A tweedily dressed man with a singsong, upper-crust voice and a face like an animated currant bun, Powell could charm you out of your socks. As he jawed, joked and reminisced about one of the most illustrious careers in British cinema—only David Lean and Alfred Hitchcock left thumbprints as large—two things emerged.

One: this man was a maverick whose every movie was a "rogue project," rather than a stone carefully placed in a monumental oeuvre. Two: for all his country-squire voice and claret waistcoats, Powell would never be the darling of any establishment, because he shot down pomposity wherever he saw it.

So (no surprise) he never got the knightood he deserved, unlike Sir Alfred H. and Sir David L. But in the last decade of his life, he got accolades just as precious, from his film-industry peers. And when he died on February 19, 1990, obituary writers went down to their word cellars to dust off vintage superlatives.

What was special about Powell? That he went his own sweet way. That he didn't give a damn, except about good art and good cinema. And that he kept surprising everyone, most of all himself.

"I only discovered what my films were about while making them," Powell once said. "When Alex Korda [the producer], who was the power in British cinema back in the '30s, married Emeric and me, it was the beginning of a rather special period." (Emeric Pressburger was Powell's Hungarian-born partner between 1939 and 1956.) "No filmmakers ever had such a run of original scripts. And they sort of grew as we made them. I was running around filming location sequences for *The Invaders* (aka, *49th Parallel*), with a double for Larry Olivier, while Emeric was still writing the first pages of the script."

To the filmgoing world, this twinning of talents seemed symbiotic, not to say Siamese. "Written, produced and directed by Michael Powell and Emeric Pressburger" proclaimed the credits over the picture of an arrow thudding into a target. (They had christened their production company The Archers.)

"I suppose the reason we shared the credits was the wartime atmosphere. Team spirit and all that. Also, we both had a very visual background. I loved American cinema and was very influenced by it. Emeric had worked for UFA in Germany in its heyday—with their fantastic visual effects—until Hitler came along, and then he popped over here. So we were a team, and we shared responsibility, even though Emeric did the scripts and I was the one behind the camera. He had a great knack with words. Of course, I wouldn't have let him direct a foot!"

Powell's own greatest knack was for pulling beleaguered projects out of any fire they might fall into. When Olivier, serving in the Fleet Air Arm of the Royal Navy, wasn't available for the title role in *The Life and Death of Colonel Blimp*—"He was off attempting to eliminate Hitler"—Powell made a wartime star out of foghorn-voiced Roger Livesey. "I loved him! Micky Balcon [the noted British producer] hated him—that hoarse voice. But he was very suburban, Micky. That's why he made all those Ealing comedies."

When Livesey himself, appearing in a play in London, couldn't go north for location shooting in Scotland for *I Know Where I'm Going!* in which the actor costarred with Wendy Hiller, Powell used a double. Probably the most hardworking double in movie history. "People can't believe it when they see the film today," he told me once, "but Roger never went near Scotland! Ever! We picked the double for his walk, height, everything; and in each shot, we'd cut on a turn or a change of angle or even a change of thought. Then we'd use back projection in the studios and push Roger right up against the screen so he seemed to be part of the scene."

When Powell thought of the money it would cost to go to India to make *Black Narcissus,* that simmering tale of sexually repressed nuns in the Himalayas, he said, Heigh-ho, hired Deborah Kerr and shot it all on a British soundstage. The result—as designed by Alfred Junge, shot by Jack Cardiff and directed by Powell—is an expressionist masterpiece.

"They said to me, But surely you'll want to shoot some establishing shots in India? That's a very insidious phrase, *establishing shots.* They said, You can't do Mount Everest in a studio. I said, A studio is exactly where you *can* do Everest, and avalanches and Tibetan horns. Wonderful studio stuff. And if we go and shoot a lot of real stuff to cut into the studio stuff, it'll make all the studio stuff look terrible. And vice versa: if we do wonderful work in the studio, the exteriors will look like something from a documentary dragged in by the cat!"

Powell's working life followed the same pattern throughout his career. He said he wanted to do something; someone told him he couldn't; he did it. Even on *The Red Shoes,* Powell's party piece for popular cinema, the director confronted impossible technical challenges with a simple, Right, let's see how we can do this.

"One of my favorite scenes is near the end, when Moira Shearer runs down the spiral staircase and the camera follows her. What we did was rotate the staircase itself, because the camera couldn't possibly have kept up. If you look carefully, you can see the stairs revolve. And though it looks like one shot, there's actually a join; because Moira ran down so fast, we had to reshoot it to make it longer. There's a half-frame jump.

"Moira did that beautifully," Powell assessed. "It's a lovely example of movement. Most actors don't grasp that movement tends to slow down in sound film. Twenty-four frames per second is a totally arbitrary speed. I always tried to shoot scenes at different speeds, even dialogue scenes: anything from 10 to 29, although, of course, you know it'll be projected at 24 frames per second. But every shot has its own viewpoint, its own pace, its own mood. We didn't shoot Moira at normal speed in her dancing scenes onstage; it was 18 or 19.

"The camera crew loves this, once they get used to it. It means you don't have to be a slave to the dialogue. David Lean and I both learned to cut on a silent moviola. If you learn cutting on a sound moviola, you instinctively follow the bloody words. That's the last thing you want. Cinema is all about images. The words take care of themselves. You know, the actors yak away—who cares?"

But there were different Powells for different days. One day he could be this dashing cynic. Another, he could be all sweetness and courtesy to great old duffers of the British movie establishment, even to the "suburban" Balcon. Yet another time, he could be wreathed in pride and dignity as guest celebrity of the Oxford Film Festival, where the jury I was on gave him a special award—for being Michael Powell.

Another day still, one could spot his black-coated silhouette standing on a frozen Leningrad river at dawn. He had arrived early on location, was dicky with flu and resembled an undertaker surveying his latest blanched customer. (The customer here was an Anglo-Soviet stretcher-case called *Pavlova,* on which Powell advised but didn't direct.)

We even met on days when Powell the debonair artist seemed caught in a Jekyll-and-Hyde struggle with Powell the penny-pinching accountant.

"Money."

Pause.

"It's all about money," Powell said.

We were talking about studio-versus-location choices in a career that spanned everything from the soundstage India of *Black Narcissus* to field-trip actioners like *The Battle of the River Plate.*

"I'm a great believer in George Bernard Shaw's remark. He was talking to some producer who was trying to persuade Shaw to adapt one of his plays into a film. And the producer was talking about how wonderful it would be for cinema and for art. And Shaw interrupted him and said, Mr. So-and-So, the trouble is that you are talking about art and I am only interested in money." Powell roared with laughter.

"I've always been very conscious of what a film cost," he continued. "If you don't plan a film properly, which means in the studio, in the offices, on the storyboards, with the bankers, there's not going to be any future film business for us. Today in Hollywood, they're so proud when a film costs $17 million, $27 million, $37 million. But no one ever knows how these prices are arrived at: Somebody must have pocketed a great deal of money! I'm entirely in sympathy with the young American directors who've tried to get rid of the studio bosses."

Powell "got rid" of the studio bosses in his day by giving them movies so bizarre—and ones that performed so unpredictably at the box office (some flopped, some, like *The Red Shoes,* were megahits)—that all a poor mogul could do was sign the checks and keep hoping. Indeed, there were times when even Powell didn't seem to know which of The Archers' arrows truly hit their targets. "Is it well done? I didn't realize that," he burbled vaguely when I raved about his Hebridean romance, *I Know Where I'm Going!*

Powell was either a master manipulator of men and movies or was himself a human blank check on which the Muses wrote their signature. Since his conversation was made up of equal parts mischief and innocence, the sardonic and the surprised, it was almost impossible to tell. On the fuss about *Peeping Tom,* he commented with an air of injured (mock?) innocence: "They called me sick, diseased, goodness knows what. Not a jot of sympathy. I had no idea the critics led such sheltered lives."

When you held the man up to his films, you realized that this ambiguity was central to Powell's magic. Movies like *The Red Shoes* and *Black Narcissus* were spiked with antijingoist jokes, while war satires like *The Life and Death of Colonel Blimp* (on which Winston Churchill tried and failed to halt production) were sweetened with romance and lump-in-the-throat love of country.

Pinning Powell down was like trying to net a rare butterfly. The flickering beauty of his films drew you on into the chase, but you knew you would never capture them. And even if you did, they would escape at the first chance. Indeed, just when Powell seemed most docile, as man or moviemaker, he was likely to fly from your grasp with a puckish giggle of triumph.

Nothing could be more apt than that Powell, that maker of unlikely marriages between movie styles, should spend his swan-song decade forging an old-young, Brit-Yank alliance with the Turks of Hollywood. One sensed his delight that he ended his days hobnobbing with the Scorseses and Coppolas. But one also sensed his appreciation of the comic incongruity of it all: as when he spotted George Lucas in a Hollywood restaurant and popped over to introduce himself. Lucas looked at him with a shocked expression, wondering, Powell said, "who this ghastly creature was who called himself Michael Powell." The British director retreated to his meal; Lucas finished his. Then, realizing that perhaps this was *the* Michael Powell, he came over to chat. Result: an invitation to come up to San Francisco for a tour of Lucas' "facility."

"Wonderful—this fantastic cave of marbles! Matte shots, animation, every kind of wizardry! He showed me about 420 matte shots from *Empire Strikes Back.* I though, I could do anything here if I could get my hands on all this.

"And, of course, it's wonderful to see it all in the hands of a filmmaker. That's what I like so much about these young Americans. However much their films cost, they're all *personal* films. George has got all his *Star Wars* films planned away, all there in boxes. 'Little boxes on the hillside!' [singing]. And they've wrested the initiative from the studio bosses," Powell explained.

"The only future for cinema is in the personal film. It always has been. But, of course, we've lost the way so often; new things have come in and distracted people's attention. Sound came in, and for 10 years no one thought of anything but sound. Color came in and no one thought of doing anything but color—which, of course, is nonsense, black-and-white is a *style.* There have continually been gadgets and gimmicks. But personal films: that's what it must come down to in the end."

Powell may have spent a happy old age yoyo-ing round the world, meeting movie wizards, advising on movies (in Leningrad and L.A.) and even marrying a movie editor, Thelma Schoonmaker of *Raging Bull.* But if he was on the end of a yoyo, it was an umbilical one, and it was always pulling him back to Britain.

Every richness in Powell's movies is a British one: the landscapes, the pageantry, the throttled, elemental romanticism (out of Wordsworth, by the Brontës). And every tension and contradiction was British, too, between shyness and flamboyance, cynicism and innocence, nostalgia and clairvoyance. America will mourn his passing, but Britain will never forget Powell, just as Powell could never forget Britain. For the Britain—the England—he loved was a visionary, not a parochial, one.

In his words, "There are those who say that England is a little island and that we all look inwards. I don't feel that. I don't regard England even as a little island. It's a world: a world I shall, when the time comes, be sorry to leave."

INDEX

CONVERSATIONS WITH FILMMAKERS SERIES

PETER BRUNETTE, GENERAL EDITOR

The collected interviews with notable modern directors, including

Robert Altman • Theo Angelopolous • Bernardo Bertolucci • Jane Campion • George Cukor • Brian De Palma • Clint Eastwood • John Ford • Jean-Luc Godard • Peter Greenaway • Alfred Hitchcock • John Huston • Jim Jarmusch • Elia Kazan • Stanley Kubrick • Spike Lee • Mike Leigh • George Lucas • Martin Ritt • Carlos Saura • John Sayles • Martin Scorsese • Steven Soderbergh • Steven Spielberg • Oliver Stone • Quentin Tarantino • Lars von Trier • Orson Welles • Billy Wilder • Zhang Yimou